CONTENTS

Abbreviations and Acronyms		2
Introduction		2
Dramatis Personae		3
Prologue		5
1	The Soviet Navy	6
2	The Submarine	11
3	The Voyage Begins	18
4	Wednesday 28 October	41
5	The Swedes Mobilise	49
6	The Soviet Salvage Expedition	58
7	Thursday 29 October	74
8	Radiation Readings	85
Bibliography		87
Endnotes		89
About the Author		94

Helion & Company Limited
Unit 8 Amherst Business Centre
Budbrooke Road
Warwick
CV34 5WE
England
Tel. 01926 499 619
Email: info@helion.co.uk
Website: www.helion.co.uk
Twitter: @helionbooks
https://helionbooks.wordpress.com/

Text © Michael Fredholm von Essen 2025
Artworks by Tom Cooper, Renato Dalmasso and Anderson Subtil
Maps drawn by George Anderson © Helion & Company 2025

Cover image: A view of the *S-363* from behind a Swedish Parachute Rangers' GPMG position.

Designed and typeset by Mach 3 Solutions (www.mach3solutions.co.uk)
Cover design Paul Hewitt, Battlefield Design (www.battlefield-design.co.uk)

Every reasonable effort has been made to trace copyright holders and to obtain their permission for the use of copyright material. The author and publisher apologise for any errors or omissions in this work, and would be grateful if notified of any corrections that should be incorporated in future reprints or editions of this book.

ISBN: 978-1-804518-65-6

British Library Cataloguing-in-Publication Data
A catalogue record for this book is available from the British Library

All rights reserved. No part of this publication may be reproduced, stored in a retrieval system, or transmitted, in any form, or by any means, electronic, mechanical, photocopying, recording or otherwise, without the express written consent of Helion & Company Limited.

We always welcome receiving book proposals from prospective authors.

Illustrations are reproduced under the Creative Commons license or the GNU Free Documentation License (GNU FDL) coupled with the Creative Commons Attribution Share-Alike License, or derive from the author's personal collection. Photographs attributed to Medström are reproduced with the permission of this publisher. The names of photographers, unless stated, are unknown.

MAP OF EUROPE 1945–1992

Note: In order to simplify the use of this book, all names, locations and geographic designations are as provided in *The Times World Atlas*, or other traditionally accepted major sources of reference, as of the time of described events.

ABBREVIATIONS AND ACRONYMS

ASW	antisubmarine warfare	**hp**	horse power
BALTOPS	Baltic Operations (exercise)	**IFF**	identification friend or foe
CIA	Central Intelligence Agency (U.S.)	**KGB**	*Komitet gosudarstvennoy bezopasnosti* (Committee for State Security)(Soviet)
ELINT	electronic intelligence		
EW	electronic warfare	**kts**	knots (nautical miles per hour)
FOA	*Försvarets forskningsanstalt* (Defence Research Establishment)(Swedish)	**NATO**	North Atlantic Treaty Organization
		nm	nautical mile(s)
FRA	*Försvarets radioanstalt* (Defence Radio Establishment)(Swedish)	**RPS**	*Rikspolisstyrelsen* (National Police Board)(Swedish)
		Säk	*Säkerhetsavdelningen* (Security Department)(Swedish)
GRU	*Glavnoye razvedyvatel'noye upravleniye* (Main Intelligence Directorate)(Soviet)	**SIGINT**	signals intelligence

INTRODUCTION

This book describes the events surrounding the Soviet Navy Whiskey-class submarine of the Baltic Fleet which ran aground on 27 October 1981 on the south coast of Sweden, close to Naval Base Karlskrona, one of the largest Swedish military bases. The incident triggered a grave diplomatic and military crisis.

Upon discovery, Swedish Navy and Army units quickly surrounded the submarine, and closed off the immediate area. Surveillance of Sweden's sea and land borders intensified. Swedish intelligence stepped up activities against the Soviet Navy and its communications. A tense diplomatic game began over the fate of the stranded submarine and its crew. The Soviets claimed that the submarine had entered Swedish waters by accident, and demanded that it be allowed to leave without inspection of the vessel or interrogation of its crew. The Swedes demanded further clarification with regard to the submarine's mission and activities. Meanwhile, Swedish technical intelligence concluded that the submarine carried nuclear weapons, ultimately identified as torpedoes with nuclear warheads. The submarine crew took measures to blow up the submarine, in case Swedish special forces would storm the vessel – a contingency that the Swedish Armed Forces indeed prepared for.

To exacerbate the political and military crisis, Swedish intelligence and naval reconnaissance noted the unannounced arrival of a task force of Soviet ships which anchored just outside the 12-nautical-mile (22km) line that delimited Sweden's territorial waters. The Soviet task force, commanded by Vice Admiral Aleksey Kalinin on the *Obraztsovyy*, a large antisubmarine warfare ship described as a destroyer by NATO, eventually may have consisted of more than 10 Soviet Navy vessels. In response, Sweden's Prime Minister Thorbjörn Fälldin ordered the Armed Forces to defend the border, should the Soviets attempt a rescue of the stranded submarine. Vice Admiral Kalinin's task force was indeed prepared for such an eventuality, and for a few critical hours, Swedish and Soviet air, naval, and ground forces prepared to engage in battle – something that went unnoticed by the national and international media which monitored and reported the incident.

At the time, Swedish and international media saw the incident as evidence of extensive Soviet underwater activities in Swedish waters. The Swedish Armed Forces concluded that this violation was deliberate and part of illegal activities directed against Sweden. Yet, others argued that the violation was due to incompetence and substandard technical equipment rather than a conscious policy of aggression. Meanwhile, the Swedish government's response to the incident at times appeared as if from another world, particularly when a perceived need to pander to domestic party-political rivalries and a deeply-rooted distrust of anything Russian raised the stakes instead of reducing tensions. We will see that the crisis was a severe blow to the sense of security that for years had dominated Swedish politics, debate, and public opinion. It is in this light we must understand the Swedish actions during the crisis, which otherwise often come across as overly hostile and even provocative.

From an intelligence perspective, the incident shows how prejudices and mirror-imaging affect intelligence assessments in a detrimental way.

Although the paranoia and its manifestations in hindsight appear comical, the crisis brought a very real and enduring risk that the confrontation between Soviet and Swedish military units, each armed to the teeth and each deeply suspicious of the other, might escalate into bloodshed. Wars have started for lesser provocation than this.

The stranded submarine being a Whiskey-class submarine, the incident is popularly known in the West as 'Whiskey on the Rocks'.

DRAMATIS PERSONAE

Soviet Union

Andropov, Yuriy Vladimirovich, Chairman of the intelligence service KGB.

Arkhipov, Mikhail (patronym undisclosed). Senior Lieutenant. Chief engineer of the *S-363*.

Avrukevich, Iosif Fyodorovich, Captain First Rank. Chief of staff of 157th Submarine Brigade, Paldiski, Soviet Estonia. Joined Gushchin onboard as mentor because it was the captain's first independent command of a submarine of Project 613.

Baltuška, Raimundas Saulius, Captain First Rank. Lithuanian who served as head of the Baltic Fleet's Navigation Directorate.

Basov, Nikolay (patronym undisclosed). Electrician, rating of the engineering section of the *S-363*.

Belkin, Nikolay (patronym undisclosed). Rating of the Osnaz (Electronic Warfare, EW) section of the *S-363*.

Besedin, Vasiliy Vasil'yevich, Captain-Lieutenant. Political officer and deputy commander of the *S-363*.

Brezhnev, Leonid Il'ich, General Secretary of the Communist Party and supreme leader of the Soviet Union.

Buchak, Ivan Vasil'yevich, Captain First Rank. Commander of 157th Submarine Brigade, Paldiski, Soviet Estonia.

Dolgov, Pyotr (patronym undisclosed), Warrant Officer. Bosun of the *S-363*.

Gorshkov, Sergey Georgiyevich, Admiral of the Fleet of the Soviet Union. Supreme Commander of Soviet Naval Forces.

Grigor'yev, Boris Nikolayevich, Second Secretary, Soviet Embassy in Stockholm. Clandestine KGB officer who spoke fluent Swedish.

Grishin, Vladimir 'Volodya' (patronym undisclosed), Warrant Officer. Head of the sonar section of the *S-363*.

Gushchin, Anatoliy Mikhaylovich, Captain Third Rank. Commanding officer of the *S-363*. The voyage that ended up in Swedish waters was his first as submarine commander.

Kalinin, Aleksey Mikhaylovich, Vice Admiral. First Deputy Commander of the Baltic Fleet.

Kapitanets, Ivan Matveyevich, Vice Admiral. Commander of the Baltic Fleet.

Korostov, Anatoliy 'Tolya' Ivanovich, Senior Lieutenant. Chief navigator of the *S-363*. The voyage that ended up in Swedish waters was his first as chief navigator.

Lyakin, Viktor Fyodorovich, Captain Third Rank. Commander of the large missile ship *Prozorlivyy*.

Morozov, Aleksandr (patronym undisclosed). Rating of the signals section of the *S-363*.

Navoytsev, Pyotr Nikolayevich, Admiral. First Deputy Chief of the Central Staff of the Naval Forces.

Nejland [Neyland], Nikolay 'Nick' Vasil'yevich, KGB officer and Deputy Foreign Minister of Soviet Latvia.

Novikov, Anatoliy Ivanovich, Second Secretary, Soviet Embassy in Stockholm.

Pershin, Vladimir (patronym undisclosed), Senior Lieutenant. Head of the department for mines and torpedoes of the *S-363*.

Prosvirnin, Yuriy Gennad'yevich, Captain First Rank. Officer of the military intelligence service GRU and naval attaché accredited to Sweden. Having served in Norway's capital Oslo, he spoke fluent Norwegian which also enabled him to understand and communicate in Swedish, two closely related languages.

Rymko, Yevgeniy Potapovich, Chargé d'Affaires, Soviet Embassy in Stockholm.

Savchenko, Pavel (patronym undisclosed), Senior Sailor. Rating of the signals section of the *S-363*. Called **Sergey Kovalchuk** in Besedin's memoirs.

Shkanov, Boris Petrovich, Captain First Rank. First officer of the operations command within the Central Staff of the Naval Forces.

Starostenko, Aleksey (patronym undisclosed), Lieutenant. Physician of the *S-363*.

Stepanov, Igor' (patronym undisclosed), Warrant Officer. Head of the signals section of the *S-363*.

Tarasov, Mikhail (patronym undisclosed), Warrant Officer. Cook of the *S-363*.

Volodin, Aleksandr (patronym undisclosed), Warrant Officer. Head of the sonar section of the *S-363*.

Ustinov, Dmitriy Fyodorovich, Marshal of the Soviet Union. Despite his military rank, more a defence industry official than a soldier. Replaced Marshal of the Soviet Union Andrey Grechko as Defence Minister of the Soviet Union.

Yakovlev, Mikhail Danilovich, Ambassador Extraordinary and Plenipotentiary of the Soviet Union to Sweden.

Yakovlev, Viktor S. (patronym undisclosed), Senior Lieutenant. Executive officer of the *S-363*. No relation to Ambassador Yakovlev.

Zakharov, Gennadiy Ivanovich, Captain First Rank. Commander of the Baltic Fleet's 561st Independent Maritime Intelligence Post.

Zeibots, Gaidis Andrejs, Captain Second Rank (?). Latvian who served as deputy chief of staff of 128th Missile Ship Brigade in Baltiysk and accordingly was a member of Vice Admiral Kalinin's staff on the *Obraztsovyy*.

Zemskov, Igor' Nikolayevich, Deputy Foreign Minister of the Soviet Union responsible for relations with the Scandinavian countries.

Sweden

Charles XVI Gustavus, King of Sweden.

Abrahamsson, Bengt. Police constable.

Adelsohn, Ulf. Chairman of the opposition conservative Moderate Party.

Andersson, Gerth. Radar ground controller at Low Altitude Filter Centre S2S Myran.

Andersson, Gunilla. Owner and manager of Hotel Aston, Karlskrona.

Andersson, Jan, Captain. Commander of 1st Squadron of Bråvalla Air Wing (F 13) at Norrköping.

Andersson, Karl, Commander. Chief of staff at Naval Base Karlskrona.

Åström, Christer. Television reporter.

Åström, Leif, Major. Commander of 2nd Squadron of Västgöta Air Wing (F 6) at Karlsborg.

Beckman, Lars. Nuclear weapons expert at the Defence Research Establishment (Swedish: *Försvarets forskningsanstalt*, FOA).

Berg, Jan-Åke, Lieutenant Colonel. Chief press officer, Defence Staff.

Bjäre, Bertil, Brigadier General. Air Force officer who served as military attaché, Moscow.

Björling, Percy, Commander. Operations section (Op 2), Defence Staff. Former submariner.

Bjurman, Christer, Lieutenant. Commander of the torpedo boat T 134 *Varberg*.

Borg, Lennart, Lieutenant Colonel. Head of the Security Department at the Defence Staff (Swedish: *Försvarsstabens säkerhetsavdelning*, Fst/Säk).

Bruzelius, Nils, Lieutenant Commander. Commander of the submarine *Neptun* on the eve when the *S-363* stranded on Torumskär.

Carlsson, Sven 'Sven-Calle', Commander. Chief press officer, Navy Staff.

Danckwardt, Jean-Carlos, Brigadier General. Commander of Blekinge Coastal Artillery and Karlskrona Defence District (Fo 15), and accordingly all land forces in the operation.

De Geer, Carl, Ambassador Extraordinary and Plenipotentiary of Sweden to the Soviet Union.

De Geer, Lars-Erik. Nuclear weapons expert at the Defence Research Establishment (Swedish: *Försvarets forskningsanstalt*, FOA).

Eckerberg, Lennart. Head of the Foreign Ministry's Political Department.

Edwardsson, Rolf, Lieutenant Commander. Operations Department, Naval Base Karlskrona.

Elming, Torbjörn, Lieutenant Colonel. Head of the Swedish Parachute Ranger School at Karlsborg.

Elmstedt, Claes, Minister of Communications.

Eriksson, Leif 'Ecka', Captain. Coastal Ranger officer, commander of Boarding Team 1.

Fagö, Thomas, Lieutenant Commander. Commander of the torpedo boat T 136 *Västervik*.

Fälldin, Thorbjörn, Prime Minister. Farmer in northern Sweden and chairman of the agrarian Centre Party, who won political power largely because of his anti-nuclear stance.

Felin, Dag, Police Commissioner, Karlskrona.

Forsberg, Tore, Chief Superintendent. Head of the Soviet Section of the Security Service.

Forsman, Lennart, Commodore. Commander of Naval Base Karlskrona.

Gisselsson, Jan, Captain. 1st Squadron of Bråvalla Air Wing (F 13) at Norrköping.

Gudmundsson, Per. Journalist at the tabloid *Kvällsposten*.

Gunnarsson, Per-Olof. Journalist at the tabloid *Kvällsposten*.

Gustafsson, Bengt, Colonel. Commander of Svea Engineer Regiment (Ing 1). Played no role in the *S-363* crisis, but in 1986 succeeded Lennart Ljung as Supreme Commander of the Armed Forces.

Gustafsson, Torsten, Minister of Defence. Farmer on the island of Gotland and elected representative of the agrarian Centre Party.

Hamilton, Björn, Lieutenant. Acting commander of the submarine *Neptun* during the crisis.

Hellborg, Ragnar, Reader, Department of Physics, Lund University. Specialist on neutron radiation measurement.

Hellstedt, Lars, Lieutenant. Commander of the maritime surveillance centre in Karlskrona.

Helmerson, Klas. Interpreter.

Hirdman, Sven, State Secretary and the senior official of the Ministry of Defence. Career diplomat with long experience of the Soviet Union who in military service had learnt Russian at the Armed Forces School of Interpreters.

Hjälmroth, Sven-Åke. Head of the Security Department (Swedish: *Säkerhetsavdelningen*, Säk) of the National Police Board (*Rikspolisstyrelsen*, RPS) which was responsible for counterespionage and accordingly constituted Sweden's Security Service.

Hovgard, Gunnar, Colonel. Commander of Västgöta Air Wing (F 6) at Karlsborg.

Jansson, Nils-Ove, Lieutenant Commander. Played no role in the *S-363* crisis, but later assumed a leading position in the military intelligence service.

Jansson, Per. Interpreter.

Jansson, Ulf. Commander of the civilian tugboat *Karlshamn*.

Johansson, Sven, Detective Inspector.

Klintebo, Roderick, Captain. Experienced submarine officer and commander of 1st Submarine Flotilla. Born in Scotland to a Swedish merchant marine officer, he retained dual British-Swedish citizenship for the duration of his life. Klintebo also participated in the history project of the Swedish submarine arm.

Kviele, Bengt. Acting County Prosecutor.

Leifland, Leif, Cabinet Secretary and the senior official of the Foreign Ministry. Career diplomat.

Lindén, Rolf, Major. Head of the Operations Section at Blekinge Coastal Artillery and Karlskrona Defence District (Fo 15).

Lindquist, Lennart, Captain. Karlskrona Coastal Artillery Regiment (KA 2).

Ljung, Lennart, General. Supreme Commander of the Armed Forces since 1978.

Lundquist, Nils-Henrik, Director General of the Defence Research Establishment (Swedish: *Försvarets forskningsanstalt*, FOA).

Magnusson, Arne, Coastal Customs Commissioner. Commander of the Coast Guard vessel *Tv 281* from Kalmar. His rank roughly approximated that of an army major or a navy lieutenant commander.

Malm, Rolf, Lieutenant Colonel. Tactics and Intelligence Department, Navy Staff.

Malmgren, Anders, Commander. Commander of 13th Patrol Boat Division at Gålö in the Stockholm archipelago.

Mattsson, Gunnar, Inspector of Maritime Safety, Swedish Maritime Administration, Kalmar.

Mattsson, John, Coastal Customs Commissioner. Commander of the Coast Guard vessel *Tv 103* from Simrishamn.

Nilsson, Sonnie. Director of the Karlskrona Tourism Board.

Nord, Olle. Veteran engineer at the Defence Research Establishment (Swedish: *Försvarets forskningsanstalt*, FOA).

Nygren, Erik, Major General. Commander of 1st Strike Wing (E 1).

Ohlsson, Rolf. News editor at the regional newspaper *Sydsvenska Dagbladet*.

Olson, Sven-Olof 'Sven-Olle', Lieutenant General. Air Force officer who served as the commander of Military District South.

Olsson, Brian. Former sailor who in 1931 ran away from a Swedish ship in the Black Sea port of Poti and then lived for four years in Soviet Ukraine, learnt Russian, and after his return to Sweden functioned as volunteer police interpreter.

Öfverberg, Kjell, Major. Commander of 1st Squadron of Västgöta Air Wing (F 6).

Palme, Olof. Chairman of the opposition Social Democrat Party.

Peine, Elisabeth. Staff assistant, Karlskrona maritime surveillance centre.

Rasmusson, Gunnar, Commander. Press officer of Naval Base Karlskrona.

Schuback, Bengt, Vice Admiral. Chief of the Defence Staff.

Sjöberg, Magnus, National Prosecutor.

Söderholm, Conrad, Coastal District Commissioner. Chief of Blekinge Coast Guard District and commander of the Coast Guard vessel *Tv 253* from Karlshamn.

Sollin, Per. Fisherman Ingvar Svensson's son-in-law.

Sönnerstedt, Erland, Lieutenant Commander. Intelligence Department at the Defence Staff (Swedish: *Försvarsstabens underrättelseavdelning*, Fst/Und).

Sturkman, Bertil. Fisherman.

Svensson, Emil, Commander. Head of the Navy's Analysis Group and outspoken hawk on the Soviet Union and Russia.

Svensson, Eric. Civilian maritime pilot from Karlshamn.

Svensson, Ingvar. Fisherman.

Svensson, Rolf. Radar ground controller at Low Altitude Filter Centre S2S Myran.

Theutenberg, Bo Johnson, Ambassador. Advisor on international law to the Foreign Ministry and outspoken hawk on the Soviet Union and Russia.

Tjäder, Thomas. Interpreter.

Törneryd, John, Harbour Master in Karlshamn. In command of the tugboat *Karlshamn* during the final salvage operation.

Törnwall, Bengt, Commander. Commander of the 13th Torpedo Boat Division and commanding officer on the torpedo boat T 138 *Piteå*.

Ullsten, Ola, Minister for Foreign Affairs. Chairman of the Liberal People's Party, which had formed a coalition government with Thorbjörn Fälldin's agrarian-based Centre Party.

Wallroth, Bengt, Colonel. Head of Operations Section 5 (Swedish: *Operationssektion* 5, Op 5) of the Defence Staff, that is, military intelligence and security.

Walter, Jan Erik, Assistant Master of the Armed Forces School of Interpreters. An expert linguist who among other achievements reformed and modernised the traditional teaching of Russian grammar.

Wickström, Gun-Britt. Secretary employed by the County administration.

Widell, Thor 'Tosse', Commander. Master of Equipment (Swedish: *ekipagemästare*) at Naval Base Karlskrona and responsible for salvaging the stranded submarine.

Wieloch, Tadeusz. Interpreter. The son of Polish immigrants, Wieloch was at Lund University where he pursued a career as a neuroscientist.

PROLOGUE

Colonel Oleg Pen'kovskiy visited London in April 1961. Pen'kovskiy was an officer of the GRU, the Soviet military intelligence service. Among other tasks, he had previously served as military attaché and GRU resident in Turkey. Pen'kovskiy enjoyed the support of Marshal of Artillery Sergey Varentsov, the commander of artillery and rocket forces, and was a friend or at least acquaintance of Army General Ivan Serov, head of the GRU. He had access to numerous highly classified Soviet documents. Presently, Pen'kovskiy was also deputy head of the State Committee for Science and Technology. He had offered his services to U.S. and British intelligence already in 1960, and the relationship was formalised during his stay in London. Pen'kovskiy began to spy on behalf of the British Secret Intelligence Service (SIS, popularly known as MI6), which henceforth ran him in a joint operation with the U.S. Central Intelligence Agency (CIA). Over the next 18 months, Pen'kovskiy delivered more than 5,000 secret Soviet documents to the SIS. As far as is known, no other spy ever revealed classified Soviet documentation to the West in such great quantities – and of such great value.

The documents covered many subjects. Those deemed to be of the greatest long-term interest to Western intelligence in the 1960s concerned technical details and launch procedures of Soviet intercontinental and intermediate-range ballistic missiles, for which Marshal Varentsov was responsible. Of even higher immediate value was the information that Pen'kovskiy handed over with regard to the Soviet buildup in Cuba. The documents provided showed that the Soviet Union was unprepared for war with the United States over Cuba. This information was of crucial importance to U.S. President John F. Kennedy because it gave him the confidence to face down his Soviet counterpart Nikita Khrushchev during the Cuban Missile Crisis in 1962 with reasonable hope of success. And Kennedy's gamble worked, since Khrushchev acted rationally – which is why the Cuban Missile Crisis is almost universally regarded as an American success story. Fortunately for the world, Nikita Khrushchev was not his predecessor Joseph Stalin, who on the eve of Germany's invasion

Colonel Oleg Vladimirovich Pen'kovskiy at his trial for espionage and treason in 1963.

of the Soviet Union two decades earlier refused to trust available intelligence on Hitler's Germany and ignored his advisors. Had Khrushchev been less rational, less well-informed about U.S. combat readiness, or convinced that he held an advantage, the outcome might have been a nuclear war.

Yet, Pen'kovskiy delivered numerous documents on other topics as well. Some of them concerned Soviet naval doctrine, a subject which by then was virtually unknown in the West. Although nobody paid much attention to these documents at the time of the Cuban Missile Crisis, U.S. naval intelligence analysts later on realised that they revealed the thinking behind the transformation of the Soviet Navy that currently was ongoing. Moreover, without the secret documents delivered by Pen'kovskiy, we would lack the means to understand the background of the incident, two decades later, when a Soviet Whiskey-class submarine ran aground in Swedish waters in 1981. Pen'kovskiy's documents reveal the background of the submarine's mission order, without which its actions and armament do not make sense.

The use of Pen'kovskiy's reports is particularly appropriate because there are conflicting interpretations of the submarine incident. The Soviets, at least in public, regarded it as a commonplace naval mission accidentally gone wrong. The Swedes, and most Western observers, were utterly convinced that the submarine was on an intelligence mission and under the control of the GRU.

1
THE SOVIET NAVY

Imperial Russia had maintained a navy since the seventeenth century and often used it to good effect. However, after the Russian Revolution in 1917, the new Soviet power focused its attention on the Red Army (until 1946 its formal name), and not the Navy. The Soviet fleets were merely tasked with territorial defence, the protection of those regions of the Soviet Union that were vulnerable to assault from the sea. This was quite understandable, since several Western powers, including Britain and the United States, landed intervention forces in the Soviet state during the civil war which followed the Revolution. The German invasion during the Second World War, too, showed the Soviet leadership the importance of fielding a strong army. For the early Soviet leaders, including Joseph Stalin (1878–1953), the best use of a navy was in support of the army, which in their view provided the real fighting force.

However, with the onset of the Cold War requirements changed. Now a nuclear superpower, the Soviet Union could no longer ignore the oceans that surrounded its great landmass. Henceforth, the Navy's missions would still include territorial defence against amphibious assault and enemy bombardment. The Navy would also continue to provide support to the Ground Forces. However, to these missions was added a new one: the mission to provide area defence against incursions into Soviet sea-space by enemy surface vessels and submarines – including, most importantly, those carrying strategic bombers armed with nuclear free-fall bombs and, somewhat later, missiles armed with nuclear warheads. With increasing ranges of engagement, it was no longer sufficient to adopt a defensive posture close to the shore. The Navy realised that enemy incursions of the new type would have to be met already on the high seas, at some distance from the Motherland. This became particularly urgent after the death of Stalin in 1953. His successor Nikita Khrushchev (1894–1971) ameliorated many of the destructive policies of his predecessor. No transformation of the Navy had been possible under the leadership of Stalin, who when it came to naval matters simply favoured more and larger conventional cruisers, destroyers, and medium-range submarines of the kind which had served him well during the war against Germany. It had not helped that Stalin also had a history of executing those who questioned his policy decisions.

Khrushchev knew that it was necessary to transform the Navy in line with the increased responsibilities gained under the conditions of the Cold War. Unlike Stalin, Khrushchev also saw the need to rely on missiles for national defence. He also wanted to improve the lives of ordinary citizens through a series of economic and agricultural reforms. For these two reasons, Khrushchev ordered major cuts in conventional forces. We know quite a lot about Soviet doctrine during the Cold War, because the Soviets published their naval doctrine from 1960 onwards in a special classified series of documents prepared by the top military command and intended only for army commanders or equivalent and officers above this level. This was the Special Collection of the premier Soviet military journal, *Voyennaya Mysl'* (Military Thought). The Central Intelligence Agency (CIA)

Nikita Sergeyevich Khrushchev, First Secretary of the Communist Party of the Soviet Union and Chairman of the Council of Ministers, that is, supreme leader of the Soviet Union until 1964.

Sergey Gorshkov, Admiral of the Fleet of the Soviet Union.

acquired a copy of the classified series of doctrinal documents, which the Agency then translated and analysed. Many of the early issues (1960–1962) were handed over by the aforementioned spy Oleg Pen'kovskiy. Parts of the translation have been declassified by the CIA, but the originals remain classified by the Russian Armed Forces.[1] In January 1956, Khrushchev appointed Sergey Gorshkov (1910–1988), a veteran of the Second World War, Admiral of the Fleet of the Soviet Union and Supreme Commander of Soviet Naval Forces. Gorshkov commanded the Navy until 1985. During his time in office, Gorshkov oversaw a massive naval buildup of surface and submarine vessels of new types and armaments and the expansion of the Soviet Navy into a modern force with a global presence. Gorshkov was the chief architect of the naval transformation and modernisation that henceforth took place in the Soviet Union.

The Carrier Threat
Gorshkov and his team early on realised that in the 1950s, the primary naval threat to the Soviet Union derived from U.S. carrier task forces which could move long-distance bombers armed with nuclear weapons into range of the Soviet landmass. The bombers onboard could reach deep into Soviet territory which enabled the bombing of most Soviet cities with nuclear weapons. The Soviets estimated that each U.S. carrier attack force would consist of three carriers, and that each carrier would carry some 140 nuclear bombs, which would be used during the first 72 hours of open warfare. Even if the Soviets managed to destroy 50 percent of the U.S. bombers, they still expected some 200 U.S. nuclear bombs to reach their targets on Soviet soil.[2]

Since the conventional naval set-up which derived from the Second World War was insufficient to counter the new threat, Gorshkov and his team introduced the first change in direction of the Soviet Navy since the Revolution: the introduction of what is best termed the anti-carrier programme. Realising that it would be difficult to shoot down every hostile strategic bomber, Gorshkov and his team instead chose to concentrate on weapon systems that would be able to destroy the aircraft carrier itself, before it arrived in range of the Soviet Motherland and the carrier's bombers could be ordered into the air. To destroy a carrier was, of course, no easy task, since carriers were huge warships and well-protected by the other ships of the carrier task force.

Gorshkov accordingly abandoned the construction of conventional cruisers, destroyers, and medium-range submarines in favour of the introduction of warships armed with missiles. While the new mission was added to the Navy's existing missions, all of which remained, the requirements of modern war meant that the Soviet design bureaus had to introduce new types of armament that would enable the anti-carrier role. For this reason, anti-ship missiles armed with nuclear warheads became a key component of the anti-carrier programme.

Moreover, Gorshkov re-built Naval Aviation around a new large force of land-based strategic bombers armed with anti-ship missiles. Henceforth, enemy carrier task forces would be met by a hard-hitting combination of, from the air, long-range Naval Aviation units armed with nuclear anti-ship missiles, from the surface, surface warships likewise armed with nuclear missiles, and from below, submarines armed with nuclear missiles as well as torpedoes with nuclear warheads.[3]

There would be no time for Soviet units to attack enemy naval bases or support vessels. During the very first hours of open warfare, Soviet Naval Aviation must focus on the enemy aircraft carriers. Soviet doctrine from this time onwards accordingly emphasised strategic jet bombers armed with anti-ship missiles with nuclear warheads as the key weapons system to deploy in the initial phase of combat. While submarines equipped with nuclear-armed torpedoes were important, too, they might not arrive in range in time to strike.

Gorshkov's reforms did not include the scrapping of already-existing and functional naval assets, only a re-focus in the construction of new ones. Torpedo-armed submarines remained potent weapons against U.S. carrier task forces, and especially so if they carried torpedoes with nuclear warheads. Henceforth, this became the primary mission of older types of diesel-electric submarines, including the type that the North Atlantic Treaty Organization (NATO) gave the reporting name Whiskey and which would play such a prominent part in the incident described in this book.

The Polaris Threat

A new major threat arose in the early 1960s. The mission remained the countering of seaborne nuclear delivery systems, yet the focus began to change. In 1960, the first submarines armed with submarine-launched ballistic missiles (SLBM) entered service with the U.S. Navy. This was the Ethan Allen-class submarine, with an armament of 16 Polaris missiles. The first unit was declared operational in November 1960. Henceforth, the Soviets realised, it was no longer sufficient to interdict and destroy the U.S. aircraft carriers; it would also be necessary to locate and destroy the U.S. missile-armed submarines which operated beyond Soviet sea-space, notably in the Norwegian Sea, the northern reaches of the North Sea, and the eastern Mediterranean.

Gorshkov and his team responded by initiating another major defence programme, that of antisubmarine warfare (ASW).

In the words of Captain Robert B. Bathurst of the U.S. Naval War College:

> The history of Soviet ASW efforts does not begin until the late 1950s because until then there was no real ASW problem. There was no requirement to protect convoys in coastal zones and there was not any great prospect of a submarine threat. Because there was no need to protect shipping on the high seas there was no concept of sea control except for the defensive rings in the Baltic, Black and Okhotsk seas. The Polaris threat abruptly forced the Soviet Navy to expand its operational art. New classes of ships, submarines, and airplanes were developed and became operational in the second half of the 1960s as the Soviets, to meet the threat, adopted an operational doctrine of combined systematic employment of all existing forces for antisubmarine warfare.[4]

Bathurst, a Second World War veteran, had followed Soviet naval affairs for years. He had served as assistant naval attaché in Moscow, was the former professor of intelligence (Layton Chair of Intelligence, 1972–1975) at the U.S. Naval War College, and presently served as professor of national security affairs at the same institution. We will return to his conclusions.

Soviet naval theorists based the antisubmarine warfare programme on previous experiences, in particular those of the Second World War. This led to them to conclude that antisubmarine warfare depended on the combined employment of all platforms for combating submarines, including a combination of surface vessels and aircraft.[5] Ultimately, the Soviet Navy also developed submarines suitable for antisubmarine warfare.

Moreover, the Soviet Navy began regular deployments of naval units to the aforementioned regions where submarines with Polaris missiles operated, which hitherto had not formed part of the traditional Soviet defensive zone. The antisubmarine warfare programme consisted of both naval and air assets. It also gave rise to a new major construction effort of new classes of surface ships. The Soviet Navy was less traditional and more willing to adapt to the new circumstances than most Western navies. For instance, with the introduction of guided missile armament, Gorshkov's team also abandoned the traditional system of ship classification in favour of a more descriptive system based on armament and mission type. Henceforth, a surface warship was referred to as a 'missile cruiser' (Russian: *raketnyy kreyser*, RKR), 'large missile ship' (*bol'shoy raketnyy korabl'*, BRK), or 'small missile ship' (*malyy raketnyy korabl'*, MRK), if she operated as a platform for surface-to-surface anti-ship missiles. If her role was antisubmarine warfare, she was instead called an 'antisubmarine warfare cruiser' (*protivolodochnyy kreyser*, PKR), 'large antisubmarine warfare ship' (*bol'shoy protivolodochnyy korabl'*, BPK), or 'small antisubmarine warfare ship' (*malyy protivolodochnyy korabl'*, MPK). Unlike the more tradition-bound Western navies, the Soviets no longer talked about destroyers and frigates. For this reason, Western naval analysts for years dithered over whether a given Soviet warship should be designated, say, a destroyer, missile destroyer, or frigate. Incidentally, Soviet ship classes were principally designed for offensive operations against either surface ships or submarines. Thus, they were primarily, or exclusively, armed with surface-to-surface missiles (SSM), not surface-to-air missiles (SAM). Neither of these classes were primarily intended for air defence operations, which was more efficiently handled by land-based air units.

Gorshkov explained his thoughts in his book on the sea power of the Soviet state:

> In the quest for ways of developing our navy, we avoided simply copying the fleet of the most powerful sea power of the world [the United States]. The composition of the navy, its weapons, ship designs, and organization of forces were determined primarily by the missions which the political leadership of the country assigned to the armed forces and consequently also to the navy, by the country's economic resources, and also by the conditions under which the navy had to accomplish these missions.[6]

Defence Zones

Western naval analysts often failed to understand Gorshkov's reforms. Instead, and despite Gorshkov's words, they assumed that the Soviets merely copied the navies of the West, and in particular the U.S. Navy. One of few Western naval analysts who did perceive what happened in the Soviet Union, the aforementioned Robert Bathurst, noted that

> The United States has been concerned in a traditional way with its ability to maintain sea lines of communication to Europe for the resupply of NATO. The Soviets … understood this as simply part of the overall strategy of preparing for the decisive war to destroy the socialist camp. Consequently, Soviet tactics involved moving out the perimeter of their defense in accordance with a strategic theory of defense zones… In the West it was not assumed that the Soviets really believed what they were saying about our intention to unleash a war for the destruction of the socialist camp. Other explanations were required, and most often they centered on the assumption that the Soviets themselves were preparing for an aggressive war, primarily one to break our sea lines of communication. The fact that they did not construct ships that seemed suitable for that mission was a constant mystery… As the Soviets could not be credited with believing the reality of their own positions – it was assumed that they were operating with perceptions that fit our assumptions and not theirs – it was

widely believed that they could not be serious about what they said. That assumption underlay much of our strategic and political thinking.⁷

What Bathurst argued against was the tendency to assume that Soviet plans and strategies were based on the same assumptions as those in the West – an analytical cognitive trap known as mirror-imaging. He also, correctly, argued than any analysis based on mirror-imaging was faulty. Soviet naval developments were never quite as slow as was commonly believed in the West. To cite Bathurst again:

> The Soviets were the first to begin building submarines modularly (that is in sections that were then welded together); in the early fifties the Soviets perfected the air-to-surface missile carried by the *Badger* bomber and introduced by 1956 a reconnaissance and strike aircraft with a range of 3,500 miles without refueling; in 1956 the Soviet *Zulu*-class submarine put to sea with a 250-mile ballistic missile to be followed by the first of a series of nuclear-propelled ballistic missile submarines, the *Hotel* class; in November 1957 the first *Sputnik* flew, and it was obviously designed for military, including naval reconnaissance uses. It was not until 1959 that *George Washington*, the United States first nuclear submarine FBM, was launched with sixteen 1,100-mile Polaris A1 missiles. The world's first surface-to-surface missile on a surface ship appeared on the *Kildin* which became operational in 1959. The first submarine with surface-to-surface missiles was the *Whiskey* class that appeared in 1958 and went through some modifications before the more sophisticated version, the *Juliet*, appeared in 1962.
>
> Furthermore, it should be recalled that the Soviets had begun writing about the revolution in military science at least as early as 1960. They were quite obviously oriented to the technical and operational changes that the possibility of missiles had introduced into naval warfare long before some Western navies, including our own, fully accommodated them.⁸

To the Soviets, coastal defence involved a layered defensive strategy. Missile cruisers and large missile ships would, together with the large submarine fleet, defend against enemy surface intrusions in open waters and with a particular emphasis on carrier task forces. In a similar manner, antisubmarine warfare cruisers and large antisubmarine warfare ships would defend against sub-surface intrusions in the same waters. Closer to the shore, small missile ships would engage surface intruders, while small antisubmarine warfare ships handled the sub-surface environment. Meanwhile, fast, mobile units of yet smaller vessels, each known as a 'missile boat' (*raketnyy kater*, RKA) or 'torpedo boat' (*torpednyy kater*, TKA), would operate in support, often in conjunction with vessels of similar or slightly larger size, each designated as a patrol ship (*storozhevoy korabl'*, SKR). Most of the vessels intended for operations close to the shore were capable of minelaying in addition to their primary mission. Meanwhile, land-based air units would handle general reconnaissance as well as antisubmarine warfare duties, provide air defence, and with regard to intruding carrier forces, carry out air strikes with missiles armed with nuclear warheads. Any intruder would meet a multifaceted, hostile environment.

By the mid-1970s, Gorshkov's initiatives to reform the Soviet Navy were mostly completed. The anti-carrier programme and the subsequent antisubmarine warfare programme had expanded the Soviet Navy into a powerful, modern ocean-going force. The Soviet Union possessed a powerful fleet of submarines, including many armed with ballistic missiles, a couple of helicopter cruisers, and a soon-to-be operational aircraft carrier. At this time, Gorshkov wrote, clearly with some pride, about the utility to the Soviet state of his blue-water navy:

> We may assert that a state bounded by the sea, which does not have a navy corresponding to its importance in the world, thereby shows its relative economic weakness. Thus, each ship of a navy is a relative indication of the level of development of science, technology, and industry in a given country and an indicator of its real military might.⁹

Nonetheless, the Navy's emphasis remained on coastal defence of the Motherland. For this purpose, a major share of the force consisted of missile cruisers, missile ships, and submarines on the one hand and antisubmarine warfare cruisers and antisubmarine warfare ships on the other. These were supplemented and supported by the aforementioned fast missile boats and torpedo boats.

While Western navies were slow to pay attention to Gorshkov's reforms, U.S. intelligence had by the mid-1970s mostly understood Gorshkov's doctrine. In 1975, the CIA summarised the Soviet naval stance:

> The principal forces to be employed were cruise missile and torpedo attack submarines and missile-equipped strike aircraft. These were to establish a defense in depth against Western carrier task forces attempting to penetrate to within striking range of the USSR. Defense against Western ballistic missile submarines was to be accomplished by a combination of antisubmarine barriers and area searches by submarines and aircraft.¹⁰

U.S. intelligence had also noted that the Soviet Union and the Warsaw Pact invariably would employ nuclear weapons against enemy carrier task forces and ballistic missile submarines, even in a war that possibly began with a phase of conventional warfare. These targets were simply too dangerous to leave alone, since

> The enemy [NATO], under conditions of a critical situation, may go over to the employment of nuclear weapons … Therefore, it is necessary to use all means [already during a possible conventional phase] to destroy his launchers and nuclear delivery aircraft … engage in joint operations of naval and long-range aircraft to destroy the main forces of the enemy fleet, especially missile submarines … [and] aircraft carriers … ¹¹

Bathurst has summarised Soviet naval strategy during the Cold War in the following terms:

> …there have been, roughly, three periods of postwar Soviet strategy. The first was the initial aftermath of the war when the Soviet Union was in a condition of strategic and economic inferiority. The Soviet Navy was limited to the mission of protecting the flanks of the army and of patrolling Soviet waters and coastlines because of extreme shortages in manpower and in the economy… After 1953, planning for a change in missions was begun. It was based upon the adoption of nuclear power and heavy emphasis on missile warfare. Tactics

were developed for moving the defense perimeter further out to sea. The threat from aircraft and naval ballistic missile submarines had led to the need to establish zones of defense further from Moscow, even at the 1,500 kilometer mark, to develop successful antisubmarine warfare and to provide air cover for theaters of action from Soviet air bases.

With the successful development of missiles and rockets – the revolution in military affairs that the Soviets emphasize constantly – they began introducing new tactics for the destruction of Western fleets in specific areas and new strategies for winning, or at least breaking up and neutralizing, the Third World.[12]

Fleet Organisation

There were subtle differences between the four Soviet Fleets. The Northern Fleet, based in Severomorsk in the Arctic Kola Peninsula, focused on ocean-going antisubmarine warfare units and was also the home of most nuclear-powered submarines. The Black Sea Fleet, with headquarters in Sevastopol, had begun operations in the Mediterranean. In comparison, the Pacific Fleet, based in Vladivostok, which had developed into a blue-water fleet under Stalin remained geographically hemmed in by the Japanese islands and the Korean Peninsula. For this reason, it by this time received few modern ocean-going warships.

The oldest of the Soviet Fleets, the Baltic, with its headquarters in Kaliningrad and primary port in Baltiysk, remained focused on coastal defence against the Soviet Union's host of enemies on the Western front. It did not openly display the same interest in ocean-going antisubmarine warfare operations as did the Northern Fleet. Nor did its units regularly deploy to foreign waters, as the Black Sea Fleet did in the Mediterranean. It happened, but comparatively seldom. NATO observers frequently dismissed the Baltic Fleet as a 'mere coastal defence force'.[13] Indeed, U.S. intelligence focused elsewhere, which would suggest that the Baltic held little of interest. Yet, the comparative inattention displayed by U.S. intelligence in the Baltic was not a sign of neglect, but of the existing close cooperation between U.S. intelligence on the one hand and the intelligence services of partner countries such as West Germany, Denmark, and last but not least, Sweden, with which the United States since 1952 maintained a secret alliance according to the terms of which the Americans treated Sweden on a parity basis with the NATO member-states.[14]

Within a Fleet, the vessels were divided into what might best be translated squadrons (*diviziya*, pl. *divizii*; a former term still in occasional use was *eskadra*, pl. *eskadry*), brigades (*brigada*, pl. *brigady*), divisions (*divizion*, pl. *diviziony*), and detachments (*otryad*, pl. *otryady*). A squadron consisted of a large number of vessels of different classes, which were under the same command and expected to operate together. For this reason, the different vessels of the squadron generally had similar characteristics with regard to speed and range. The squadron was commonly subdivided into brigades, each of which consisted of from two to four divisions. A division typically consisted of three or four surface warships of the same, or similar, class, although a submarine division could consist of about 10 submarines. It follows that a division's vessels also concentrated on one specific mission, such as missile attack or antisubmarine warfare. A detachment, finally, customarily consisted of a small group of vessels – a task force – which temporarily operated together, for instance during an exercise.

A Fleet consisted of other organisational components, too. Its integral Naval Aviation component has already been mentioned, but the Navy also included integral Naval Infantry, with each Fleet having an allocated Naval Infantry force of at least regimental strength. Furthermore, the Navy included coastal missile and artillery units in some locations. A Fleet's naval bases constituted independent units, as did the various support services, including signals, emergency rescue service, and so on.

The Navy and RYaN

The next major change came in 1981. While Gorshkov's reforms were completed during the period of détente that occurred in the 1970s, the détente was followed by heightened tensions between the two pacts – a period sometimes called the Second Cold War. The Soviet intervention in Afghanistan in 1979 was only one of several consequences of this.[15] The leadership of the Soviet Union, the Politburo, suspected that Ronald Reagan, who became U.S. president in 1981, planned a surprise first strike with nuclear weapons. The Politburo and Yuriy Andropov, the chairman of the intelligence service KGB who within less than two years would become General Secretary of the Communist Party and thus supreme leader of the Soviet Union, therefore formulated a covert response. They ordered the KGB and its military counterpart, the GRU, to follow up, within the framework of a joint, covert intelligence operation against what was termed RYaN (*Raketno-Yadernoye Napadeniye*, nuclear missile attack) any signs of such attack plans from the United States and NATO member-states. The operation began in May 1981 and did not wind down until the summer of 1984 – and RYaN reporting continued until 1989. Indeed, similar operations continued right up to the dissolution of the Soviet Union in 1991.[16] If signs of imminent nuclear attack were identified, the combat readiness of the Soviet nuclear forces was naturally raised in turn. The Motherland must be able to fight back, and with immediate effect. There was therefore always a risk that some incident might trigger a pre-emptive nuclear attack.

These activities, of course, in turn worried the Western powers, including Sweden. In short, every action resulted in countermeasures, which in turn increased suspicion between the two blocs. As Bengt Gustafsson, Swedish supreme commander 1986–1994, observed: 'Nobody could fail to notice the increasing tension between the pacts from the late 1970s onwards.'[17]

Operation RYaN was little, if at all, known in the West by October 1981. When the Soviet Whiskey-class submarine *S-363* left port in mid-September 1981, the KGB and GRU were heavily involved in setting up, and delivering, RYaN reporting. Yet, they had only been engaged in this task for four months, and it remains unclear how much the new reporting strategy at this point had influenced naval operations. Besides, operation RYaN did not target Sweden, since Sweden had no nuclear first strike weapons.

2
THE SUBMARINE

The *S-363* was an attack submarine of the class that the Soviet Union designated Project 613. In the West, the class was better known as Whiskey, which was its NATO reporting name. The *S-363* was built in Leningrad (in post-Soviet Russia again St. Petersburg) in 1956 at the Ordzhonikidze Shipyard, which was the official Soviet name for what once had been (and in post-Soviet Russia again is) the Baltic Iron Ship Building and Engineering Company (*Baltiyskiy zavod*). The Soviet Union referred to the *S-363* as a medium-sized diesel-electric submarine. The *S-363* was not a modern submarine. It was one of 215 vessels of its class built from 1951 to 1957, and the submarine had been in service for 24 years. Some of its crew were not yet born when the *S-363* entered into service. The design was even older. The class known as Project 613 derived from the German Type XXI submarine, a design developed during the Second World War. The first XXI unit was completed in 1944. The Soviets made the captured staff at the Schichau Yard in Danzig (modern-day Gdańsk) finish the five units which already had been laid down and then moved the production facilities and skilled staff to the Soviet Union for further development.

The Type XXI was a very successful design, which similarly inspired other countries, too. Major features of the design were copied during the development of the American *Tang*, British *Porpoise* and *Oberon*, French *Narval*, and Swedish *Hajen III* classes of submarines. Sweden developed the *Hajen III* independently, having salvaged its own Type XXI, the U 3503 which by the end of the war was abandoned and scuttled by its crew off Gothenburg.

The submarine design employed both diesel engines and electric engines. Diesel engines demanded a plentiful air supply, so were used only when the submarine was surfaced or could rely on the snorkel tube for air intake. The diesel engines were also very noisy, which obviously made them unsuitable from a stealth perspective. The two small high-rotation propellers produced plenty of sound, too, but this was unavoidable with the configuration (in comparison, Sweden built submarines with only one large, low-rotation propeller to reduce sound). During combat operations, the submarine relied on its electric engines to maintain silence to the extent that this was possible.

TECHNICAL CHARACTERISTICS OF THE S-363

Designation: *S-363*
Vessel type: Medium-sized diesel-electric attack submarine
Soviet project designation ('class'): Project 613
NATO reporting name: Whiskey
Bort number at the time of the incident: 137
Builder: Ordzhonikidze (formerly Baltic) Shipyard No. 189, Leningrad
Laid down: 12 January 1956
Launched: 16 November 1956
Commissioned: 17 September 1957

Service:
- Red Banner Northern Fleet: 26 September 1957
- Twice Red Banner Baltic Fleet: 20 August 1966
- Mothballed in Daugavgriva, Soviet Latvia: 21 September 1968
- Overhaul in Liepaja, Soviet Latvia: 29 November 1979 to 24 February 1981
- Re-entered service: 24 February 1981
- Organisation: 75th Submarine Division, 157th Submarine Brigade, 14th Submarine Squadron
- Military unit: v/ch 56084
- Home port: Liepaja, Soviet Latvia
- Decommissioned: 17 July 1988 (crew disbanded on 1 October)
- Scrapped: probably in late 1988 in Tallinn

Displacement:
- Surface displacement: 1,048 tons
- Underwater displacement: 1,345 tons

Dimensions:
- Length: 76 metres
- Beam: 6.3 metres
- Height: 11 metres
- Draught: 4.55 metres

Speed:
- Surfaced: 18.25kts
- Submerged: 13.1kts
- Economy mode (submerged): about 2.5kts

Operating depth: 170 metres
Maximum regulation depth: 200 metres
Maximum range: 12,000 to 15,000nm
Operational radius: 3,000nm
Fuel: 115 tons
Autonomy: 30 days
- Propulsion:
- 2x 2,000hp 37D diesel engines
- 2x 1,350hp PG-101 electric main engines
- 2x 50hp PG-103 electric engines for economy mode
- 2x 112-cell 46SU batteries
- 2 propeller shafts

Navigation:
- Kurs-3 gyrocompass (installed 1956)
- GON magnetic compass (installed 1956)
- LR-5 log, that is, pressure speedometer (installed 1957)
- ARP-53 radio direction finder (from 1972)
- PIRS-1 receiver for signals from the commercial Decca Navigator System (installed 1980/1981)

Electronics:
- MRK-50 Flag (NATO reporting name Snoop Plate) surface surveillance radar (probably installed 1956/1957)
- NEL-5 echo sounding unit in bow for active sonar (from 1978)
- MG-10M hydrophone listening array in bow for passive sonar
- Nakat radar warning receiver
- Fakel-MO-1 mutual warning and identification (IFF) system
- HF radios of unknown type and VHF radios R-811 and R-903
- Underwater telephone of unknown type

Armament:
- 4x forward and 2x aft 533mm torpedo tubes
- 14 torpedoes, as follows:
  * 2x SAET-60M nuclear torpedoes
  * 2x SAET-60M conventional torpedoes
  * 6x SET-53M anti-submarine warfare conventional torpedoes
  * 4x 53-65K conventional torpedoes

Personal weapons for crew:
10x AKM (Kalashnikov) 7.62 x 39mm assault rifles
1x RPK (Kalashnikov) 7.62 x 39mm machine gun
1x PM (Makarov) 9 x 18mm pistol per officer, individually issued

Crew: 52 (standard)
       56 (in October 1981)
       59 (according to the Swedish reading of the vessel's logbook)

Based on various, sometimes conflicting sources.
   Note that distances at sea are measured in nautical miles (nm) and cable lengths. One nautical mile equals 1,852 m. One tenth of a nautical mile (185.2 m) constitutes one cable length.

Submarines of the Project 613 class. Notable are very different modifications of the sail introduced over the time on different vessels from this series, as well as the process of loading torpedoes via a hatch in the forward deck. (Author's collection)

Most of the navigation equipment and some electronics were old. Some of the original gear from 1956 remained in operation. Later observers, including Swedish officers, described them as rusty, scratched, and in poor condition.

Older types of submarines such as those of Project 613 were employed for combat duties that were complementary to that of more modern vessels, yet corresponded to established doctrine. We have seen that Soviet doctrine regarded U.S. aircraft carrier groups as a serious threat, because the bombers onboard were armed with nuclear weapons and could reach deep into Soviet territory. As a countermeasure, the Soviet Navy therefore primarily intended to use aircraft-borne nuclear-armed anti-ship missiles to destroy large ship targets at sea, such as these U.S. aircraft carriers.[1]

Yet, Soviet doctrine still envisaged a combat role for submarines. Most attention was given to nuclear-powered missile-armed submarines, since these clearly held an advantage over older types. Already by the 1960s, the Soviet Navy realised that diesel-electric attack submarines were extremely limited in combat capabilities with regard to carrier groups. This particularly concerned closed sea theatres, such as the Baltic. For this reason, they proposed that the tactics of 'lying in wait' and barrier patrols were the best deployment of this type of submarine. Moreover, the Soviets increased their combat capability considerably through the widespread use of torpedoes with nuclear warheads.[2] This role suited the old diesel-electric submarines, including those of Project 613. The former head of the Pacific Fleet, the highly experienced Admiral Yuriy Panteleyev (who joined the navy in 1918 and became a submariner already in 1925), wrote in 1961:

> The submarine fleet possesses incomparably great capabilities for combat with the aircraft carrier strike units [Russian: AUS, *Avianosnoye udarnoye soyedineniye*]. It may be deployed in complete secrecy, during the period of exacerbation of the military-political situation, to those very areas of the ocean or sea, designated by the enemy as zones for the deployment of his forces for a strike against our installations. And it may very well be that the enemy aircraft will not have time to take off for the delivery of a strike, as they will go to the bottom together with their 'airfield' after being attacked by nuclear weapons of the submarine forces which had been covertly deployed beforehand in the appropriate areas of the ocean or sea.[3]

Admiral Panteleyev continued:

> … submarine forces can occupy necessary waiting positions and from them conduct covert and prolonged observation of the enemy.[4]

Some NATO member-state navies noted that Soviet submarines of the Project 613 class from the Baltic Fleet in the 1960s and 1970s regularly exited the Baltic Sea on 30-day missions to take up this kind of waiting position off naval bases such as Clyde (Faslane) in Scotland, the home of U.S. and British nuclear submarines, and Brest in France, which at the time developed to service U.S. aircraft carriers and also housed nuclear submarines. At some point, these navies informed Swedish naval intelligence that the orders of this recurring 'Whiskey patrol' was to report the departure and arrival of their submarines and, in case of war, to carry out attacks with nuclear-armed torpedoes.[5]

In the Baltic Sea, the bottleneck formed by the Straits between Denmark and Sweden gave the U.S. Navy little choice for the selection of deployment zone. Any carrier group, or indeed any other naval task force, that wanted to penetrate the Soviet defences from this direction would have by bypass the Danish island of Bornholm, located between the Swedish and German shores. For this reason, the waters just northeast and southeast of Bornholm formed the preferred killing zone for Soviet submarines of Project 613. There, they could patrol or lie in wait until their target finally appeared, revealing itself. The submarine did not have to employ fancy sensors to locate a target, it only needed to stay hidden. As an additional boon, this task also enabled the old Project 613 submarines to contribute to the antisubmarine warfare mission by participating in the increasingly important mission to detect hostile submarines moving into the Baltic Sea. Baltic Fleet submariners designated the two overlapping patrol areas as P-1 and P-2. They had the following coordinates:[6]

Area P-1
55°20'0"N 16°43'0"E
55°13'0"N 16°49'0"E
54°51'0"N 15°33'0"E
54°58'0"N 15°27'0"E

Area P-2
55°21'0"N 16°53'0"E
55°14'0"N 16°50'0"E
55°22'0"N 15°29'0"E
55°29'0"N 15°32'0"E

When displayed on a navigational chart, areas P-1 and P-2 looked like a pair of trousers. For this reason, Baltic Fleet submariners nicknamed the two areas 'the trousers'. When they began the mission, they customarily said that they 'went into the trousers'.

In addition to submarines, the Soviet Navy always deployed a surface vessel as a picket and forward observer at the entry point to the Baltic Sea, which in Navy terminology was called the DOZK-57 line (from Russian: *korabel'nyy dozor*, 'ship patrol'). The picket was located in-between Bornholm, Rügen in East Germany, Møn in Denmark, and Trelleborg (Smygehuk) in Sweden. Each vessel so deployed remained on this duty for about a month, frequently anchored, and was then relieved by another vessel. The Soviet Navy called a ship with this assignment *brandvakhta* (an old term meaning 'fire-watch'), but Soviet sailors, fully aware of what the duty meant to them, gave such a ship the nickname 'green boredom' (*zelyonaya toska*). Swedish sailors customarily referred to the Soviet picket vessel as *vakthunden* ('the watch-dog').

It takes time to change an existing military doctrine and introduce new weapon systems. It easily takes 10 years or more from decision to completion of a new warship or combat aircraft. In 1981, major parts of the Soviet Armed Forces, in particular its older components, remained dimensioned after the threat as it was perceived during the 1960s. Baltic Fleet Headquarters knew that diesel submarines like Project 613 were obsolete. Nobody in his right mind would give one of these old submarines a high-priority mission that might determine the fate of the Motherland. The Soviet Union had more modern submarines and strike aircraft for operations in the Atlantic and Arctic. Yet, the Project 613 submarines formed part of the fleet and accordingly received missions that conformed to established doctrine, yet were within their capabilities. These mission types are detailed in the Combat Regulations of the Soviet Navy.[7] Predictably, the Combat Regulations emphasise the threat from ballistic missile submarines:

When at sea, every submarine (surface ship, aircraft, helicopter) with the means to detect and destroy submarines must, regardless of the task to be performed, be ready to conduct combat actions to destroy enemy submarines independently, within a large unit (group), and in cooperation with other types of forces of the Navy... Prior to the initiation of military actions, the search for enemy submarines is carried out in the course of antisubmarine search operations and systematic search actions.[8]

We will see that by 1981, the antisubmarine warfare mission had become routine and was even pre-printed in the Soviet Navy forms used for filling in mission orders. Another routine precaution was that each mission order by then specified how the chain of command would be implemented if a given unit was obliged to embark upon an antisubmarine warfare mission. The Combat Regulations provide the details:

The direct control of ASW forces in one area (on one line) is exercised by the commander of the search forces, designated from among the commanders of the surface ship large units. The commander of the search forces exercises control over attached ships and aircraft (helicopters) after they cross a specified line and two-way communications are established.[9]

Yet again, the limited capabilities of the Project 613 submarines were well known. The Combat Regulations make clear that they should not really be employed in high-threat environments, such as in the Atlantic and Arctic:

Diesel submarines conduct combat actions in areas with a weak ASW defense and also on the approaches to our own coast.[10]

When it came to the original high-priority mission, that of combat against U.S. carrier task forces, the Combat Regulations emphasised the need to search for the enemy in the assigned area (or line) in a concealed manner.[11] The Combat Regulations reiterated the need to destroy enemy aircraft carriers:

Enemy aircraft carriers in transit to combat action areas at the outbreak of war must be destroyed by strikes from submarines, naval missile-carrying aviation, and long-range aviation before the carriers reach the point where the attack aircraft based aboard them can take off... In order to destroy aircraft carriers located in combat maneuver areas at the outset of war, submarines operate from their tracking positions... tasks are also performed to ... prevent the entry of additional enemy ship groupings into seas and ocean areas contiguous to our shores, blockade straits ...[12]

In short, there were plenty of tasks to carry out even for obsolete submarines, whether the targets were aircraft carriers that penetrated the Baltic Sea through the Great Belt in Danish waters (for instance, the HMS *Bulwark* (R08) in 1971 and 1973 and USS *Intrepid* (CVS-11) in 1971 and 1972) or other high-value warships such as amphibious landing fleets or battleship task forces. Swedish signals intelligence (SIGINT) reporting from the years 1945 to 1951 demonstrates that the Soviets then perceived Western landing fleets, including those that might set out from Swedish ports, as a serious threat, and documents brought to the West by Colonel Ghulam Dastagir Wardak, an Afghan defector, show that the Soviet General Staff Academy as late as in the mid-1970s still considered this a threat.[13] In short, Moscow fully expected NATO to launch an invasion of Soviet territory as soon as the time was ripe. While the looming threat of intruding carrier groups grew increasingly unlikely over time, in 1985 U.S. President Ronald Reagan sent the huge battleship USS *Iowa* (BB-61) with a task force into the Baltic Sea as part of the large NATO exercise BALTOPS (short for Baltic Operations) as if to confirm the Soviet threat assessment.

A Swedish source also seemingly confirms that the carrier threat in 1981 still dominated the threat perception in the submarine arm of the Baltic Fleet. A retired representative of Swedish Armed Forces intelligence years later claimed that an unidentified former Soviet naval officer had told him that the *S-363* carried a new type of nuclear-armed torpedo which was developed for use against various, unspecified types of enemy vessels.[14] Perhaps the unidentified source was the *S-363*'s political officer Vasiliy Besedin, who quite openly seems to have mentioned the new type of torpedo nuclear warhead to a journalist from a Swedish daily in 2006.[15] But before then, in a discussion with Swedish officers in Karlskrona already in 2001, Besedin hinted at which targets the nuclear torpedoes were designed for. He said that their submarine had to carry nuclear torpedoes because their guidance systems were poor and the targets so 'big' that maximum explosive power was required.[16] The Swedish officers jumped to the conclusion that Naval Base Karlskrona was the intended target. However, it seems obvious to the author of this book that what Besedin described was a carrier group. Besedin's comment accordingly confirms the expected tasks of the old submarine.

First compartment of the Project-613 class, left side, including torpedo controls. (1979; Author's collection)

Second compartment, signals section. (Corporal V. L. Afanas'yev, 1969; web site www.submarines.narod.ru)

Fifth compartment: The two 37D diesel engines. (Author's collection)

Hatch between sixth and seventh compartments. (1979; Author's collection.)

The Crew

The *S-363* belonged to 75th Submarine Division of 157th Submarine Brigade, under Captain First Rank Ivan Buchak with his command post in Paldiski, Soviet Estonia.[17] The vessel's home port, however, was Liepaja (now Liepāja) in Soviet Latvia.

The four senior officers of the command crew of a submarine of Project 613 were the commanding officer, the political officer who because of his loyalty to the Communist Party simultaneously served as deputy commander, the executive officer, and the chief engineer.

The senior command crew of the *S-363* were mostly new appointees to their respective positions. This was neither a coincidence nor surprising. We have seen that the old submarine was mothballed for more than 10 years, from September 1968 to November 1979. The *S-363* was then taken out of storage and overhauled, only re-entering service on 24 February 1981. Since the old submarine then had no command crew, it was natural to man it mostly with up-and-coming officers awaiting their first command.

The commanding officer of the *S-363* was Captain Third Rank Anatoliy Gushchin (b. 1946).[18] He was the son of farmers near Tambov in Russia. Trained at the Higher School of Outgoing Boats in Leningrad, Gushchin was accepted for independent command of a submarine of Project 613 in 1977. He was appointed to this position in December 1980, and took formal command of the *S-363* on 20 January 1981, an appointment that became effective when the submarine re-entered service in February 1981. He was then the youngest commander in 157th Submarine Brigade. Gushchin was married, with a daughter and a baby son. The voyage that ended up in Swedish waters was his first as submarine commander. Possibly because of this lack of experience, Gushchin often came across as silent and introspective, bordering on morose.

The political officer and deputy commander of the *S-363* was Captain-Lieutenant Vasiliy Besedin (b. 1952).[19] A political officer had special responsibility for the political education, morale, and spiritual well-being of the crew.[20] Invariably a Communist Party member, the political officer was tasked with ensuring that the crew followed socialist dogma as decided by the Party leadership in Moscow. He supervised the Party organisation and conducted party political work within his unit. The political officer also lectured the crew on Marxism-Leninism, the Party's view of international affairs, and the Party's tasks for the armed forces. Besedin, a Ukrainian, received initial navigation training at the Kiev Higher Military-Political School, from which he graduated in 1974. Like Gushchin, he was appointed to this post during the overhaul of the *S-363* before the mission. Most of what we know about the daily activities onboard the *S-363* derive from later interviews with Besedin, who also published his memoirs about the incident. Besedin seems not to have been overly zealous with regard to socialist dogma, and appears to have been outgoing and made friends easily. He comes across more as a counsellor to the crew than a political worker. Besedin was married, with two young children.

Senior Lieutenant Viktor Yakovlev served as executive officer of the *S-363*.[21] Very little information has been released about Yakovlev. This is unsurprising; while he was a senior member of the command crew, for formal reasons he was little more than an aide to the commanding officer and certainly not his deputy in the chain of command. The executive officer on a Soviet naval vessel was a career naval officer. Unlike the political officer, who reported to the chief of the Political Directorate of the Navy, the executive officer answered to the regular chain of command. Of course, most officers were members of the Communist Party, since this in all but name was a prerequisite for a successful career as a military officer. Yet, Yakovlev's job was first and foremost that of a naval professional.

Then there was the chief engineer.[22] The command structure for a warship encompassed a number of shipboard departments, each known as a combat unit. Engineering was such a department, and it was headed by the chief engineer. On the *S-363*, this position was held by Senior Lieutenant Mikhail Arkhipov. He was responsible for engines and most technical systems onboard the submarine. Very little information has been released about him, too.[23]

The same goes for Senior Lieutenant Vladimir Pershin, head of the department for mines and torpedoes on the *S-363*. Very little information has been released about Pershin. Being a key officer for the submarine's combat duties, he formed part of the officers who headed the respective four-hour duty shifts. Each kept watch twice a day in the submarine's central command post (when the boat was submerged) or on the upper deck bridge (after surfacing) At sea, Besedin, Yakovlev, and Pershin took turns for this task, mostly but not invariably according to the following schedule: Midnight to 4:00 a.m.: Besedin; 4:00 a.m. to 8:00 a.m.: Pershin; 8:00 a.m. to 12 a.m.: Yakovlev; 12:00 a.m. to 4:00 p.m.: Besedin; 4:00 p.m. to 8 p.m.: Pershin; and finally, 8:00 p.m. to midnight: Yakovlev.

Because the voyage was Captain Gushchin's first as submarine commander, he was accompanied by a mentor: Captain First Rank Iosif Avrukevich (b. 1940), the chief of staff of 157th Submarine Brigade in Paldiski. Avrukevich, a Belarusian, was an experienced submariner. Accepted for independent command of a submarine of Project 613 in 1969, he held such commands until he was appointed to the position of chief of staff in August 1976, after graduation from the Naval Academy. His previous position was that of deputy commander of the Paldiski Submarine Brigade. Avrukevich was the highest-ranking officer onboard, but he was not in formal command; this position was held by Gushchin. Besedin later claimed that Gushchin from the outset in word and deed showed that it was he, not Avrukevich, who was in command, and that Avrukevich addressed Gushchin as 'chief'.[24] In his position as chief of staff and mentor, Avrukevich occasionally took part in submarine missions in the Baltic, North Sea, and Atlantic. He was well versed in navigation, but perhaps his skills were a bit rusty. He was apparently the only man onboard who had a working knowledge (limited as it was) of German and English. Avrukevich was married with two daughters. He was confident and vociferous. Avrukevich was somewhat older than the other officers. Yet, Swedes who met Avrukevich described him as 'youthful' in behaviour and intellect.[25]

Avrukevich's presence on the *S-363* may have made Gushchin feel safer and more confident, but it also meant that one of the four officers of the senior command crew had to give up his narrow cabin in the second compartment to the mentor. This became Besedin, who had to move to a crewman's bunk in the seventh compartment. He chose the seventh compartment since it contained an emergency exit hatch. The submarine had a total of seven compartments, divided by strong waterproof bulkheads.

A key role for the mission was for obvious reasons played by Senior Lieutenant Anatoliy Korostov, the chief navigator of the submarine.[26] The chief navigator was important for mission success but not a member of the senior command crew. He was more of a technical specialist. Korostov was appointed to the position in August 1979 and accepted for independent command in this position in March 1981. The voyage that ended up in Swedish waters was his first as chief navigator.

From this description it is obvious that most command-level officers were new in their positions, having been appointed in early 1981 when the *S-363* re-entered service. It was really only Avrukevich who had the required prior experience of independent command, and his task was that of a mentor, not a commander or navigator. Besides, he had spent the last five years as chief of staff, with only limited forays at sea.

Most of the crew consisted of young conscripts. Some had only recently concluded their first dive, an event which in the Soviet submarine fleet by tradition was celebrated with the presentation and drinking of a mug of undiluted seawater. Commander Karl Andersson of the Swedish Navy, who eventually would handle most daily negotiations with the Soviet crew, in old Navy manner described the conscripts as 'farmhands' and said that they appeared awkward and inexperienced. He said that of those Soviet submariners whom he met regularly, only Avrukevich and Besedin seemed to know what they were doing.[27]

The S-363 having re-entered service, the crew's first task was to make sure that the vessel was fully functional. This was also a means to test the command crew. The overhauled submarine's first mission of the year was accordingly a trial voyage followed by routine training exercises. All went well. Having accomplished the initial trial voyage, the submarine and crew participated in an exercise in which the submarine successfully identified a 'hostile' ship and, without being detected by the antisubmarine warfare ships nearby, simulated the launch of a torpedo at the target. By the end of the summer, all systems were assessed as operational, and Captain Gushchin and his crew were deemed ready to set out from Baltiysk on a live mission.

Captain Anatoliy Gushchin. (Medström)

3
THE VOYAGE BEGINS

On the night before Captain Gushchin and the officers of the S-363 embarked upon their first live mission together, they celebrated the coming voyage in the Golden Anchor, a popular Baltiysk restaurant. They toasted in vodka in the traditional manner of Soviet submariners, expressing their hope that the number of surfacings would equal the number of dives.[1]

Mission orders were to patrol the customary area east of the Danish island of Bornholm in submerged position between 16 September (with a scheduled departure at 6:00 p.m.) and 5 November 1981 (with a scheduled return to base at 8:00 a.m.), while maintaining permanent combat readiness to launch torpedoes against designated targets.[2] They were forbidden to go closer to foreign territorial waters than five nautical miles (nine km).[3] Neither the Soviet Navy nor, later, the political officer Besedin ever released additional details on the mission, such as which were the designated targets or exactly from which position they hoped to accomplish this. Such details were, for obvious reasons, highly classified. However, based on the type of submarine, known mission parameters, and the known mission types of Soviet diesel-electric submarines like the S-363 it seems highly likely that the mission strictly followed doctrine, that is, to patrol the killing zone east of Bornholm in readiness to launch torpedoes with nuclear warheads against an intruding U.S. carrier group or similar high-value target, in case war broke out during the mission. Notably, combat against U.S. carrier groups remained a key task as late as in the 1986 Combat Regulations of the Soviet Navy.[4] We also know that the S-363, like virtually all combat units of the Navy, had the detection of hostile submarines as the secondary (although in 1981 admittedly far more likely) mission. This was known as 'Monitoring of foreign submarines in patrol areas' and was indeed pre-printed on the mission order form then employed by the Navy.

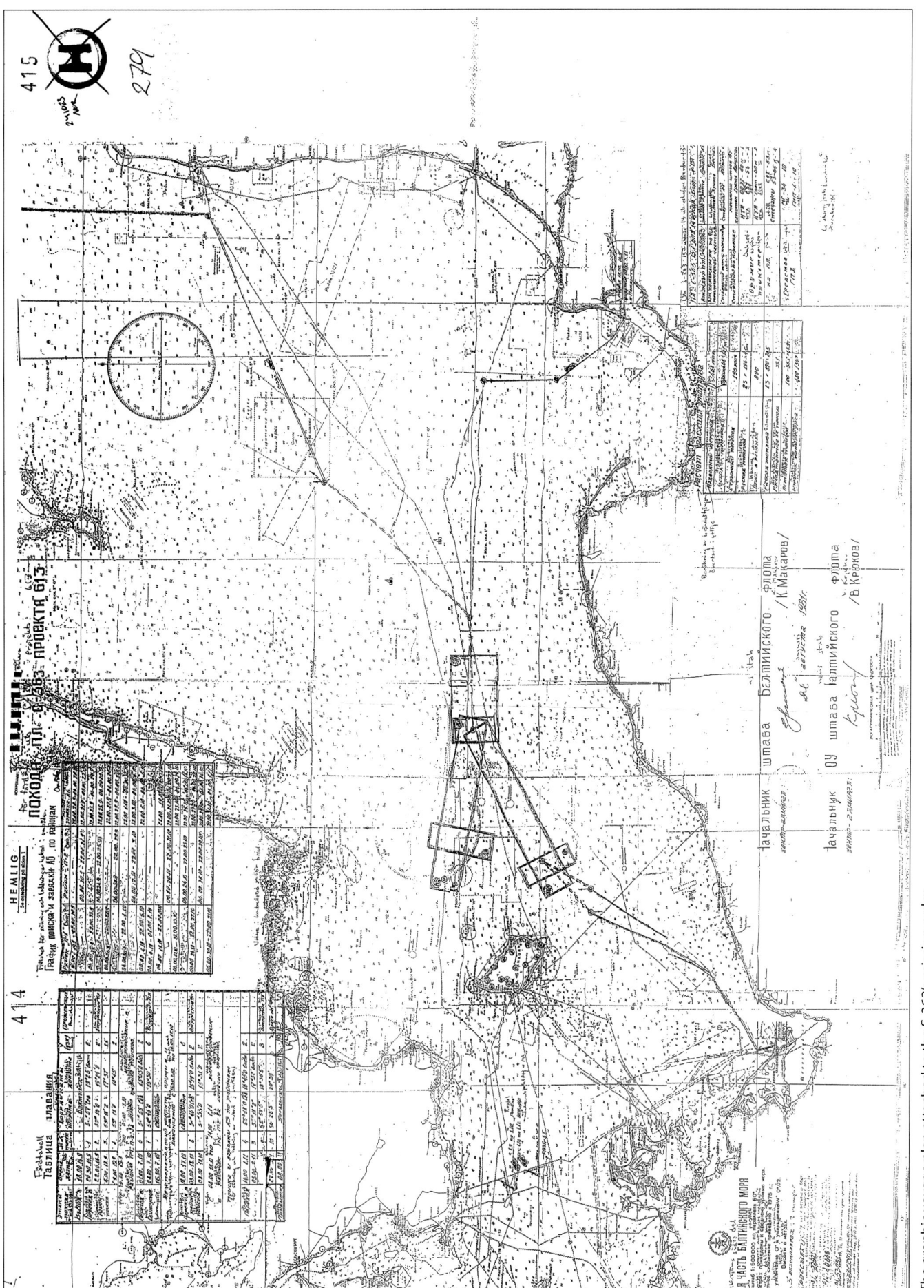

The graphic voyage plan attached to the S-363's mission order.

Экз. № 2

КОМАНДИРУ ПЛ "С-363"

**ШТАБ
ДВАЖДЫ
КРАСНОЗНАМЁННОГО
Балтийского флота**
"28" 08. 1981 г.
№ 3/00105
Гор. Калининград, 100

**БОЕВОЕ РАСПОРЯЖЕНИЕ
БАЛТИЙСКОГО ФЛОТА
№ 0033/ОП**

г. Калининград
(Время московское) "27" августа 1981 г.

Карта № 21003
Издания 1975 года

*Дано разрешение на
выход ЗАС №3750/КП
от 11.9.81г.
Ком-гр Радкевич
14.9.81г.*

1. Деятельность ВМС иностранных государств в Балтийском море в соответствии с разведывательной картой и информацией КП БФ.

2. Боевую службу несут:

в Балтийском море мрзк "Редуктор" с 5.9 по 3.11.81
ПЛ "С-345" с 18.8 по 17.9

на линии ДОЗК-57 мт "С. Рошаль" с 1.9 по 1.10
мпк-140 с 1.10 по 1.11

3. З а д а ч и :

а) основная:
Поиск и слежение за иностранными подводными лодками в районах П-1; П-2

б) дополнительные задачи:
- разведка деятельности ВМС иностранных государств;
- выявление деятельности исследовательских судов;
- выявление интенсивности судоходства и рыболовства;
- совершенствование элементов задач Л-2, Л-3 КПЛ-75г.

Снята копия в одном экз.
3 3 92

- 2 -

5

408

4. Подводной лодке "С-363" выйти в море в 18.00 16.9 осуществить переходы и патрулирование в районах П-1; П-2 согласно графическому плану перехода.

Межпоходовый ремонт и отдых личного состава в Свиноустье

с 07 октября по 17 октября с.г.

Возвратиться в базу Палдиски 0800 5 ноября

Районы патрулирования:

№ П-1

Ш = 55°20'0 сев   Д = 16°43'0 Вост
Ш = 55°13'0   Д = 16°49'0
Ш = 54°57'0   Д = 15°33'0
Ш = 54°58'0   Д = 15°27'0

№ П-2

Ш = 55°21'0 Сев   Д = 16°53'0 Вост
Ш = 55°14'0   Д = 16°50'0
Ш = 55°22'0   Д = 15°29'0
Ш = 55°29'0   Д = 15°32'0

Способ маневрирования в районах на прямых и обратных галсах. Цикл патрулирования – 48 часов, поиск – 40 часов, зарядка АБ – 8 часов. Зарядку АБ осуществить в районах

№ ЗА

Ш = 55°10'5 Сев   Д = 16°40'0 Вост
Ш = 55°24'0   Д = 16°40'0
Ш = 55°24'0   Д = 17°19'0
Ш = 55°10'5   Д = 17°19'0

Режим особой скрытности.

С получением информации об ожидаемом переходе иностранной ПЛ из восточной части Балтийского моря в зону Балтийских проливов, поиск вести по приказанию КП БФ в районах:

№ 618.

6
409

- 3 -

№1
Ш = 54°52'6 Сев   Д = 15°52'0 Вост
Ш = 55°03'0   Д = 15°31'0
Ш = 54°50'2   Д = 15°42'0
Ш = 55°06'0   Д = 15°41'0

№2
Ш = 55°11'5 Сев   Д = 15°56'5 Вост
Ш = 55°12'5   Д = 15°44'0
Ш = 55°30'0   Д = 15°57'0
Ш = 55°28'5   Д = 16°03'0

№3
Ш = 55°11'5 Сев   Д = 16°57'0 Вост
Ш = 55°11'5   Д = 16°39'0
Ш = 55°23'5   Д = 16°39'0
Ш = 55°23'5   Д = 16°57'0

При обнаружении иностранных ПЛ осуществлять за ними слежение до потери контакта. При слежении принимать меры по недопущению опасных ситуаций, могущих привести к столкновению. При возникновении возможности опасного сближения с иностранной ПЛ, для уточнения обстановки активно использовать гидролокатор. С потерей контакта данные по обнаружению и слежению донести на КП БФ в соответствии с требованиями приказа ГК ВМФ № 0060-72г. и директивы НГШ ВМФ № 728/0295-78 года.

С прибытием в район слежения надводных кораблей установить связь на УКВ р/с 811 ЗАС или по ЗПС с кораблем командира сил поиска, дать ему последние данные по иностранной ПЛ и действовать по его указанию.

С прибытием в район противолодочного самолета (вертолета) при необходимости установить с ним связь на УКВ в р/с 903, передать ему последние данные по слежению и действовать по его указанию.

5. На подводную лодку принять полный боекомплект оружия: торпеды: САЭТ-60М -2, СЭТ-53М, САЭТ-60М-2, 53-65К-4
Вариант загрузки показан на графическом плане похода.

6. Все виды обычного оружия применять:

- по приказу ГК ВМФ или командующего БФ, переданному условным сигналом или шифром;

- по решению командира корабля на самооборону при вооруженном нападении иностранных кораблей или самолетов. Ядерное

— 4 —

410

оружие применять только по специальному приказу (сигналу) Министра обороны СССР.

7. В личном сейфе командира ПЛ иметь пакеты:
- № 1
- № 4
- № 14 (БС)

С получением сигналов, указанных на пакетах, или специального приказания, вскрыть пакет с соответствующим сигналом и действовать согласно вложенному в него боевому распоряжению.

8. Связь осуществлять согласно распоряжению по связи штаба БФ № 034 от 26 августа. Исходная программа связи № 83АС,8, вариант программы № 2, опорный сеанс связи № 1 документов "Янтарь-5", переход на другие программы связи по приказанию КП БФ.

Прием политической информации производить в соответствии с документами "Янтарь-5" в сеанс с 01 часа 02 минуты до 01 часа 17 минут ежесуточно.

С выходом на боевую службу доносить НЕМЕДЛЕННО:
- о случайных или несанкционированных выстрелах торпед;
- прочих инцидентах с оружием (потерях, повреждениях торпед);

В минимально возможные сроки с учетом конкретно сложившейся обстановки:

а) О действиях иностранных вооруженных сил:
- пусках ракет иностранными ракетными ПЛ, НК и с береговых установок;
- ядерных взрывах, о которых не было оповещений, обнаружении радиоактивного и биологического заражения;
- инцидентах с ядерным оружием в иностранных вооруженных силах;
- массовом взлете палубной авиации (20-25 самолетов в течение 15-20 минут с авианосца);

4

— 5 —

411

— полёте большой группы иностранных самолётов (более 10) в одиночных (групп) самолётов стратегической авиации в направлении границ СССР;

— провокационных действиях ВМС и авиации иностранных государств;

— нарушении государственной границы СССР иностранными кораблями, судами, самолётами;

— фактических боевых действиях ВМС и авиации иностранных государств, постановке мин самолётами, кораблями (судами), высадке десанта и диверсионных групп, боевых столкновениях между вооружёнными силами иностранных государств;

— слежении за подводной лодкой противолодочными силами иностранных государств, когда она не может от них оторваться;

— сигналах тревог и переводе вооружённых сил иностранных государств в повышенные боевые готовности;

— обнаружении в море отдельных надводных кораблей и корабельных группировок за пределами постоянных районов их деятельности, боевой подготовки и базирования;

— применении средств активных и пассивных помех иностранными кораблями и самолётами для подавления электронных средств;

б) Об авариях корабля и аварийных происшествиях:
— столкновениях;
— посадке на мель и касании грунта;
— потере винта, обломе лопастей винтов;
— пожарах;
— пробоинах и трещинах в прочном корпусе ПЛ, а также больших поступлениях забортной воды внутрь прочного корпуса;
— ударах о неподвижные или плавающие подводные препятствия;
— проваливании ПЛ на глубину, превышающую рабочую;

в) Об авариях вооружения и техники:
— несанкционированных (случайных) потерях или повреждениях торпед;

- 6 -

9
412

- взрывах паров масла с разрушением ресивера дизеля;
- гидравлических ударах в цилиндрах двигателей;
- взрывах водородной смеси в аккумуляторных ямах и отсеках ПЛ;
- возгорании элементов АБ ПЛ в количестве 25% и более от общего числа элементов в данной группе;
- других авариях вооружения и техники, устранение которых связано с прекращением подводной лодкой выполнения задач боевой службы;

г) О чрезвычайных происшествиях и заболеваниях личного состава:
- о случаях гибели личного состава;
- измене Родине, покушении на измену;
- антисоветской пропаганде и агитации;
- преднамеренном убийстве и покушении на убийство начальников подчиненными, других умышленных убийствах военнослужащих;
- неповиновении, неисполнении приказа;
- массовых или единичных заболеваниях особо опасными инфекционными заболеваниями, тяжелых травмах;
- хищениях, утратах секретных и сов.секретных документов;

д) О пропуске радиограмм в адрес ПЛ и о всех других случаях, которые командир ПЛ считает важными;

е) О всплытии в точке № 9 Ш= 55°58'Сш Д= 18°36'Вост

9. Управление ПЛ с КП БФ.

Старший на походе *начальник штаба 157бпл капитан 1 ранга Аврукевич И.Ф.*

Подводной лодке запрещается приближаться к территориальным водам иностранных государств ближе 5 миль.

Плавание в подводном положении в темное время суток в период всего похода осуществлять с включенными ходовыми огнями

— 7 —

личное наблюдение за внешней обстановкой ЗАПРЕЩАЕТСЯ.

При обнаружении корабля (судна), терпящего бедствие, донести на КП, оставаться в его районе, ведя скрытное наблюдение до получения соответствующего указания с КП флота.

В случаях гибели корабля (судна) всплыть, принять меры к спасению людей и оказанию им необходимой медицинской помощи. Последующая доставка спасенных людей в порт или передача их на другой корабль — только по указанию КП БФ.

При плавании по ФВК, при подходах к полигонам БП, в сложной навигационной обстановке запрещается использовать РЛС в активном режиме.

10. Аварийно-спасательное обеспечение осуществляет СО БФ.

11. Документы на поход, после возвращения в базу и составления отчета, уничтожить установленным порядком.

ПРИЛОЖЕНИЕ: графический план похода, р/л № 2009 на одном листе, сов.секретно.

КОМАНДУЮЩИЙ БАЛТИЙСКИМ ФЛОТОМ
ВИЦЕ-АДМИРАЛ   И.КАПИТАНЕЦ

НАЧАЛЬНИК ШТАБА БАЛТИЙСКОГО ФЛОТА
КОНТР-АДМИРАЛ   К.МАКАРОВ

The *S-363*'s mission order without appendices, declassified in Russia in 1994 but only declassified in Sweden in 2024. As can be seen from the reprinted original, the order was handwritten on a pre-printed or at least photocopied form.

THE S-363'S MISSION ORDER

The following is a translation into English. A few words relating to nuclear weapons seem to have been redacted in the Soviet original.

Twice Red Banner Baltic Fleet Headquarters
28 August 1981
No. 3/001051
Kaliningrad, 180

Copy No. 2
For the commander of the submarine *S-363*

COMBAT MISSION ORDER for Baltic Fleet No 0033/OP[5]
Kaliningrad, 27 August 1981
(Moscow time)

Permit for exit from ZDS [base area] *No. 3750/KP, 11 September 1981*[6]
[handwritten on form, with unreadable signature by a *Captain First Rank, 14 September 1981*]

Card No. 21003
Edition of 1975

1. Activities of naval forces of foreign states in the Baltic Sea in accordance with the intelligence card and information of Baltic Fleet Headquarters.

2. Combat mission carried out by:
   In Baltic Sea,
   the MRZK [intelligence collection ship] *Reduktor* from 5.9 to 3.11 1981,
   Submarine [of Project 613] *S-345* from 18.8 to 17.9.
   On patrol at the entry to the Baltic Sea line [DOZK-57],
   Minesweeper *Semyon Roshal'* from 1.9 to 1.10,
   MPK-140 [small antisubmarine warfare ship of Project 12412, NATO reporting name Pauk, with No. 140] from 1.10 to 1.11.

3. Tasks:
   a) Primary:
      Monitoring of foreign submarines in patrol areas
      P-1, P-2
   b) Additional duties:
      – reconnaissance with regard to activities of naval forces of foreign states.
      – monitoring activities of oceanographic vessels.
      – monitoring of intensity in shipping and fishery.
      – training of [combat] tasks L-2, L-3 from KDPL-75g.[7]

4. Submarine S-363 will set out at 6:00 p.m. on 16 September, carry out voyages and patrols in areas P-1, P-2 according to graphic plan. Repairs during the voyage and rest for the crew in Świnoujście from 7 October until 17 October this year.
   Return to base Paldiski at 8:00 a.m. on 5 November.

   Patrol areas:

Area P-1	Area P-2
55°20'0"N 16°43'0"E	55°21'0"N 16°53'0"E
55°13'0"N 16°49'0"E	55°14'0"N 16°50'0"E
54°51'0"N 15°33'0"E	55°22'0"N 15°29'0"E
54°58'0"N 15°27'0"E	55°29'0"N 15°32'0"E

   Patrol method is straight legs forwards and backwards. Patrol cycle: 48 hours, including search 40 hours and recharging of batteries 8 hours. Recharging shall take place in areas:

Area 3A
55°10'5"N 16°40'0"E
55°24'0"N 16°40'0"E
55°24'0"N 17°19'0"E
55°10'5"N 17°19'0"E

Stealth regime should be followed.

If information is received about an expected movement of a foreign submarine from the eastern Baltic Sea towards the Strait [between Denmark and Sweden], upon order from KP BF [Baltic Fleet Headquarters] a search is to be carried out in areas:

Area 1	Area 2	Area 3
54°52'6"N 15°52'0"E	55°11'5"N 15°56'5"E	55°11'5"N 16°51'0"E
55°03'0"N 15°31'0"E	55°12'5"N 15°44'0"E	55°11'5"N 16°39'0"E
54°50'2"N 15°42'0"E	55°30'0"N 15°51'0"E	55°23'5"N 16°39'0"E
55°06'0"N 15°41'0"E	55°28'5"N 16°03'0"E	55°23'5"N 16°51'0"E

When observing foreign submarines, these must be monitored until contact is lost. When monitoring, measures must be taken to avoid dangerous situations that could lead to a collision. If there is a risk of collision with a foreign submarine, active sonar must be used to clarify the position. When contact is lost, data on observation and surveillance shall be reported to the Baltic Fleet Headquarters in accordance with the requirements of Order No. 0060 of the year 1972 of the Supreme Commander of Naval Forces and Directive of the Chief of the Central Staff of the Naval Forces No. 728/0295 of the year 1978.

Upon the arrival of a surface vessel in the surveillance area, the submarine shall establish contact by encrypted high-speed radio on VHF with radio transmitter R-811 or by underwater telephone with the flagship of the anti-submarine force, give the latest information about the foreign submarine to the vessel, and act upon its orders.[8]

When an anti-submarine aircraft (helicopter) arrives in the area, if necessary establish contact with it on VHF using the radio transmitter R-903, give it the latest information regarding surveillance, and act upon its orders.

5. The submarine shall carry a full complement of the following weapons:
Torpedoes: SAET-60M [with nuclear warhead] -2 pcs; SET-53M; SAET-60M -2 pcs; 53-65K -4 pcs[9]
The ordered weapon load option is displayed on the graphic voyage plan. [It states two SAET-60M torpedoes and two SET-53M torpedoes in the forward torpedo tubes, as well as two SAET-60M torpedoes in the aft torpedo tubes. In addition, four sets of SET-53M and four sets of 53-65K torpedoes were carried onboard. The SAET-60M was a torpedo intended for use against surface ships, could carry a nuclear warhead, and was the primary weapon against large ship targets. The SET-53M was an anti-submarine torpedo. The 53-65K was a conventional torpedo used against surface ships.]

6. All types of customary weapons shall be used:
   – by order of the Supreme Commander of Naval Forces or the Commander of the Baltic Fleet, which is communicated by agreed signal or cipher;
   – by decision of the vessel's commander in self-defence in the event of an armed attack by a foreign ship or aircraft. Nuclear weapons must only be used on a special order (signal) from the Ministry of Defense of the Soviet Union.

7. In the captain's personal safe, the following packages must be stored:
   – No. 1
   – No. 4
   – No. 14 (secret)[10]
Upon receipt of the signals specified on the package, or a special order, the ship's commander must open the package with the corresponding signal and act in accordance with the combat instruction placed therein.

8. Communication must take place in accordance with the communication instruction of Baltic Fleet Headquarters No. 034 of 26 August. Initial communication programme No. 8 encrypted high-speed transmission, No. 8, programme alternative No. 2, auxiliary communication contact No. 1 in the documents 'Yantar'-5', transition to other communication programmes according to orders from Baltic Fleet Headquarters.

Reception of political information must take place in accordance with the documents 'Yantar'-5' when contacted from 1:02 a.m. to 1:17 a.m. every day.

During combat missions, reporting must take place IMMEDIATELY:
– about random or unsanctioned torpedo launches;
[– line apparently redacted, presumably because of reference to nuclear weapons]
– other incidents with [probably: nuclear] weapons (losses, damage to torpedoes);

As soon as possible in view of the concrete situation:

a) On the activities of foreign armed forces:
   – missile launches from foreign missile submarines, surface ships, and coastal batteries;
   – unannounced nuclear explosions, observation of radioactive or biological contamination;
   – incidents involving nuclear weapons in foreign armed forces;
   – mass take-off of aircraft from flight deck (20-25 aircraft in the course of 15-20 minutes from aircraft carriers);
   – flight of a large group of foreign aircraft (more than 10) in single (groups of) aircraft from strategic aviation in the direction of the border of the Soviet Union;
   – provocative actions by naval forces and aviation of foreign states;
   – violation of the state border of the Soviet Union by foreign ships, boats, aircraft,
   – actual combat actions of naval forces and aviation of foreign states, mine laying from aircraft, ship (boat), landing of troops or diversionary groups, combat clashes between armed forces of foreign states;
   – surveillance of the submarine by the anti-submarine forces of foreign states, when the submarine is unable to move away from them;
   – alarm signals and heightened combat readiness of the armed forces of foreign states;
   – observation at sea of individual surface ships and groups of ships that are outside their regular areas of operations, combat training, and basing;
   – use of active and passive electronic countermeasures by foreign ships and aircraft;
b) On shipwrecks and emergencies:
   – collisions;
   – going aground and hitting the seabed;
   – loss of propeller, breakage of propeller blades;
   – fire;
   – holes and cracks in the submarine's pressure hull and in case of large intake of water into the pressure hull;
   – collisions with fixed or floating underwater obstacles;
   – if the submarine sinks to a depth that exceeds its working depth;
c) In the event of damage to armaments and equipment:
   – unsanctioned (accidental) loss of or damage to the torpedoes;
   – oil vapor explosions with breakage of the diesel engine vapor collector;
   – hydraulic shocks in the engines' cylinders;
   – hydrogen mixture explosions in the submarine's battery bays and battery bulkheads;
   – ignition of the battery elements of the submarine to the number of 25% or more of the total number of elements of this group;
   – other failures of armament and equipment, the prevention of which means that the submarine must abort its combat mission;
d) In case of extraordinary events and illness among the crew:
   – about deaths in the crew;
   – treason, attempted treason;
   – anti-Soviet propaganda and agitation;
   – premeditated murder or attempted murder of an officer by subordinates, other premeditated murder of military personnel;
   – disobedience, failure to carry out orders;
   – mass sickness or isolated cases of particularly dangerous infectious diseases, severe injuries;
   – theft, loss of secret and top secret documents;
e) On gaps in radio telegrams to the submarine and on all other cases that the vessel commander considers important;
f) On assuming surface position in point No. 9, Lat 55°58'5"N Long 18°36'5"E.

9. Command of the submarine from Baltic Fleet Headquarters
The senior officer onboard is the chief of staff of 157th Submarine Brigade, Captain First Rank I. F. Avrukevich.

The submarine is prohibited from going closer than 5 nautical miles to the territorial waters of foreign states.

Voyage in submerged position [illegible words in available copy] time must be done with lit navigation lights throughout the voyage.

… [illegible words] reliable observation of the situation outside IS PROHIBITED.

When observing a ship (boat) in distress at sea, a report must be made to Headquarters, and the submarine must remain in the area and conduct covert observation until appropriate instructions are received from Navy Headquarters.

In the event of a ship (boat) sinking, the submarine must surface, take measures to rescue people and provide them with the necessary medical assistance. Afterwards, bringing rescued people into port or handing them over to another ship may only take place on instructions from Baltic Fleet Headquarters.

When traveling in monitored military fairways, when approaching a training area for combat training, and under complicated navigational conditions, it is permitted to use radar.

10. Rescue services are provided by the rescue department of the Baltic Fleet.[11]

11. Voyage documents must, after returning to base and debriefing, be destroyed in the established order.

    ATTACHMENT: Graphic voyage plan, Working Paper No. 2009, on one sheet, classified secret.[12]

Commander of the Baltic Fleet
Vice Admiral
[signature] I. Kapitanets

Chief of Staff of the Baltic Fleet
Rear Admiral
[signature] K. Makarov

The small antisubmarine warfare ship *MPK-140* carried no name beyond her numerical designation. She belonged to the class known as Project 12412, NATO reporting name Pauk. NATO called ships of this class missile corvettes. The first vessels of the class entered service in 1979. In 1980, this particular vessel was observed with bort number 250, but it is unknown if she still retained it in October 1981. At an unknown date, she was also observed with bort number 210. (Photo. U.S. Department of Defense, 1985)

MRZK [small intelligence ship] *Reduktor*, a SIGINT collection ship of the class for which NATO used the reporting name Okean. Built to resemble a civilian trawler, the *Reduktor* was primarily a SIGINT collector. However, she carried out other intelligence-related tasks as well. On 21 August 1972, KGB Chairman Andropov presented a plan known as SPLASH to the Central Committee of the Communist Party of the Soviet Union. It was entitled 'Plan for the Operation of a Shipment of Weapons to Irish Friends', by which was meant the Official IRA, a paramilitary group with Marxist leanings. The KGB sent a first shipment of two machine guns, 70 automatic rifles, 10 Walther pistols, and 41,600 cartridges, all of non-Soviet manufacture. The pistols were lubricated with West German oil and the packaging was taken from several countries around the world by KGB agents so that the weapons could not be traced back to the Soviet Union. The arms, in waterproof wrapping, were dumped on the Stanton sandbank at a depth of about 40 metres some 90km off the coast of Northern Ireland. A few hours after the delivery, a fishing boat belonging to the Official IRA arrived to haul up the weapons (Andrew and Mitrokhin, *Mitrokhin Archive*, p.502). The *Reduktor* remained in service until 1992. (Author's collection)

The minesweeper *Semyon Roshal'*, built in 1967 and entered into service in 1970, was the first ship of the class known as Project 266 M Akvamarin, NATO reporting name Natya. Many remain in service in various countries, including this one in the Russian Navy. (Author's collection)

Combat readiness was the unpleasant everyday reality of the Cold War. East and West stood in permanent readiness to annihilate the other, in case war seemed imminent. Andrey Grechko, Marshal of the Soviet Union and Minister of Defence, described the meaning of combat readiness in the Soviet military in the following terms:

> Combat readiness is no motto or high-flown phrase, but a totally concrete concept. It is that state of the Armed Forces in which they are capable of repelling and disrupting aggression at any moment and under the most difficult conditions of the situation, no matter what the source or the means and methods used, including nuclear weapons.[13]

Yet, for the submariners there was nothing new in the balance of terror between East and West. Like their counterparts in the West, they had all grown up under these conditions. Nobody expected World War III to break out on their watch. Most of the officers and crew probably preferred not to think about it at all. Tasked to defend the Motherland, they accepted the mission, and so far, nothing was out of the ordinary. The mission parameters appeared much the same as on most other occasions.

The *S-363* left port on 16 September 1981, at 6:05 p.m. (Moscow time, always used within the Baltic Fleet), departing from quay position No. 74 in the closely guarded Naval Base Baltiysk under electric power. Having entered the windy Bay of Gdańsk, Captain Gushchin switched to diesel power, which was used to bring the submarine to the position where its underwater voyage began. Having reached the predetermined position, the captain ordered Warrant Officer Igor' Stepanov, head of the signals section, to send a telegram to the Baltic Fleet Headquarters confirming that they had reached the position, and would dive according to orders. During the rest of the mission, there would be few opportunities to contact Fleet Headquarters. Then the submarine switched to electric power and descended to a depth of 40m. The mission was underway.

Following standard practice, Captain Gushchin henceforth allowed the crew to grow beards and moustaches. To make the voyage more enjoyable, he promised a prize – a serving of pirozhki, a traditional Russian pastry – to the crew member who had the longest beard when the mission concluded.[14]

Into the Trousers

Besedin was on duty when the *S-363* on 17 September entered its traditional patrol areas P-1 and P-2 east of Bornholm. He marked the time as 09:00 a.m. (Moscow time) for when the *S-363* 'went into the trousers'.[15]

In the patrol area, the submarine followed a plan which ensured that it always was combat ready, and also was as difficult to detect as possible. Certain depths were assigned to the submarine for combat service. As a rule, the submarine would patrol at a depth of at least 30m, so as not to be discovered by antisubmarine warfare aircraft and not to collide with any surface ship. But the submarine must also retain a distance of at least 10 to 15m from the bottom of the sea, so as not to hit the seabed. For these reasons, the *S-363* usually maintained a depth of 40m. Moreover, the submarine would not move fast. In the submerged position, the submarine usually moved at a speed that Soviet submariners called 'cat steps' (catwalk in other navies), in which the two 50hp PG-103 electric engines worked in economy mode, propelling the submarine with a speed of about 2.5 knots. Under these conditions, the submarine did not need to surface to recharge its batteries for three days. Even so, in order to ensure a reserve of electric power, many submariners charged the batteries after two days of operations. Not so Captain Gushchin, however. Based on the testimony of Besedin, he strictly followed mission parameters, charging batteries every third day, usually around 09:00 or 10:00 p.m. when it already was dark so as to minimise the risk that somebody observed the submarine. It was Gushchin's first independent mission, and he was under the eyes of his mentor, Avrukevich.

At regular intervals, at most once per day, Gushchin would order the submarine to perform the manouevre called clearing the baffles. A submarine tracking another submarine can take advantage of its target's baffles, that is, the area in the water directly behind a submarine that is a blind spot for a hull-mounted sonar, to follow at a close distance without being detected. Gushchin would order a turn of usually 30 degrees port or starboard to listen with the sonar for a few minutes in the area that was previously blocked by the baffles. This became a routine procedure. No hostile submarine was ever found.[16]

For safety and security reasons, while submerged the crew was not permitted to move from one section of the submarine to another without permission from the duty officer. The submarine was built with watertight compartments, each separated by pressure bulkheads provided with watertight pressure-resistant doors. When submerged, the compartments were closed and only the submarine's four senior officers were allowed to move from compartment to compartment: the commander, the political officer, the executive officer, and the chief engineer. On the *S-363*, we can assume that Avrukevich, in his role as mentor and highest-ranking officer, was added to this number. It was also important to avoid unnecessary sounds. It was not allowed to play music, nor to make loud noises by tapping or banging hatches.

To brighten the monotony of life under water, Besedin, along with other officers, would hold a quiz before surfacing, asking questions prepared from a variety of issues including technology, geography, culture, and so on. He would ask the questions through the loudspeaker, separately for each compartment. The officers would form a jury that determined the winner in each compartment. The winners would be the first to go upstairs to the long-awaited smoke break. Other prizes consisted of food and chocolates.

By tradition, the vessel's commanding officer was always the first to open the upper hatch. Then powerful fans were turned on to drive fresh air into the compartments. It took four hours to recharge the batteries, and during this time period, the crew was allowed up the submarine's tower or fairwater (a structure technically known as sail in American usage or fin in British usage) for four minutes each to smoke or breathe fresh air. The ban on transition from one compartment to the other was temporarily cancelled. The standard procedure was to run one diesel engine to move the submarine forwards with a speed of seven knots, while the other diesel engine was used to recharge the batteries. The crew also took the opportunity to dump garbage and depleted air purification filters overboard. The men could finally take showers, since water was then taken from the cooling system of the diesel engine in the fifth compartment. The entire crew had to use the same water outlet.[17] It was not permitted to surface to recharge batteries within the patrol areas, so special positions for this had been allocated outside of them. To save electricity, the submariners would have only one or at most two light bulbs lit in each section, and even the electric system that guided the vertical rudder was turned off. The rudder was instead handled manually from the stern.

Collision

The mission plan stated that after three weeks on patrol, the submarine would sail into the Polish port of Świnoujście to give the crew a few days of rest. However, on the seventeenth day of the mission, a problem occurred. At 6:10 p.m. on 2 October, the *S-363* patrolled in area P-1 at the location of 55°09'N 16°07'E, at a depth of 40m.[18] While passing through a customary fishing ground for Polish fishermen, the submarine crew suddenly heard the rattle of metal. The submerged *S-363* had collided with a fishing trawl. Finding no trace of the fishing vessel, the crew at first worried that they had caught and dragged the trawler below the surface, causing it to sink with all hands. They had all heard rumours of such incidents taking place with submarines. Fortunately, the submarine proceeded steadily in the water, without signs of strain from attached debris. No trawler had been dragged under, then. Yet, the crew had heard none of the characteristic sounds of trawlers before the collision. Warrant Officer 'Volodya' Grishin, the head of the sonar section, swore that he had not slept on his post.[19] Ultimately, the submariners concluded that the trawler must have been adrift, without engine running. Or, perhaps the trawl itself was adrift. The submariners never found out.

Running submerged within the patrol area, the crew dared not surface to look for damage. This would have to wait until 4 October, when the *S-363* surfaced at night according to plan to recharge batteries. In the darkness, they saw the most obvious consequences of the collision. Half of the metal-and-plexiglass windbreaker on the deckhouse railing was demolished. In addition, even at night the trace of the trawl cable was clearly visible on the tower. Far worse was that the collision had bent the antenna, designated RPN-47-03, for the ARP-53 radio direction finder. This was significant damage, since the direction finder was the primary means used for navigation on Project 613 submarines. Besedin related how this was a bad surprise for Anatoliy Korostov, the chief navigator, since he used the ARP-53 unit to determine the position for where to surface to recharge the batteries. Was the *S-363* even in the right position for surfacing, outside the patrol area? Korostov could not be certain. Moreover, the NEL-5 echo sounder too began to fail at this time (more on which below). Henceforth, the submariners would have to use fallback methods for navigation. Captain Gushchin decided that they would calculate the position of the submarine with the Western commercial Decca Navigator System. A receiver for the Decca radio signals of the type called PIRS-1 had been installed on the submarine shortly before the mission.[20] This was the first version of a Soviet-produced receiver designed to take advantage of the Decca signals without actually subscribing to Decca's commercial services.

The Decca Navigator System was a hyperbolic radio navigation system that allowed ships and aircraft to determine their position by using radio signals from a dedicated system of static radio transmitters. While the Decca greatly facilitated navigation and was one of the best commercial systems of its time, its accuracy depended on several technical factors, which were beyond the control of the navigator. These included the width of the lanes (blue, red, or violet), angle of cut of the hyperbolic lines of position, instrumental errors, and propagation errors (for instance, skywave or skip, that is, the propagation of radio waves reflected or refracted back towards Earth from the ionosphere, a phenomenon particularly prevalent at night). By day these errors could range from a few metres on the baseline up to a nautical mile at the edge of coverage. At night, skywave errors were greater and, on receivers without multipulse capabilities, it was not unusual for the position to jump a lane, sometimes without the navigator knowing.

Since the Decca Navigator System was a commercial system, the company did not usually sell Decca receivers outright, instead leasing them to users, which produced a significant amount of income. Unwilling to lease a commercial Western system for their military vessels, the Soviets had to develop their own receivers for making use of the Decca signals. The PIRS-1 receiver worked with the Decca Navigator System, but lacked automatic lane identification. This complicated the work of Soviet navigators, who first must determine their general position by other means. The PIRS-1 was intended as a backup system, not the primary means of navigation.

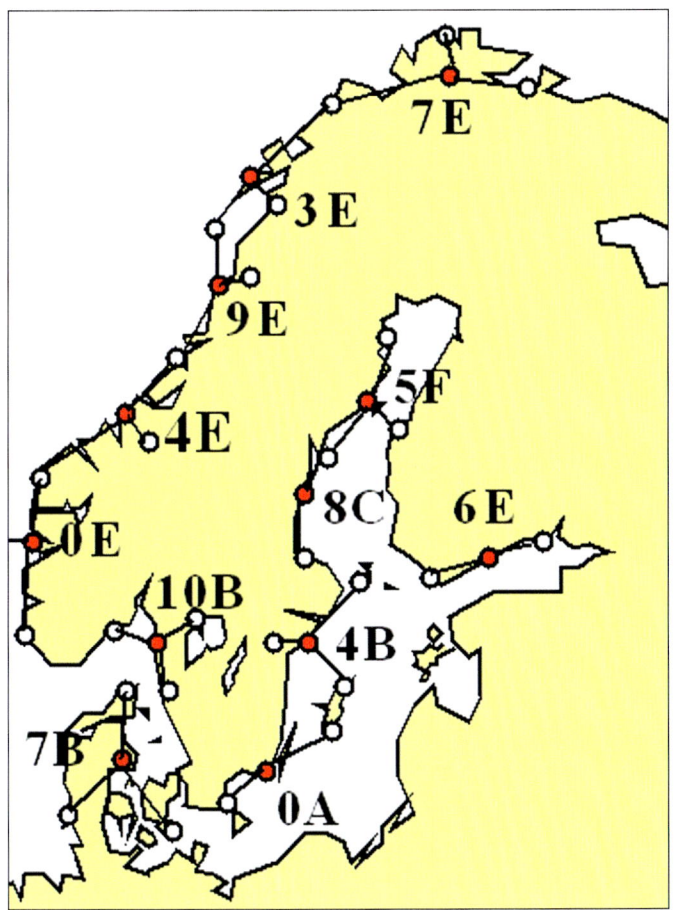

The Decca chains in Scandinavia. Under normal conditions, the waters off Karlskrona were well covered by the Southern Baltic Decca chain, which opened in 1970. (Map: Leif Elsby)

Despite this uncertainty, the *S-363* surfaced at 09:30 a.m. (Moscow time) on 7 October more or less as planned not far from the Soviet base in Świnoujście, Poland.[21] The first phase of the mission completed, the submarine set a course to Świnoujście, where they would replenish fuel, fresh water, and food. They sailed the remaining distance on the surface, in daytime, which also enabled them to inspect the damage from the collision with the trawl cable. With half of the metal-and-plexiglass windbreaker on the deckhouse fence demolished, the crew had to cut off the rest with a hacksaw. They painted over the scratch mark from the trawl cable clearly visible on the tower with regular black paint. What looks like the effects of these repaired damages are faintly visible in Swedish photographs of the *S-363*.[22] Yet, there was nothing they could do about the windbreaker and the bent antenna of the ARP-53 radio direction finder. These items could only be repaired at a naval base.

The *S-363* sailed into the Soviet base in Świnoujście at 1:30 p.m. on the same day.[23] In port, the crew expected a ten-day leave. The submarine would only set out again on 17 October. However, there were political tensions in Poland caused by the emergence of the Solidarity movement. Beginning in 1980 as a trade union protest against the communist government's failed economic policies, the growing Solidarity movement's seemingly interminable strikes and demonstrations inexorably drove the country, already in deep recession, towards bankruptcy. In December 1981, the political turmoil would ultimately lead to the imposition of martial law, but so far, the situation had not yet got that much out of hand. However, there were tensions, so the crew was advised for their own safety not to leave the base alone.

While in Świnoujście, the base mechanics repaired the ARP-53 antenna. The Soviet base in Świnoujście hosted 24th Missile and

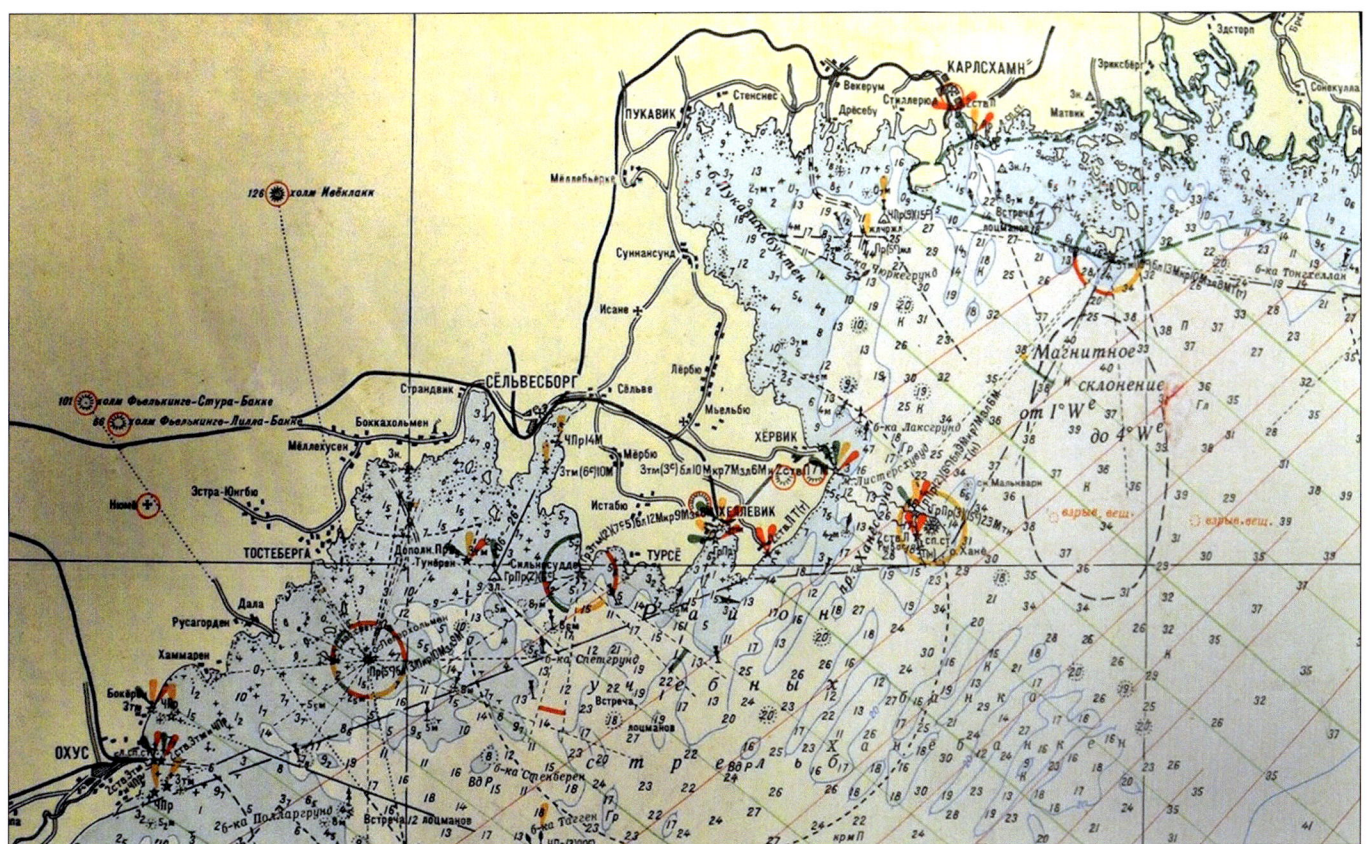

Soviet navigational chart over the western Blekinge archipelago, depicting the red and green Decca lanes, 1980. Although found while scrapping a Soviet submarine, the chart is of civilian origin. (Photo: Medström)

The state of the tower when the *S-363* stranded on the Swedish coast. (Author's collection)

Left: ARP-53 radio direction finder. Right: Cover for the Kurs-3 gyrocompass. (Author's collection)

Torpedo Boat Brigade, so there were repair facilities. Besides, the Polish Navy, too, operated Project 613 submarines, and the two navies cooperated closely. After six days, the system was reinstalled into the submarine. However, Besedin related that the repairs were unsuccessful. The radio direction finder gave the impression of working, but readouts were wrong. Apparently, it still functioned yet produced a fairly constant error of a few degrees which the operator must know to get a reasonable reading. The base technicians then recommended the submarine crew not to use it for the rest of the mission.[24]

Gushchin reported this problem to Fleet Headquarters in Kaliningrad. On 16 October, the day before the mission was to recommence, he discussed the matter on the phone with the head of the Baltic Fleet's Navigation Directorate, Captain First Rank Raimundas Baltuška (1937–2016). Gushchin reported that the PIRS-1 receiver worked satisfactorily with the commercial Decca Navigator System. Yet, the Decca was only intended as a backup system. Could the mission continue with this navigation system alone? Gushchin reported his willingness to continue. He was informed that the First Deputy Commander of the Baltic Fleet, Vice Admiral Aleksey Kalinin (1928–2004), would decide on the matter, and get back to him in the morning next day.

Besedin later related that he asked Gushchin why he declared his willingness to continue without the ARP-53. According to Besedin, Gushchin responded that he at first had planned to say no, but he thought that such a message to Fleet Headquarters would harm his career. Having considered this, Besedin agreed with Gushchin's assessment.[25] The Soviet Navy was built for war, and personal safety was not an overriding priority. Submarine commanders were expected to put the mission first, regardless of the odds. Although the Soviet Union had a large submarine fleet, the number of senior officers was no higher than enabled most of them to know each other. If Gushchin had stated that the mission could not continue because of maritime safety, it might not have ended his career as a submarine officer. Yet, it likely would have stuck to him, giving him a reputation for unwillingness to face and overcome risks.

Was Gushchin's and Besedin's career concerns that serious? Possibly. According to the U.S. naval intelligence officer Bobby Ray Inman, who around 1965 served as assistant naval attaché in Stockholm, U.S. intelligence at that time had determined that Whiskey-class submarines operated in the Swedish outer archipelago, because

> … young Soviet Naval officers being assigned to nuclear submarines, who would be going on extended cruises, standing officer on the deck, watches, they were trained in the Baltic on those diesel submarines. Getting them close to the Swedish was to let them understand and learn what it was like

to operate near but not quite inside territorial waters, before they would then report to the Northern Fleet, to nuclear submarines, and to deploy for reconnaissance missions off the East Coast of the United States.[26]

Was the U.S. assessment correct? We do not know. We have seen that the mission order prohibited Gushchin from going closer to foreign territorial waters than five nautical miles, so his was certainly not a mission in the Swedish outer archipelago. Yet, on his first independent assignment as a submarine commander, and under the sharp eyes of his mentor Avrukevich, it was perhaps understandable if Gushchin hoped that the present mission would be a stepping stone to that of the prestigious position of commander of a modern, nuclear submarine.

While the submarine remained in port, Senior Lieutenant Anatoliy Korostov, the chief navigator, tested the PIRS-1 receiver with the Decca system again. He found that everything functioned well, and judged that the level of error was well within what could be tolerated.[27] Was Korostov's assessment wrong? Like Gushchin, who was on his first voyage as submarine commander, Korostov was on his first voyage as chief navigator. If Gushchin worried about the impact on his career if he aborted the mission, Korostov likely shared his captain's concerns. For both men, it was easier to report their willingness to continue than to cause difficulties by pointing out technical problems. Besides, in hindsight Besedin noted that the decision to continue to some extent was the effect of the Russian national character. It was best to set out to sea regardless of any malfunctioning systems. Perhaps everything would go well. And if problems occurred, perhaps the crew could resolve them.[28] Avrukevich, trained in the same culture as his younger colleagues, supported Gushchin's decision to continue the mission.

At 12.40 p.m. (Moscow time), the order to continue the mission arrived by telegram to the Soviet base in Świnoujście. Captain Gushchin was instructed to set out on the same day (17 October), at 6:20 p.m. The mission was the same as before, patrolling areas P-1 and P-2 in submerged position while maintaining combat readiness.[29]

The *S-363* set out as planned. At 9:45 p.m., the submarine reached its point of diving. The *S-363* submerged to a depth of 40m, and proceeded towards area P-1.[30]

Crash Dive

Nothing unusual seems to have happened for three days.[31] On 20 October, the *S-363* surfaced as planned outside the patrol area to recharge batteries in the darkness. While the crew, as usual, took advantage of the slow surface run to ascend the tower to get some fresh air and smoke cigarettes, the rating of the *S-363* Osnaz section Nikolay Belkin at 8:50 p.m. suddenly detected the radar signals from what likely was an antisubmarine warfare aircraft with the Nakat radar warner and raised the alarm. The Osnaz section was responsible for Electronic Warfare (EW), which primarily meant Electronic Intelligence (ELINT).

Following standard procedures, Captain Gushchin ordered the diesel engines shut down, switched to electric engines, and initiated an immediate crash dive. They at once submerged to a depth of 30m. Gushchin was satisfied; a Project 613 submarine was expected to be able to dive within 60 seconds. This time, the crew made it in 45 seconds.[32]

While the sudden dive in response to an antisubmarine warfare aircraft can be described in terms of an exercise with the intention to maintain a state of alert, it also showed the importance given to the task of staying undetected by potentially hostile aircraft. Although the submarine was outside the patrol area, the *S-363* was on an operational mission, not a training mission. It was still a mission to defend the Motherland against intruding U.S. carrier groups and similar high-value targets, should one penetrate into the Baltic Sea with hostile intention. Following Soviet doctrine, the *S-363* formed part of the important forward defence zone. A successful defence of the Motherland depended on the *S-363*'s ability to stay undetected until it could launch torpedoes against a hostile intruder.

The incident with the antisubmarine warfare aircraft may have been important for another reason as well. Besedin later recalled that following this incident, he noticed the first signs that the submarine was in trouble. According to Besedin, he overheard Gushchin and the chief navigator, Korostov, discussing their position on a navigational chart. Gushchin told Korostov that the location could not be correct and that he must have calculated it wrongly. Korostov replied that he had acquired the position based on signals from the PIRS-1 receiver while they recharged the batteries, but this had needed extra work since the PIRS-1 receiver did not receive a stable signal. Besedin noted that Korostov had not climbed the tower while the submarine was surfaced. He had apparently been too busy working with the receiver. And now Korostov's calculation said that the submarine was more than 10 nautical miles from the assigned area to recharge batteries. Besedin later reminisced – when writing or possibly when he later edited his diary for publication – that something was obviously wrong. Either way, Besedin related that Gushchin upon further calculations concluded that Korostov's position was wrong, and that this mistake derived from a problem with the PIRS-1 receiver.[33]

Two days later, on 22 October, while the *S-363* remained in patrol area P-2, the plan said that the submarine at 10:30 p.m. would ascend to periscope depth for three minutes so as to receive a radio message from Fleet Headquarters. Afterwards, the submarine again would dive to a depth of 40m. At periscope depth, Gushchin gave Korostov a short moment to retrieve Decca signals through the PIRS-1 receiver. Korostov was only able to receive the signals once. He again calculated their position, and again the result was strange.[34]

The message from Fleet Headquarters informed Gushchin that certain NATO countries on the following day (23 October) would carry out an antisubmarine warfare exercise with its own submarines in patrol area P-1.[35] This was unpleasant news for the *S-363* crew. They would perhaps have felt yet more worried, had they known that the NATO antisubmarine warfare exercise was no minor undertaking, but the U.S.-led BALTOPS, which was the largest NATO naval exercise held in the Baltic Sea. Several NATO member-states participated, and in 1981 Denmark hosted the exercise.[36] On the following day (23 October), the *S-363*'s batteries reached a dangerously low level. Suddenly, the hydrophone operator reported engine sounds. While the hydrophone specialist believed the distance to be too great for the surface ship to discover the *S-363*, Gushchin decided to leave the patrol area to allow the *S-363* to recharge and to avoid being discovered by active sonar. He ordered evasive action, with constantly changing course, speed, and depth, so as to avoid potentially hostile antisubmarine warfare units. In the words of Besedin, the resulting route, as laid out on the navigational chart, looked absolutely insane (and this is indeed the immediate impression when looking at it, as becomes clear from the map included in this book). Moreover, the frequent course changes depleted the already-low batteries, so the submarine now had to surface to recharge them.[37]

Meanwhile, Besedin later related, he increasingly often noticed Avrukevich, Gushchin's mentor, discussing the submarine's position with Korostov. This is also obvious from the submarine's logbook, in which the recorded positions are struck through, corrected, and as a whole suggest a deep uncertainty of where the submarine exactly was located. Two days later (25 October), the submarine again left the patrol area, aiming to surface to recharge the batteries. All was quiet, so the crew assumed that the NATO antisubmarine warfare exercise now was over. Meanwhile, Gushchin and Korostov worked with the PIRS-1 receiver for a whole hour to get Decca signals that could be used to determine the vessel's real position. However, Avrukevich did not accept the result based on the signals that the PIRS-1 received from the Decca system. He finally told Gushchin that the PIRS-1 receiver was too unstable to be trusted. Instead, Avrukevich suggested, they should use the traditional method with a sextant. However, the persistent cloud cover prevented the use of this means to determine the submarine's position before it must dive again.[38]

Besedin wrote in his diary that the characteristics of the sea felt vaguely different from previously. Previously, they had frequently encountered fishing trawlers. Now these were gone, he remembered. Instead, they found a large cargo transport.[39] Gushchin was apparently worried, too. He went so far as taking the submarine up to periscope depth in the middle of the day to observe the surface. Seeing nothing, he ordered the crew to raise the radio antenna. Korostov again worked the PIRS-1 receiver to retrieve Decca signals. After three minutes, Korostov claimed that he had ascertained their position. The PIRS-1 receiver apparently worked this time. The location of the *S-363* deviated eight nautical miles from what he had expected. Gushchin agreed that this was conceivable, considering the frequent course changes of the previous days.[40]

Gushchin thought that the position determined with the help of PIRS-1 and Decca seemed correct. He then ordered the submarine to descend to a depth of 40m, after which the vessel continued its mission in what they assumed was patrol area P-1.[41]

Sailing Blind
Unfortunately, Avrukevich now openly disagreed with Gushchin on their geographical position. He went to check the details for himself. Obviously dissatisfied, Avrukevich late in the evening of 26 October ordered the submarine again to ascend to periscope depth. Avrukevich had apparently determined that the *S-363* probably was near the Danish island of Bornholm. By going to periscope depth, he hoped to find a well-known lighthouse on Bornholm, which would confirm the position. The submarine ascended to periscope depth at 9:24 p.m. to monitor surface conditions and receive telegrams (none reached them). Unfortunately, Avrukevich never found the lighthouse. In his opinion, the poor visibility was to blame. The Baltic Sea is notorious for poor weather, and autumn conditions are often abysmal. Irritated, Avrukevich at 9:45 p.m. ordered the *S-363* again to descend to a depth of 37m.[42]

Later in the night, at 2:40 a.m., Avrukevich decided that since the echo sounder, too, had broken down, they would have to risk descending to the seabed to measure the water depth as a means to determine the real location. This was an extremely risky manoeuvre; they all knew that the Baltic Seabed was generously littered with forgotten old mines and containers full of chemical warfare agents dumped or lost during the two world wars, or indeed later. Descending onto any one of these hazards might spell disaster. The seabed was also full of other garbage, dumped or lost there over the centuries. For this reason, we have seen that Soviet submariners were instructed never to descend deeper than 10 to 15 metres from the seabed. Yet, Avrukevich had the submarine descend all the way to the bottom, so that he could measure the depth with the depth meter – which at this spot showed 51m. Had the mission been a mere training exercise, he could have used the surface radar for navigation, but this was forbidden during the mission so as to avoid detection by hostile ships, as was indeed the use of active sonar. We have seen that the mission order actually permitted the use of radar in complicated navigational circumstances, but probably nobody wanted to admit that they actually were lost. Having determined the depth of the sea, Avrukevich found a location on the navigational chart that corresponded to the determined depth. This must be the real location, he concluded.

Besedin later reminisced that the use of such risky manoeuvres showed that nobody on the vessel, neither navigator, captain, nor even the captain's experienced mentor, really was sure of their present position.[43]

From this point in time, Avrukevich effectively assumed control of the submarine's navigation. Years later, Gushchin said that he regretted not entering this in the vessel's logbook, but at the time he had too much respect for the higher-ranking officer.[44] Avrukevich henceforth worked with Korostov, who did not question the senior officer, and ignored Gushchin's comments. Technically, Gushchin remained in command, but it was obvious that he, too, preferred not to question Avrukevich on the issue of navigation.

On 27 October, Korostov again worked with the PIRS-1 receiver for a long time to get Decca signals, at this time probably together with Gushchin. Afterwards, at 2:15 p.m. they again ascended to periscope depth. Normally, the *S-363* would only ascend when it was dark. They worked with the PIRS-1 receiver until 2:46 p.m. to get a Decca signal.[45] Apparently, this did not go well. At 5:20 p.m., the *S-363* again was on a course to what they estimated to be the location for surfacing and recharging batteries. Gushchin was then quite worried, and soon ordered an ascent to periscope depth to check the PIRS-1 receiver again. Meanwhile, Gushchin surveyed the horizon through the periscope. He found neither ships nor signs of aircraft. Korostov did the PIRS-1 readings of the Decca, and recalculated their position. He told Gushchin that the receiver worked fine, and that they were only 14 nautical miles from the planned position.[46]

Gushchin accepted the position, and ordered Korostov to calculate a course to the planned location for recharging batteries. Korostov planned a course through what he estimated to be patrol areas P-1 and P-2 towards the north, where they would recharge. They continued at a depth of 40m, in an area which the charts said had a total depth of from 70 to 80m.[47]

But for some reason, Gushchin continued to worry about the location of the submarine. At 6:55 p.m., he again ordered an ascent to periscope depth. Having raised the periscope, they could observe several fishing vessels.[48] Soon, he saw a blinking light ahead of the submarine. Even though the sonar section could not confirm the propeller sound of any fishing trawler, Gushchin assumed that the blinking light derived from a trawler. It must have been far away, he reasoned. Gushchin ordered a detour around the trawler, and a descent to 30m.[49]

At 8:04 p.m., Gushchin ordered the *S-363* to surface to recharge batteries and a course to avoid the fishing vessels. Four minutes later, at 8:08 p.m., the submarine surfaced. Gushchin ordered the lighting up of the submarine's navigation lights to show any surface vessels that it was underway.[50] The submarine henceforth used the starboard diesel engine for propulsion. Meanwhile, the port engine was used to recharge the batteries. The noise was heard far and wide. Climbing

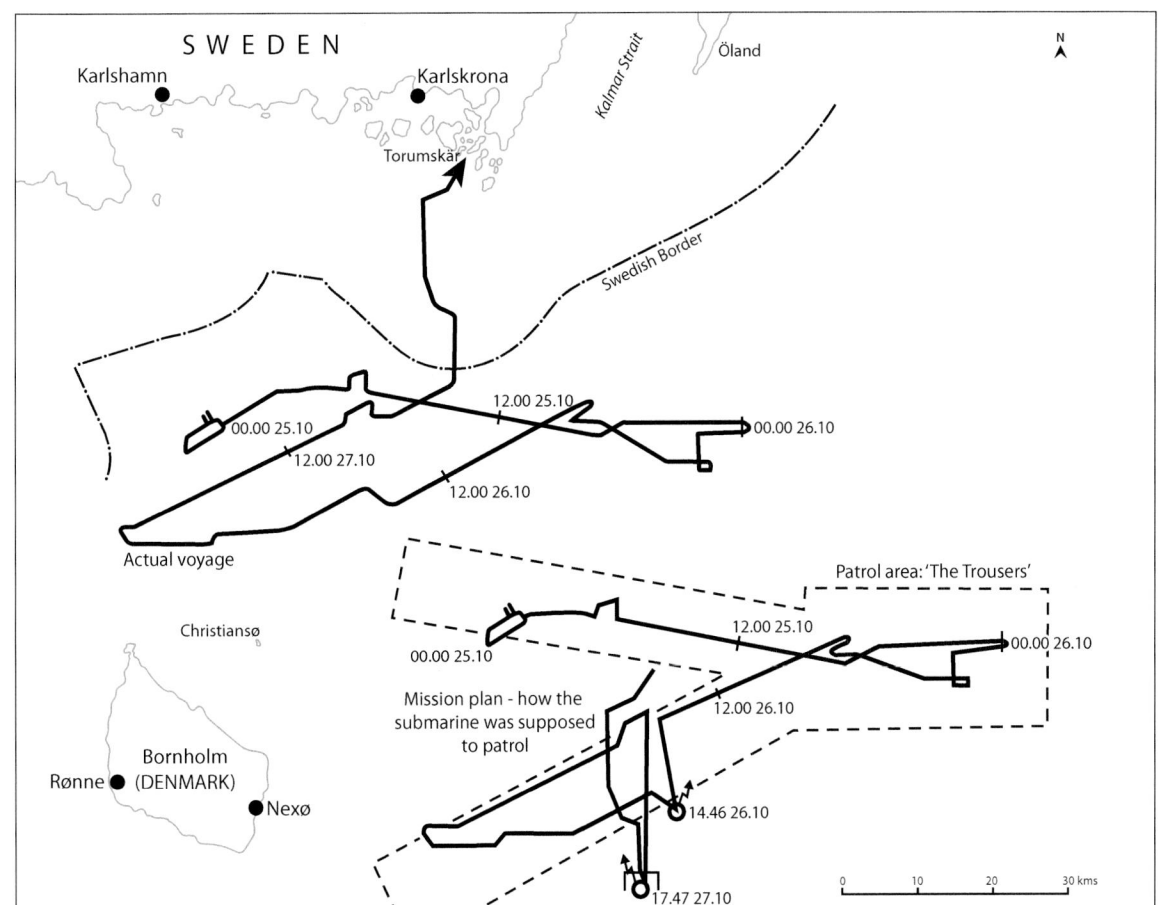

Submarine's mission plan and actual voyage. (Map by George Anderson)

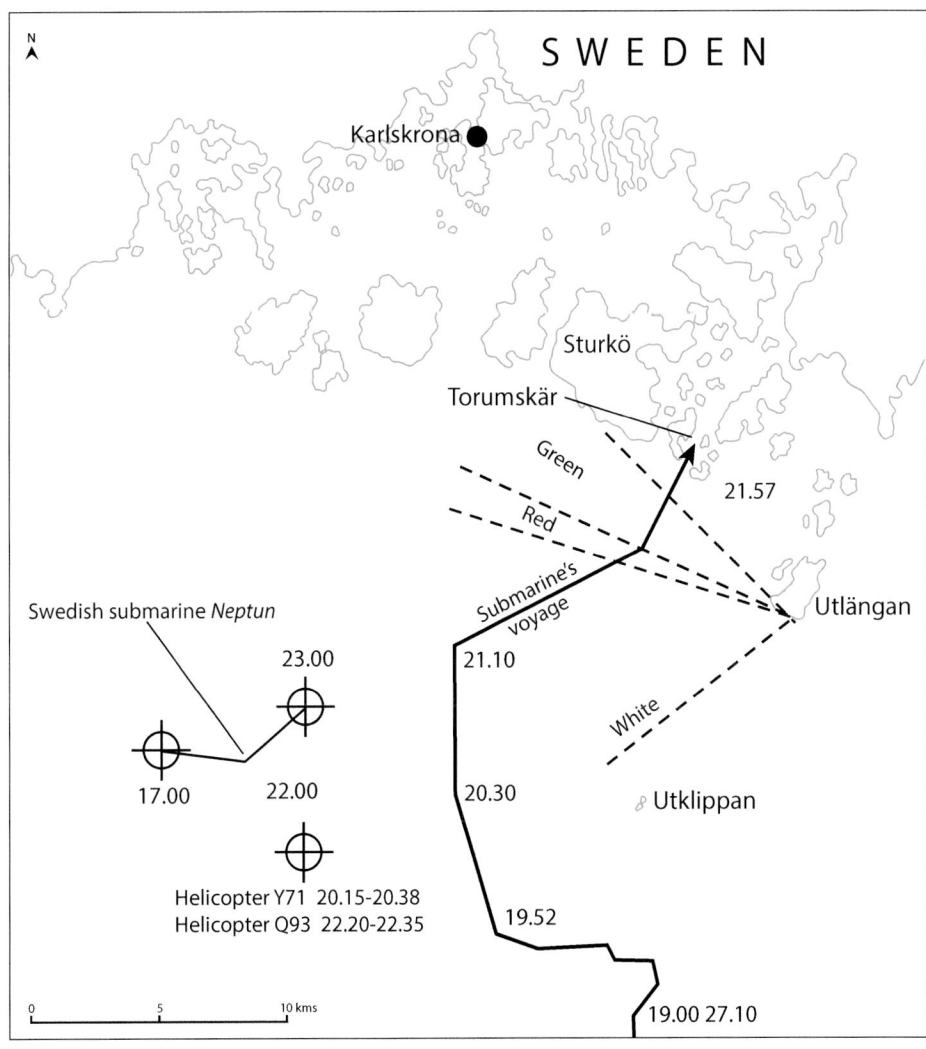

Submarine's voyage into Swedish waters. All times are Moscow time. (Map by George Anderson)

up in the tower, Gushchin and Besedin (who had relieved Pershin as duty officer at 8:00 p.m., although nobody remembered to enter this into the vessel's logbook) could see a faint white light in the distance, which Gushchin again interpreted as a fishing vessel. At this point, the rating of the Osnaz (EW) section Nikolay Belkin, manning the Nakat radar warning receiver, reported the discovery of a coastal radar station. When Gushchin said that this was impossible, Belkin got nervous and changed his report to a ship's navigation radar. Gushchin interpreted the discovered radar signal as linked to the fishing vessel with the faint white light. (The Soviet commission of inquiry report found that Gushchin identified the radar as that of a West German destroyer; see Appendix 1.)

Soon afterwards, the crew also noted what they believed to be black oil spills on the water surface. At night, visibility was far from great in the darkness and mist, but Besedin later retold that they found this odd.[51]

What the submarine crew did not realise was that they had already entered Gåsefjärden ('Goose Firth') Bay deep inside Swedish territorial waters and within a restricted military area, closed to all foreign nationals. What they thought were oil spills were skerries, the coastal radar station was indeed a coastal radar station, and the faint white light that Gushchin interpreted as a fishing vessel was light emanating from settlements on land.

At 9:31 p.m., the signals section received a telegram from Fleet Headquarters. There is no logbook entry that suggests that the S-363 responded to the telegram. Twenty-six minutes later, at 9:57 p.m. (Moscow time, or 7:57 p.m. Swedish time), the S-363 ran aground on the skerry known as Torumskär, just off a military fairway, or approach channel, leading into Naval Base Karlskrona, which was only 12km away.[52]

Stranded

Both Gushchin and Besedin were in the tower when the S-363 stranded on the Torumskär rock. The suddenness of the accident caused Gushchin to fall and hit his chest badly on the fairing for the magnetic compass. Besedin almost fell overboard as the bow of the S-363 first rose into the air, and then sharply turned to port. Yet, Besedin was fortunate; he only hit a rubber-covered edge. The diesel engine was still working, so the entire submarine shook as the vessel lodged itself firmly on the rock. Eventually, but not before they were back home on the base, it was discovered that a stone from the skerry had lodged itself into the broken hydrophone fairing in the submarine's bow and still remained there. The submarine leaned 11 degrees to port, and 3 degrees to stern. Despite the pain in the chest, Gushchin managed to grab the microphone to the loudspeaker system, ordering the engine room to turn off the engine.[53]

The submarine had run aground in the surface position, with a speed of around eight knots. The impact had been significant. Normally, a submarine would not have travelled at such a high speed in an unknown archipelago environment. However, it was a reasonable cruising speed out at sea, where the submariners indeed believed that they were at the time. Later, we will see that the Swedish naval officer Karl Andersson assessed that the speed must have been at least eight knots, the same speed (8.5 knots) as the vessel's navigational logbook states.

Avrukevich then ran up into the tower, asking what had happened. Since nobody had a clue, Gushchin ordered Senior Sailor Pavel Savchenko, the signalman and lookout, to turn on the searchlight and aim it on the bow. The sudden light illuminated a large white mass perhaps 10m ahead of the bow. Because of the dense mist, they could not grasp what it was. Savchenko suddenly suggested that the white mass looked 'like ice'. The executive officer Yakovlev attempted a joke, chuckling to the rating: 'Don't say that you tell me we've reached the North Pole!'[54] Only later in the night did they understand that what the torch illuminated was a slab of bare rocks above the water.

When they finally understood that they had ran ashore, and no longer were out in the open sea, their first thought was that the landmass must be the Danish island of Bornholm.[55]

Gushchin and Avrukevich both agreed not to contact Fleet Headquarters yet, at least not before they had managed to determine their position and, with a little luck, get the S-363 off the rock.

The vessel's logbook shows that at 8:13 p.m. (local time; which henceforth will be used unless stated otherwise), Gushchin ordered the navigation lights that showed the submarine as underway to be turned off. Instead, the anchor lights that showed it as stationary were turned on. At 9:00 p.m., somebody made an entry into the vessel's logbook that having analysed the situation, Gushchin had concluded that they had stranded near Christiansø, a Danish island northeast of Bornholm with a well-known old lighthouse. An hour later, the S-363's logbook listed Besedin as having become duty officer (which meant a double shift, perhaps unavoidable in the confusion since the department heads were needed elsewhere).[56]

The diesel engines could not reverse, so the crew attempted to use the electric engines to get off the rock. The crew continued to recharge the batteries until about 1:00 a.m. However, even with recharged batteries they could not move the submarine off the rock. Then the batteries were empty and must be recharged. The chief engineer, Arkhipov, had the crew attempt to get off the rock by pumping water back and forth between the ballast tanks, since this would change the balance of the submarine.[57] Gushchin also sent down divers (one heavy and one light) to check the hull and try to ascertain how it was lodged on the rock.

They abandoned the attempt to get off the rock about 4:30 a.m. At this point, the crew needed some rest. By then, Korostov had managed to get fresh Decca signals through the PIRS-1 receiver. He now indicated a position on the Swedish coast, but not as deep in the bay as was really the situation.[58] Korostov entered the position 56°03'0"N 15°46'0"E in the S-363's logbook at 11:00 p.m., 24:00 p.m., 4:00 a.m. (and later also at 8:00 and 12.00 a.m., all Moscow time).[59]

Gushchin could not accept the new calculation, instead scolding the navigator severely. According to Besedin, many angry words were addressed to Korostov himself, his close and distant relatives, as well as the commander who released such a navigator from training school.[60] Ultimately, Gushchin and Avrukevich personally carried out a new calculation, again with fresh Decca signals from the PIRS-1 receiver. They received the same result: the S-363 had somehow managed to hit a rock on the Swedish coast.[61]

Besedin later commented that '… To be honest, at that moment I did not react so much to the stunning news as I worried for the commander and navigator. Both were extremely dejected. There was only one way to get them out of it – to distract them with work… I said to the navigator: 'Look, Tolya, you must determine where, how, and when the error appeared. It is necessary that you yourself, and not someone else, find it.'[62]

Meanwhile, the inhabitants of the surrounding islands heard the noise of engines throughout the evening and the whole night, but could not see anything in the darkness. Islands and mist hid the submarine lights, but the evening was still and sounds could be heard far over the water. Eyewitness reports from Gåsefjärden Bay mentioned the loud sound of diesel engines from at least about 6:00 to 7:00 p.m. onwards, which confirms the presence of the Soviet

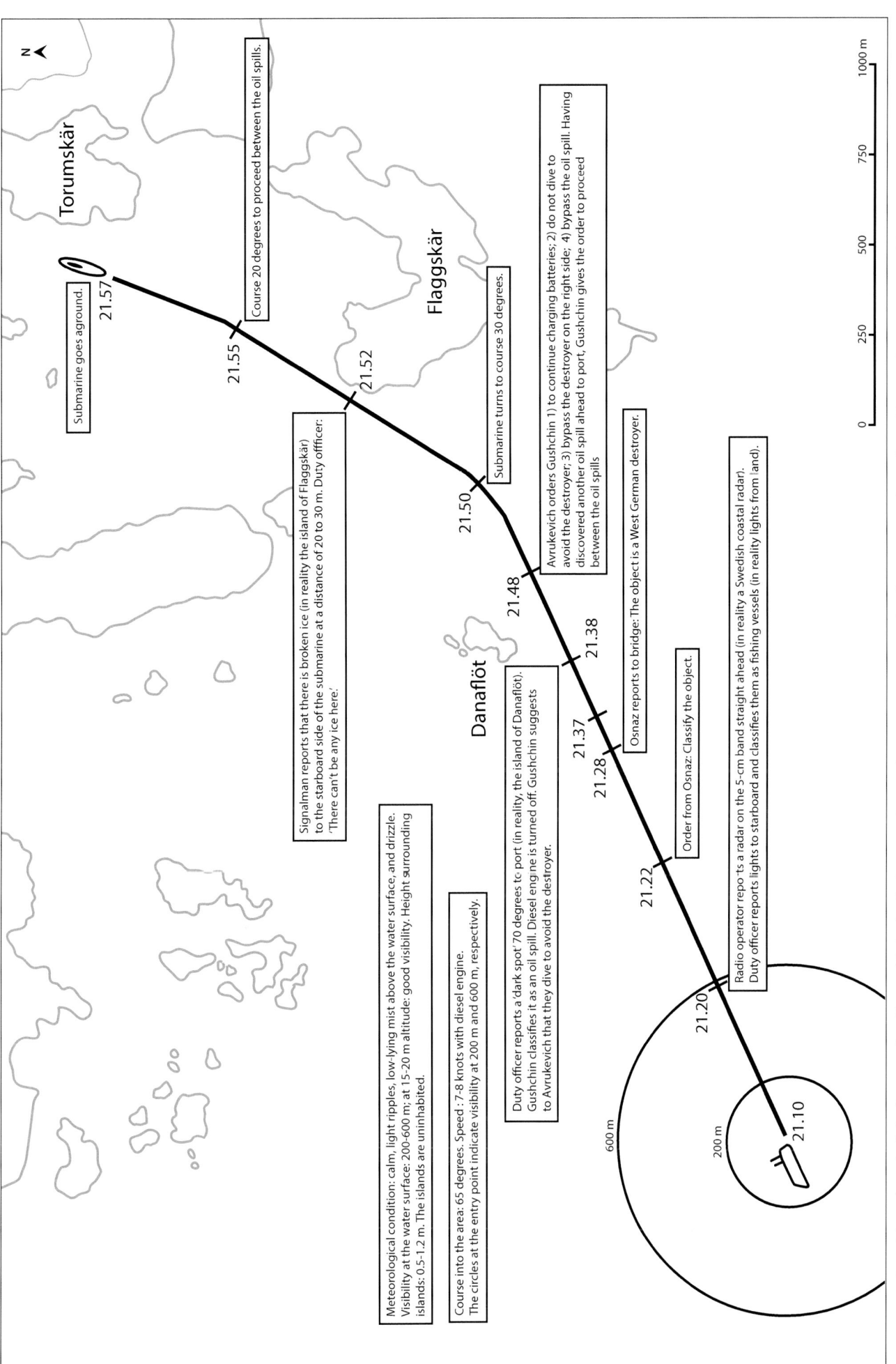

The reconstruction of the submarine's final approach to Torumskär in the Soviet commission of inquiry report. Most details are seemingly confirmed by Besedin's account and the submarine's logbook (more on which below). However, considering the state of navigational confusion and the resulting missing entries in the logbook at the final stage of the voyage, this remains, at best, a reconstruction. While it seems likely that the S-363 followed this route, we cannot be sure that all details are correctly depicted. All times are Moscow time. (Map by George Anderson)

submarine's diesel engine while underway.⁶³ Most assumed it was a naval exercise nearby, and went to bed for the night. The only one who took action was Rolf Ohlsson, a journalist who worked as news editor for the regional newspaper *Sydsvenska Dagbladet*. He lived on nearby Aspö Island, heard the persistent engine noise, and at 7:30 p.m. called the Coast Guard in Karlskrona, asking what was going on. The Coast Guard contacted Naval Base Karlskrona, where somebody reassured them that nothing was happening.

Much later, the Navy in its post-incident report concluded that Ohlsson and the others had merely heard the sound of helicopter engines.⁶⁴ The Navy initially assumed, incorrectly, that the Soviet submarine would not have employed its loud diesel engines when penetrating the Swedish archipelago, so any diesel engine sound could not have emanated from the submarine. Helicopters were indeed airborne at the time. In the same evening when the *S-363* stranded, the Swedish Navy conducted trials with a new helicopter-launched, homing antisubmarine torpedo, the *Torped* 42 (Tp 42), off the Karlskrona archipelago. The submarine *Neptun*, commanded by Lieutenant Commander Nils Bruzelius, acted as a target for the torpedo. The *Neptun*, built in 1979 as the *Neptun II* and one of the Navy's three modern Näcken-class submarines, was for the trial modified with additional lights and a powerful searchlight aimed straight upwards to enable two helicopters, first the Y 71 and then the Q 93, from the Navy's 13th Helicopter Squadron to observe her movements. Onboard the *Neptun* was also Lieutenant Björn Hamilton (b. 1950), whom we will meet again. The next morning, he would take over as acting commander of the *Neptun* – Lieutenant Hamilton's first command of a submarine.⁶⁵

Except the *Neptun* and the helicopters, no other Swedish Navy units were at sea in the area. Nor did the Coast Guard have any vessels at sea there at the time.⁶⁶ To all effects, Sweden was blind to the intrusion near one of its major naval bases. That the submarine effectively was sailing blind did not sooth Swedish feelings, when the intruder finally was discovered.

Soviet and U.S. Intelligence

The little town Karlskrona, founded in 1680, was built around Sweden's primary naval base. Then, the main threat against Sweden had been Denmark, which only a few years prior to the town's foundation had invaded southern Sweden. Three hundred years later, the primary threat against Sweden was assessed to be the Soviet Union. Hosting an important naval base, Karlskrona was frequently visited by foreign intelligence officers.

The Swedish Security Service, formally, the Security Department (Swedish: *Säkerhetsavdelningen*, Säk) of the National Police Board (*Rikspolisstyrelsen*, RPS), presumably knew that at least one Soviet agent actually was in Karlskrona on the very day when the *S-363* hit the rock. This was Nikolay 'Nick' Nejland, a Latvian KGB officer who spoke Swedish fluently since his time as Stockholm correspondent for the APN (Novosti) news agency in the years 1971 to 1978. At the time, he had taken a particular interest in the then Swedish Prime Minister, Olof Palme.

Nejland, known as Nick among his Swedish friends, had played tennis at the same tennis club as the Prime Minister. He is said to have bugged the cafe next to the tennis court in order to find out what the top Swedish political leadership were talking about. But Nejland probably did not have to go that far. Palme played tennis together with the social democrat, writer, and businessman Harry Schein. The well-known journalist Åke Ortmark and Nick Nejland played on the field next to Palme. The journalist Ortmark later remarked that 'Palme in the sauna after the tennis was a goldmine'

of information. Perhaps no technical surveillance equipment was needed, and Nejland is in any case not known to have used any.⁶⁷

Nejland apparently reported on Palme from the tennis court and the sauna but, despite the fact that the content of his reporting is not known in detail outside the KGB, probably did not create any deeper picture of Palme's world of thought. Possibly his reports nonetheless gave the KGB leadership the illusion of having found a way to the Swedish Prime Minister. However, Nejland left Stockholm in 1979 and could only return for shorter visits in 1980 and 1981.

The Swedish Security Service presumably knew about Nejland's visit to Karlskrona because he had been identified by a KGB major named Imants Lešinskis, another Latvian, who had defected to the United States in the autumn of 1978. The Americans had then secretly sent Lešinskis to Sweden to inform the Swedish Security Service about KGB agents there, which had opened their eyes to Nejland. We know about this, and that the KGB knew about Nejland's blown cover, from declassified Polish secret intelligence reporting at the time.⁶⁸

On this occasion, Nejland was in Sweden to persuade the local town council of Karlskrona to open a ferry line between Karlskrona and Riga, the capital of Nejland's native Latvia. There is no reason to believe that the KGB officer Nejland had any prior knowledge of the *S-363*, which whatever its mission was a military operation. However, the Security Service, which generally shadowed any suspected Soviet intelligence officers and by then assuredly knew about Nejland, later thought that they saw a conspiracy in Nejland's visit to Karlskrona on this very day.⁶⁹

KGB agent Nick Nejland. His attempts to get close to Swedish Prime Minister Olof Palme seem not to have irked the Security Service as much as his presence in Karlskrona on the very day that the *S-363* showed up nearby. The next year, the Security Service refused Nejland a visa and barred him from joining his country's tennis team for the 5–7 March 1982 Davis Cup tournament (UPI, 25 March 1982). (Photo: Medström)

It was not only Soviet intelligence that was represented in Karlskrona at the time. On the very morning that the *S-363* crew gave up the attempt to extricate the submarine from the rock by its own power, Naval Base Karlskrona, or the South Coast's Naval Base as was its formal name, prepared to host the U.S. naval attaché, Captain David Moss, who on this day was scheduled for a two-day visit to the base together with his assistant attaché, Commander Edmond Pope. Arriving in Karlskrona in the previous evening, more or less simultaneously with the *S-363*, and taking rooms in Hotel Aston (more on which below), the two Americans showed up at the gate of the naval base as early as around 7:00 a.m. on 28 October. They were met by the base commander, Commodore Lennart Forsman (1925-2018), who previously had been the Swedish naval attaché in Washington, DC, and Ottawa, and knew them both personally.[70] Forsman asked Commander Karl Andersson (1931–2017), his chief of staff, to give the two Americans a briefing. Andersson later related that this was the first and only time ever that American visitors turned up unannounced and without keeping the chief of staff in the loop.[71] Since Andersson had not been informed about the visit of the two Americans, their presence on the scene over time became the corner stone of another conspiracy theory, according to which the Americans were involved in the intrusion of the *S-363*, in effect luring the submarine into Swedish waters by manipulating the Decca signal.[72] It is far more likely that Moss and Pope visited the base either on a previously scheduled, routine study visit or, perhaps, because of the ongoing BALTOPS exercise, which had taken place in the previous days and concluded on 27 October – the very day when the *S-363* stranded at Torumskär.

There is no suggestion that Moss and Pope engaged in anything but legitimate intelligence collection, as befitted their diplomatic status as naval attachés. Pope left the Navy in 1994. In 2000, he was arrested in Russia for buying and smuggling classified military equipment out of the country as scrap metal on behalf of the U.S. Defense Intelligence Agency (DIA). Most leading Western countries, including Sweden, engaged in the purchase and analysis of former

Commodore Lennart Forsman with Foreign Minister Ola Ullsten in front of the torpedo boat T 134 *Varberg*, February 1982. (Naval Museum, Karlskrona; photo: Lennart Bergqvist)

Soviet military equipment in the 1990s, sometimes with good results.[73] Convicted of espionage, Pope was pardoned by the newly-elected Russian President Vladimir Putin. He has since maintained that he was innocent.[74]

4
WEDNESDAY 28 OCTOBER

Having failed all attempts to get off the rock and given up all hope to accomplish it without outside help, the submarine officers realised that they had no choice but to break radio silence. Soviet submarines were ordered to maintain radio silence at all times during operations, except according to a strict radio schedule or in response to direct orders. At around 4:30 a.m., Gushchin realised that he could no longer postpone the message to Fleet Headquarters in Kaliningrad. According to the radio schedule, he should have reported in during the night, but he had not. It was still dark, with almost two hours to go before daybreak. Gushchin sent a high-speed encrypted telegram at 4:36 a.m. with the brief message that they had stranded on the southern Swedish coast. Fleet Headquarters acknowledged the message as received five minutes later, at 4:41 a.m.[1] But there was no response to their predicament. He accordingly sent another high-speed encrypted telegram at 5:16 a.m. Five minutes later, at 5:21 a.m., Fleet Headquarters acknowledged this message as well. And soon, at 5:29 a.m., a message arrived in return. Fleet Headquarters found the location on the Swedish coast hard to believe, so they asked Gushchin to repeat the submarine's position.

When dawn broke at 6:18 a.m. on 28 October, it finally became possible for the submariners to observe their surroundings. They found only a narrow strip of water in front and behind the submarine, and saw a small island no more than 30 to 40m from the submarine. About 100m further away a larger island was visible. They could even see a yellow cottage on the island. The Soviet crew realised that it was only a matter of time before they would be found by the nearby islanders, who by now surely were in the process of waking up.

With the understanding that they could not avoid making contact with the locals, the submariners raised the ensign of the Soviet Navy. They also sent another high-speed encrypted telegram to Fleet Headquarters at 6:32 a.m. Since no response came, they repeated the message at 7:07 a.m., this time with the 'big' transmitter. The same message was repeated a third time at 7:27 a.m. Fleet Headquarters sent a technical acknowledgment at 7:35 a.m. but otherwise retained an ominous silence.

But not for long. Soon, Fleet Headquarters sent a flurry of telegrams all of which included immediate instructions. Two high-speed encrypted messages reached the submariners at 7:42 a.m. The submarine sent a high-speed encrypted response at 7:45 a.m. Fleet Headquarters acknowledged the message at 7:55 a.m. At 9:07, the submariners sent a new high-speed encrypted telegram. They repeated it at 9:21 a.m. Messages arrived at 9:25 and 9:48 a.m.[2]

Some instructions could not be carried out. Others were understandable, although the crew felt hurt by them, such as the order not to lower the naval ensign. The crew of the *S-363* did not plan to surrender.[3]

The news from the *S-363* took Moscow by surprise. Admiral Gorshkov was scheduled to chair a meeting of senior commanders at 10:00 a.m. Moscow time (8:00 a.m. Swedish time). Gorshkov had a reputation for always being on time, so the other participants of the meeting grew increasingly worried when the Admiral did not show up as planned. Gorshkov only appeared after an hour. He then informed the senior commanders that a 'disgraceful incident' had occurred in Swedish waters, and that the commander of the Baltic Fleet (in reality First Deputy Commander Vice Admiral Aleksey Kalinin) was on the way to resolve the crisis. Among the participants of the meeting was Captain First Rank Vladimir Yegorov (1938–2022) of the Baltic Fleet, then commander of 128th Missile Ship Brigade in Baltiysk but on the career track for higher posts. He later related that Gorshkov did not raise the issue of taking up arms. The focus was on salvaging the submarine, not going into Swedish waters with blazing guns.[4]

Soviet supreme leader Leonid Brezhnev (1906–1982) and Defence Minister Dmitriy Ustinov (1908–1984) at the October Revolution parade in probably 1979. Both were old at the time of the *S-363* incident, and Brezhnev was no longer the decisive leader he once had been. Both appear to have delegated responsibility for handling the *S-363* incident further down the chain of command. Ustinov, always more of a defence industry official than a soldier, had in 1976 replaced Marshal of the Soviet Union Andrey Grechko as Defence Minister. (Author's collection)

Perhaps because of this focus, Fleet Headquarters was slow to inform the commander of the Baltic Fleet, Vice Admiral Ivan Kapitanets (1928–2018), who would have been responsible for any actual combat in which his units took part. Kapitanets described in his memoirs that on the day in question he was in Moscow for a meeting at the Ministry of Defence. During the afternoon, through the usual coverage of foreign radio news, he found out that the submarine had run aground.[5] It was perhaps only then that the Defence Minister of the Soviet Union, Dmitriy Ustinov, was informed about the incident. And it was probably only after this that somebody, presumably Ustinov, reported the accident to the Soviet supreme leader, Leonid Brezhnev.

Brezhnev, Ustinov, and other senior Party officials of the Soviet Politburo could be ruthless when so was required. Yet, it is likely that on this occasion the senior Soviet leaders were more concerned over the safety of the *S-363* than the Swedes realised. Only a week previously, on 21 October, the Soviet submarine *S-178*, another vessel of the Project 613 (Whiskey) class, had sunk in the Pacific Ocean, with a loss of 32 crew. The *S-178* had collided with a commercial transport. The last survivors were rescued on 23 October in an operation undertaken by the Chief of Staff of the Pacific Fleet, Vice Admiral Rudol'f Golosov. In similarity to the *S-363*, the *S-178* too had carried the chief of staff of the submarine brigade, Captain Second Rank Vladimir Karavekov, onboard at the time of the disaster, and he was among the dead.[6]

On this day, the mood among the senior leaders in Moscow might accordingly have been one of relief that the *S-363* was safe with the crew intact instead of annoyance that it had stranded on a Swedish skerry. The international implications of the accident were sensitive, but at least their sailors remained alive. In the evening Vice Admiral Kapitanets flew back to Kaliningrad.[7]

Vice Admiral Ivan Kapitanets, Commander of the Baltic Fleet. (Author's collection)

Having received the *S-363*'s initial message, the Soviet Baltic Fleet prepared to salvage the submarine. The available salvage vessels were formed into a task force under Vice Admiral Aleksey Kalinin, First Deputy Commander of the Baltic Fleet. When ready, each left port individually, sailing towards the western Baltic Sea.[8] Most were estimated to reach the assembly point off Karlskrona in the evening.

Discovery of the Submarine

Early in the morning, two local fishermen, Bertil Sturkman and Ingvar Svensson, set out from Sturkö Island near Torumskär to retrieve their nets. They discovered that part of the surface of water in the inlet to Gåsefjärden Bay was covered with a thin film of oil.[9] The two fishermen returned to Sturkö with their catch. Svensson went home while Sturkman again set off with the boat to pick up, in a different location, some of his pike hooks. Sturkman was 58 years old and, as his name suggested, belonged to a family that had lived on the island for generations, making a living from the sea. It was misty, but Sturkman knew this part of the archipelago like the back of his hand.

To his surprise, Sturkman now noted a submarine halfway up on a rock at Torumskär. It was black and carried neither number nor visible designation. In the tower he could see three or four men looking in his direction with binoculars. They were armed with assault rifles. Sturkman noted a flag with a star, but as the white-and-blue Soviet naval ensign did not at all resemble the red national flag of the Soviet Union, he understood only that this must be a foreign submarine. Because of the star, he guessed that it came from the Eastern bloc. Sturkman quickly turned his boat around and returned home. He then called upon his neighbour Ingvar Svensson. The two consulted a flag chart, but it did not include the Soviet naval ensign.

Unsure of the identity of the submarine, Svensson at 9:54 a.m. called the maritime surveillance centre in Karlskrona.

The Navy was responsible for manning a number of maritime surveillance centres. These centres received and collated information from coastal radar stations, ships at sea, lookouts and lighthouses on the coast, the Coast Guard, and other sources (including fishermen like Sturkman and Svensson), so as to allow a good overview of all moving vessels at sea. In 1981, the centre in Naval Base Karlskrona still received and collated the information manually, essentially in the same manner as during the Second World War. Changes were on the way, but they had not yet reached Karlskrona.[10]

Elisabeth Peine, a civilian staff assistant who worked in the maritime surveillance centre, took the call from Svensson. She made a note of the time and what the call was about, and then went to fetch Lieutenant Lars Hellstedt, the commander of the centre. Hellstedt followed her back to the telephone, where Svensson remained on hold. Hellstedt asked Svensson to tell the story one more time, and then promised to investigate the matter.

Hellstedt and his staff knew that no Swedish submarine was in the area. The vague description of the submarine's naval ensign suggested that it might be Polish. While the fisherman had said white-and-blue, perhaps they meant white-and-red, the colours of the Polish naval ensign? Hellstedt's guess was surely more linked to the unusually tense political situation in Poland at the time than the description received. Might the submarine be a defector? Because of the ongoing Polish turmoil, the Swedish government had carried out some advance planning for the risk that a stream of refugees would emerge out of the turbulent country. Anyway, Hellstedt reported the matter to Lieutenant Commander Rolf Edwardsson from the Base Operations Department.

Vasiliy Besedin, dressed in a *kanadka*, the characteristic fur-lined leather jacket of Soviet submariners, signals civilian visitors to keep their distance. This was the sight that met Bertil Sturkman when he approached the submarine. (Photo: Medström)

At 9:59 a.m., the information reached the Naval Operations Department of the headquarters of Military District South, which was responsible for the Karlskrona region. The headquarters of Military District South was located in the town of Kristianstad. In 1981, the Commander of Military District South was Lieutenant General Sven-Olof Olson (1926–2021), an air force officer. He was well-liked by his subordinates, not least because he was sufficiently experienced to allow his subordinates to run their own operations, in the spirit of *Auftragstaktik* (see text box), instead of micro-managing them. This was, of course, particularly important when the military district commander personally lacked experience with, say, naval operations. Then, he would leave the naval professionals to handle operations as they saw fit, as long as they adhered to the given objective, timeframe, and forces with which to accomplish the mission.

Not knowing of any ongoing naval exercise in the area, the Naval Operations Department in turn called the Coast Guard, asking if they knew anything. At 10:00 a.m. they also called the Air Force's Helicopter Squadron at the Blekinge Air Wing (F 17) in Kallinge, in Ronneby Municipality, only a short distance from Karlskrona and for this reason also the town's nearest commercial airport. At 10:50 a.m., the search and rescue helicopter Q 93 was in the air, heading for Gåsefjärden Bay.[11]

Lieutenant General Sven-Olof 'Sven-Olle' Olson, the Air Force officer who served as the commander of Military District South. (Author's collection)

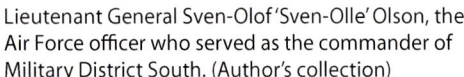

Swedish Air Force Hkp 4 search and rescue helicopter, 1978. The Hkp 4 were made first by Boeing Vertol, and later by Kawasaki Heavy Industries. (Photo: Koster)

SWEDISH ARMED FORCES AND CIVILIAN AGENCIES

The Swedish Armed Forces, formally led by the Supreme Commander and the Defence Staff in Stockholm, were strong in both manpower and technical proficiency during the Cold War. The Supreme Commander had authority over all the service branches: Army, Navy, and Air Force. However, he did not lead operations directly. By tradition, Swedish Armed Forces doctrine was based on mission-type tactics. This concept, internationally perhaps best known under its German name *Auftragstaktik* (Swedish: *uppdragstaktik*), is a method of command and delegation in which the overall commander gives each of his subordinate commanders a clearly-defined objective, timeframe, and forces with which to accomplish the objective, but leaves them freedom of planning and executing the mission independently. *Auftragstaktik* enables flexibility in execution, faster decision-making, frees the senior commanders from the need to micro-manage tactical details, and allows them to focus on strategic decisions.

In this spirit, Sweden was divided into a number of military districts, each under a military district commander responsible for all military units within the district, whether army, navy, or air force. Military district commanders were expected to display initiative and handle all operations within their respective geographical area of responsibility with available resources. If these proved insufficient, then the military district commander could request reinforcements from the Chief of the Defence Staff and the Supreme Commander, who would attempt to reassign units available in other districts.

By 1981, the Navy had severely downsized. It had only three destroyers, which indeed were being decommissioned, and no heavier warships. Instead, the Navy was assisted on land by another service branch, known as the Coastal Artillery. This organisation had originated in the nineteenth century in the system of coastal fortresses that constituted the Archipelago Artillery, which in 1902 was merged with the Marine Regiment. The result was the Coastal Artillery (Swedish: *Kustartilleriet*), which was regarded as an independent branch within the Navy. One of its two regiments was Karlskrona Coastal Artillery Regiment (KA 2), with headquarters in Karlskrona. The regiment primarily consisted of a collection of fixed and mobile artillery units located in often elaborate bunkers on islands in the archipelago. Their task was to defend the coastline against naval raids and invasion fleets. But the Coastal Artillery also included very mobile and highly trained Coastal Ranger companies. Intended for reconnaissance and raiding in a combined sea and land environment, the Coastal Rangers constituted a highly capable elite unit within the Armed Forces, comparable to the Army's Parachute Rangers. The Coastal Ranger unit belonged to Vaxholm Coastal Artillery Regiment (KA 1), based at Vaxholm northeast of Sweden's capital Stockholm.

During the Cold War, Sweden developed the concept of Total Defence (Swedish: *Totalförsvaret*), which defined a large number of civilian agencies and authorities with defence-related tasks in addition to their usual duties and how these tasks and duties should be carried out in times of crisis and war. These were known as the Total Defence Authorities (*Totalförsvarsmyndigheter*). Several of these would play prominent roles in the S-363 incident, including municipal and county authorities which were responsible for civil defence. The Customs Authority (*Tullverket*) was particularly visible during the crisis since it also incorporated the Coast Guard (*Kustbevakningen*). Customs officers were civilians, but in similarity to the police, they could serve in uniform or civilian clothes, and like police officers, had the right to carry handguns. The Coast Guard was an integral part of the Customs Office. Most Coast Guard officers, particularly at sea, wore civilian dress, although they were issued uniforms for formal occasions.

The civilian intelligence agencies also carried out defence-related tasks. Of these, the National Defence Radio Establishment (*Försvarets radioanstalt*, FRA), Sweden's national signals intelligence (SIGINT) authority, and the Defence Research Establishment (*Försvarets forskningsanstalt*, FOA), responsible for most of Sweden's technical intelligence analysis and collection with regard to platforms and weapon systems, played particularly important roles for the Swedish understanding of the S-363 incident.

Commander Karl Andersson

Meanwhile, Ingvar Svensson met his son-in-law, Per Sollin. They discussed whether to call a newspaper. There might be a monetary reward in breaking news of the foreign submarine. Yet, neither wanted to jeopardise any ongoing military operation. As a result, they agreed that Sollin first would call the maritime surveillance centre to ask if it was all right that they informed the press. A few minutes after Svensson's initial call, Sollin called the centre, where Elisabeth Peine again took the call. When Sollin asked if they could call the press, Peine connected him to the Naval Base's press officer, Commander Gunnar Rasmusson. He promised to call back within 10 minutes, after checking what was underway. Having ascertained that there actually was a report of the sighting of an unknown submarine, Rasmusson called back to Sollin, telling him that it was all right to inform the press, as long as he did not 'exaggerate too much'.[12] Knowing all too well how the press would jump on the story of a foreign submarine in the restricted military area, Rasmusson knew that he would have a busy day.

Having received a go-ahead from the Navy, at 10:30 a.m. Sollin called the tabloid *Kvällsposten* in Malmö, where two journalists, Per Gudmundsson and Per-Olof Gunnarsson, waited for something to happen. Gunnarsson took the call.[13]

Meanwhile, Commander Karl Andersson, chief of staff at Naval Base Karlskrona, had decided to look into the matter of Sturkman's report of a stranded submarine, however unlikely it seemed. Andersson was a Navy veteran who had been in the service since military high school. His wife had fled from Soviet rule in Estonia. They had two children. Andersson had just given a briefing for the aforementioned U.S. naval attaché, Captain David Moss, who as we have seen on this very morning visited the base together with his assistant attaché, Commander Edmond Pope. Andersson did not wish to call out the large torpedo boat in port based on the vague information from the telephone call. He knew that the smaller picket boat V 02 *Smyge* ('Stealthy') was available and quite suitable for the job. Originally a small torpedo boat brought into service in 1958, the *Smyge* had been rebuilt as a picket boat in 1977. She was armed with a 40mm cannon. Andersson also did not wish to call in the regular crew which most days, including this one, were engaged in the Karlskrona Naval Training Schools. Instead, Andersson suggested that he and Hellstedt set out with the *Smyge* by themselves, with only two conscript sailors and Sergeant Lars Jacobsson, an engineer, as crew. This was not unusual; in Hellstedt's role as commander of the maritime surveillance centre he had often sailed the *Smyge* when the regular crew was unavailable. True, the motley crew gathered by Andersson was too small to man the boat's cannon, but neither officer expected to need it. Having set out, Andersson noticed that the *Smyge*'s radar was malfunctioning. No matter, he knew these waters as the back of his hand, and so did Hellstedt. They could navigate them safely even in the dense fog that currently reduced visibility. It was then about 10:25 a.m.

The *Smyge* sped towards the specified location to the extent that the persistent fog and low visibility allowed. Although Andersson and Hellstedt did not expect to find any stranded submarine, they would still check Torumskär. Sturkman was an experienced fisherman, and he had surely seen something unusual over there, even if the two officers found the story about a foreign submarine unlikely in the extreme.

Swedish picket boat. (Author's collection)

At 11:05 a.m., the *Smyge* reached Torumskär, and sure enough: a foreign-looking submarine was firmly set on the skerry. Four men stood in the submarine's tower and spied towards them through binoculars. One of them was Besedin, who was on duty at this time. Behind these men, Andersson and Hellstedt could perceive a fifth crewman with an assault rifle slung over his shoulder. At the top of the tower flew the Soviet naval ensign.[14]

Somebody in the submarine command crew, presumably the duty officer Besedin, entered the arrival of the Swedish picket boat in the *S-363*'s logbook at 11:07 a.m.

At 11:09 a.m., Hellstedt reported by radio to the Karlskrona maritime surveillance centre that a submarine indeed had stranded at Torumskär. Then he and Andersson began to leaf through the navy's recognition guide to determine its class. Hellstedt identified the vessel as a Whiskey-class submarine. Andersson later said that his first thought was that it could not possibly be a real Soviet submarine on ground in a restricted military area; surely, this was a combat readiness test of some kind devised by the Defence Staff, perhaps with an old Swedish submarine disguised as a Whiskey in order to test their state of alert. Such a test would also explain the unannounced visit of the two Americans to the base, he surmised. But then Andersson noted the white-and-blue Soviet naval ensign with a red star and hammer and sickle. This was no test.

At 11:12 a.m., Andersson ordered Hellstedt to report to the maritime surveillance centre that they could confirm their initial report, and that the submarine was a Soviet Whiskey.

At 11:14 a.m., the helicopter Q 93 from the Air Wing at Kalinge in Ronneby Municipality reached the submarine.[15] Hellstedt immediately called the helicopter by radio, requesting that any radio message be reported strictly through military channels, not the non-military VHF channels that anybody could listen in to.[16]

Meanwhile, Besedin and the Soviet crew on the *S-363* observed the *Smyge*. They were surprised to see that the *Smyge*'s cannon remained covered with a canvas. Did the Swedes not expect to defend themselves, in case of trouble? The Soviet crew would, no doubt, have been yet more surprised, had they known that Andersson had not brought a gun crew.

Karl Andersson, promoted to captain and appointed commander of Karlskrona Naval Training Schools, 1986. (Naval Museum, Karlskrona)

Briefing the Supreme Commander

At this moment, Per Gudmundsson, the reporter for the tabloid *Kvällsposten*, was already on the phone to Commander Sven 'Sven-Calle' Carlsson, press officer at the Navy Staff in Stockholm. When asked, Carlsson said that he had not heard of any stranded submarine. No report had yet reached the Navy Staff from Naval Base Karlskrona. Andersson and Hellstedt were still in the process of verifying the report of the stranded foreign submarine. Carlsson then called Karlskrona, where he got hold of the press officer, Gunnar Rasmusson. He asked Carlsson to hold while he went to check with the maritime surveillance centre. He got there at almost the same time as Hellstedt's first radio report reached the centre. Three minutes later, the Soviet identity was confirmed. Rasmusson went back to the telephone, informing Carlsson about the incident.

Carlsson, in turn, contacted Lieutenant Colonel Jan-Åke Berg, chief press officer of the Defence Staff in Stockholm. At 11:15 a.m., Carlsson told Berg that a Soviet submarine had stranded in the restricted military area near Naval Base Karlskrona. Both realised that they must inform the Supreme Commander.

The Supreme Commander was General Lennart Ljung (1921–1990). He was well-liked by most officers under his command. The General saw it as his duty to safeguard their interests and those of the Armed Forces as a whole, especially in times of budget cuts. He also enjoyed the confidence of Prime Minister Thorbjörn Fälldin (1926–2016), who regarded Ljung as a key authority on military matters. However, there were complaints, including from Lieutenant General Olson in Military Region South, who argued that Ljung's style of command intruded on the customary *Auftragstaktik* employed by the Swedish Armed Forces. During the recent Soviet exercise Zapad 81, Olson said, the Supreme Commander had issued so many direct orders that his immediate subordinates at times were reduced to little more than middlemen.[17]

Soon after 11:30 a.m., Sven Carlsson, the press officer of the Navy Staff, called back to Gudmundsson, confirming the presence of a Soviet submarine. As a result, the tabloid *Kvällposten* managed to include the information in the last edition of the day.[18]

Meanwhile, reporting was also taking place according to standard operating procedures and chain of command. Having received Andersson's and Hellstedt's report that confirmed the story of the stranded submarine, and that the submarine was a Soviet Whiskey, the Karlskrona maritime surveillance centre at 11:21 a.m. sent an urgent encrypted teletype report to the Commander of Military District South in Kristianstad, with a simultaneous copy to the Operations Section in the Defence Staff (Fst/Op 2) in Stockholm. In Kristianstad, Lieutenant General Olson made sure that those who needed the information, locally as well General Ljung in Stockholm, had received the information. Following his own philosophy, he then let his subordinates do their job without his interference.[19]

Carlsson and Berg wrapped up their meeting with General Ljung soon after 11:30 a.m. Ljung ordered them to prepare a press release about the situation. As they were leaving the Supreme Commander, an officer from the Operations Section was already on his way in to the General with the urgent encrypted teletype report from Karlskrona.[20]

'My Tugboats Will Pull You Off the Rock and Then You Can Leave Our Waters'

Meanwhile, Andersson and Hellstedt on the *Smyge* approached the submarine. Coming closer, they could see that the stranded submarine surely could not get off the rock without help. They approached the submarine, intending to climb aboard.

Soon after 11:15 a.m. (at 11:10 a.m. according to the *S-363*'s logbook), Andersson climbed aboard the submarine, where a sentry armed with a Kalashnikov assault rifle awaited him. Unarmed as he was, Andersson did not believe that the Soviets would open fire as he approached. In addition to the sentry, there were three other men in the tower. Andersson tried to address them in English but no one seemed to understand what he was saying. As he tried German

one of the Soviets stepped forward. This was Avrukevich who spoke German. When Andersson asked about the name of the submarine, Avrukevich after some hesitation said that it was *U-Boot 137*, that is, submarine 137. Unwilling to reveal the submarine's permanent designation *S-363*, he gave the current but temporary bort number 137 as its designation. As a result, both the Swedes and, for this reason, the Western press hereafter referred to the submarine as the U 137. This remains its popular name in Western publications. That its permanent designation was *S-363* remained classified at the time.

Avrukevich introduced Andersson to the submarine's commander. Gushchin did not speak German. Andersson was informed that his name was Anatoliy Mikhaylovich Gushchin and that his rank was that of Captain Third Rank. Andersson attempted to write down the unfamiliar name on a piece of paper, but he only managed the first three letters: G U S. To assist, Avrukevich grabbed the pen and wrote, in German, the commander's rank and name for Andersson on the paper. Then he added 'U-Boot 137' for good measure. Avrukevich did not introduce himself at this time. Several days later, on Sunday 1 November, he told Andersson, perhaps tongue in cheek, that he was the submarine's 'navigation expert' (in German: *Ich bin der navigationsexperte*). Considering the situation, Avrukevich immediately afterwards added that he was the 'former navigation expert'.[21]

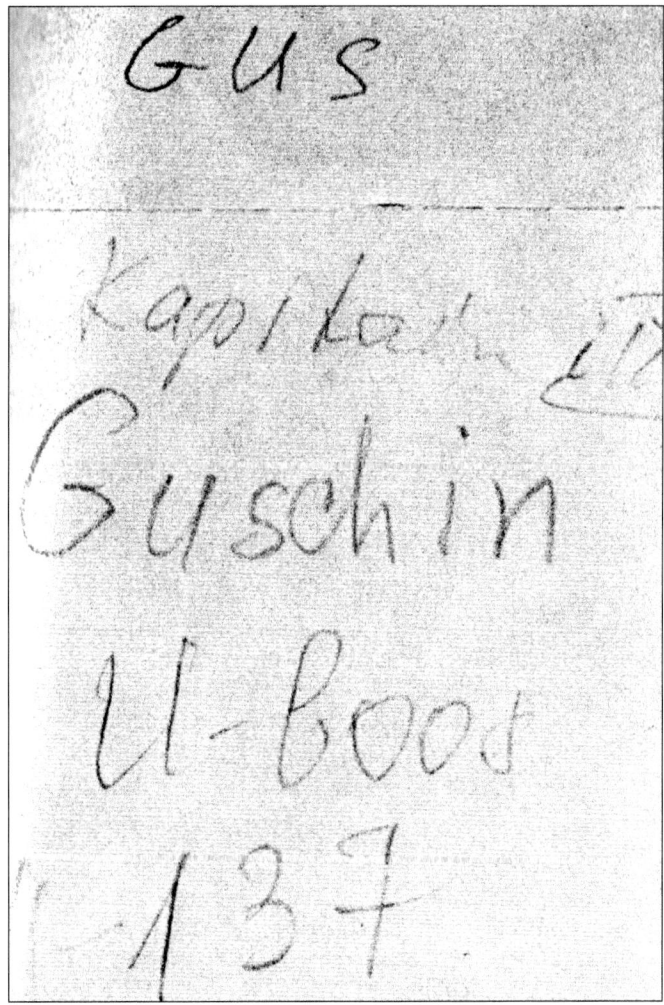

Avrukevich's handwritten note. (Author's collection)

Avrukevich now asked Andersson if he could show their exact position. He asked a crewman to bring a navigational chart. The man returned with what Andersson, from a distance and at first glance, thought looked like a detailed chart of the Blekinge archipelago. Andersson thought that it might be more detailed than the regular chart used by the Swedish Navy for navigation in the archipelago. Avrukevich quickly dismissed the chart and sent the crewman to retrieve a significantly less detailed chart of the entire southern Baltic Sea. The Soviets later denied any knowledge of the detailed chart, a fact henceforth frequently noted by Swedish representatives as evidence that the submarine was on an espionage mission. There is no way of knowing if Andersson's first impression was correct. The navigational chart was never seen again, including when the Swedes later inspected the inside of the submarine. Possibly Andersson overreacted to the unfamiliar situation. In a subsequent interview, Andersson noted that he could not really be certain that the chart covered the Blekinge archipelago. Perhaps it was another area? Andersson had only caught a brief glimpse of the rolled-up chart from a distance of two or three metres, and he had not been able to pick out any names or familiar islands on it.[22] So what was the chart? Perhaps the crewman brought a chart that indicated the submarine's secret patrol areas east of Bornholm? Avrukevich would certainly not at this stage have wanted a Swedish officer to see this information. This was a first-contact situation for both Andersson and Avrukevich, and Andersson later related that the unfamiliar situation and the language difficulties frequently caused unintended tensions.

Andersson gave them the approximate coordinates (logged at 11:10 a.m. as 56°03'09"N 15°46'0"E), and then returned to the *Smyge*.[23] The Soviets entered his departure in the *S-363*'s logbook at 11:22 a.m. Back at the *Smyge*, Andersson called Karlskrona on the radio, reporting that he just had been onboard the Soviet submarine 137 under command of Captain Gushchin. The time was 11:24 a.m. Eight minutes later, at 11:32 a.m., Naval Base Karlskrona logged that the submarine claimed a distress situation.[24]

At the latest around this time, the *S-363* received a telegram from Fleet Headquarters, informing them that assistance was on its way. Vice Admiral Aleksey Kalinin, the First Deputy Commander of the Baltic Fleet, had called up a salvage group that would be able to pull the *S-363* off the rock.[25]

Another telegram, apparently received at about the same time, ordered the crew to guard and protect the submarine, and not to allow anybody onboard. As a result, the command crew posted additional armed sentries: one in the forward torpedo compartment, two on the bridge, and two in the tower.[26]

At around 11:30 a.m., the Naval Base called the Coastal Artillery Headquarters and reported the submarine incident. A few minutes later, the Coastal Artillery ordered the duty squad – about 20 soldiers armed with old submachineguns – at Karlskrona Coastal Artillery Regiment (KA 2), to grab their weapons and move to Torumskär. The duty squad consisted of conscripts who only had been in the service for five weeks. Since nobody knew how long the mission would last, the conscripts were sent to have lunch before departure.[27] Ultimately, the soldiers were deployed on Torumskär close to the submarine, to keep it under observation but also to open fire if the Soviets acted suspiciously.

When Andersson had reported the situation, he returned to the submarine. The submarine crew entered his second visit on the day in the *S-363*'s logbook at 11:44 a.m. The submarine crew sent an encrypted high-speed telegram at 11:46 a.m.[28] Presumably, they informed Kaliningrad about Andersson's arrival. Andersson first asked about the supply situation of the submariners. Did they need food and fresh water?[29] Avrukevich said that so far, they were good.

Avrukevich and Gushchin then explained their navigational problems. The radio direction finder had malfunctioned, the gyrocompass was wrong, and the receiver for the Decca Navigator System had provided wrong signals. In addition, the hydrophone functioned poorly.

Gyrocompasses are important for navigation on ships because they have two significant advantages over magnetic compasses. First, they find and retain true north as determined by the axis of the Earth's rotation, not magnetic north as in ordinary compasses which rely on the Earth's magnetic field. Second, a gyrocompass has a greater degree of accuracy because it is unaffected by ferromagnetic materials, such as in a ship's steel hull, which distort the magnetic field. This makes the gyrocompass particularly useful within an enclosed submarine.

Avrukevich told Andersson that they expected to be salvaged by Soviet tugboats later during the day. However, Andersson said that no foreign ships were permitted into the restricted military area, and without the proper permits they would not be allowed even to cross the border.[30]

Instead, Andersson said, he would arrange for Swedish tugboats to salvage the submarine.[31] Apparently Andersson said: 'There are my tugboats. They will pull you off the rock and then you can leave our waters.'[32]

When translated, Besedin interpreted Andersson's reply as an offer to bring tugboats immediately, so that the Soviet submarine could return home. He felt deeply relieved. However, Besedin related that when they informed Fleet Headquarters, they were ordered to refuse Swedish assistance, since Soviet tugboats already were on their way.[33]

Did Commander Andersson offer to salvage and release the submarine without further hassle? It was obvious to anybody that the *S-363* was in distress. It had stranded on a rock and could not move. International law and Swedish naval instructions agreed that a foreign naval vessel in distress would be salvaged and, when safe, set on its way without further questioning or inspections. The official standing operating procedures for the Armed Forces in cases of peacetime violations of the territory, the so-called General Order for the Swedish Armed Forces in Peacetime and in a State of Neutrality of 1967, known in Swedish under the abbreviation IKFN, limited the Navy's freedom of manouevre by insisting that under these circumstances the submarine, upon discovery, should be salvaged and turned away from Swedish waters.[34] It would accordingly have been logical for Andersson to offer assistance. But the *S-363* was in a restricted military area. Did this circumstance change standing naval procedures? And if so, did Andersson take this into account? There is currently no way of knowing, since Andersson has passed away. Swedish official sources are adamant that no offer of immediate salvage was made and moreover, an offer of this kind would have been in contravention of decisions later in the day taken in Stockholm – so could not have been made. Yet, Stockholm had not yet made its decision. Andersson had only the IKFN to guide him. It does indeed seem very likely that the offer to salvage the submarine was genuine, and we will see that other evidence support Besedin's interpretation. Besides, in hindsight it is obvious that much trouble, and escalating risks of military action, would have been avoided, had the Swedish Navy accepted the presence of the Soviet submarine as the result of navigational error, and quietly assisted it in returning home.

Be that as it may, Fleet Headquarters in Kaliningrad anyway refused to accept the apparent offer of assistance. Later, rumour suggested that this refusal of assistance had less to do with international prestige than with Fleet Headquarters's realisation

In 1981, the Soviet Navy still followed the uniform regulations of 1973. Storage was limited on Whiskey-class submarines, so submarine officers brought little luggage onboard during missions. They did not bring all uniform variants. The officers of the *S-363* wore daily off-duty uniform No. 4 (with peaked cap, as illustrated here) or No. 5 (with fur cap, *ushanka*), for winter use, when they met Swedish representatives. They did not carry sidearms under normal working conditions. (Artwork by Renato Dalmaso)

When on deck during winter conditions, Soviet submarine crews customarily wore the *kanadka* ('Canadian coat'), which despite its name was the characteristic fur-lined leather jacket of Soviet submariners. Many would wear fur caps against the cold. Others simply pulled the hood over their cap, which might be a peaked cap or the ubiquitous side cap or *pilotka* ('little pilot') originally part of the Air Force uniform but because of its compact size also very popular among submariners. Most submariners carried no sidearms, but the submarine armoury contained a total of 10 standard Kalashnikov assault rifles of the AKM 7.62 x 39mm type and one RPK 7.62 x 39mm machine gun. (Artwork by Renato Dalmaso)

The S-363, commanded by Captain Third Rank Anatoliy Gushchin, was a medium-sized diesel-electric attack submarine of the class that the Soviet Union designated Project 613. In the West, the class was better known under its NATO reporting name Whiskey. The submarine was 76m long. The S-363 was built in Leningrad in 1956, as one of 215 vessels of its class built from 1951 to 1957. The submarine had been in service for 24 years, and some of its crew were not yet born when the S-363 entered into service. Its armament consisted of 14 torpedoes, which included two SAET-60M nuclear torpedoes, two SAET-60M conventional torpedoes, six SET-53M antisubmarine warfare conventional torpedoes, and four 53-65K conventional torpedoes. Doctrine designated nuclear torpedoes as the primary means to destroy enemy aircraft carrier groups and similar high-value targets. This profile is based on the sketches and descriptions compiled by Swedish military intelligence during the crisis. Other submarines of the class, and particularly the export versions, sometimes employed different configurations. (Artwork by Anderson Subtil)

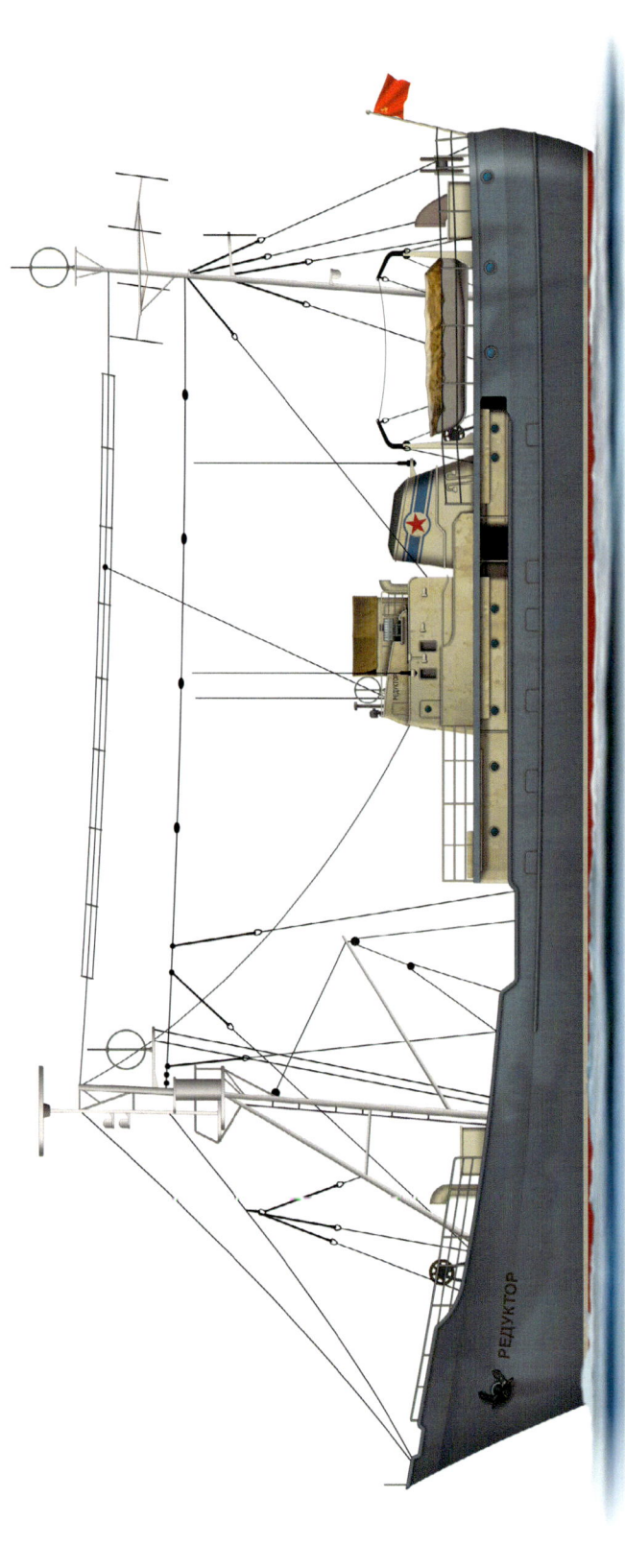

The *Reduktor* ('Reduction Gear', a name apparently chosen for no particular reason) was a small intelligence collection ship of the class for which NATO used the reporting name Okean. The name of her commanding officer, or the number of her crew, was never released. She was 50.8m long. Built on a trawler frame and with the intention to resemble a civilian trawler, the *Reduktor* was primarily a SIGINT collector. However, she carried out other intelligence-related tasks as well, including arms deliveries from the KGB to the Official IRA, an Irish paramilitary group with Marxist leanings. The *Reduktor* sported an impressive array of antennas for SIGINT collection. The tarpaulin above the bridge likely hid yet other, but more sensitive antennas. The *Reduktor* remained in service until 1992. (Artwork by Anderson Subtil)

WHISKY ON THE ROCKS VOLUME 1: A SOVIET SUBMARINE STRANDED IN SWEDISH WATERS, 1981

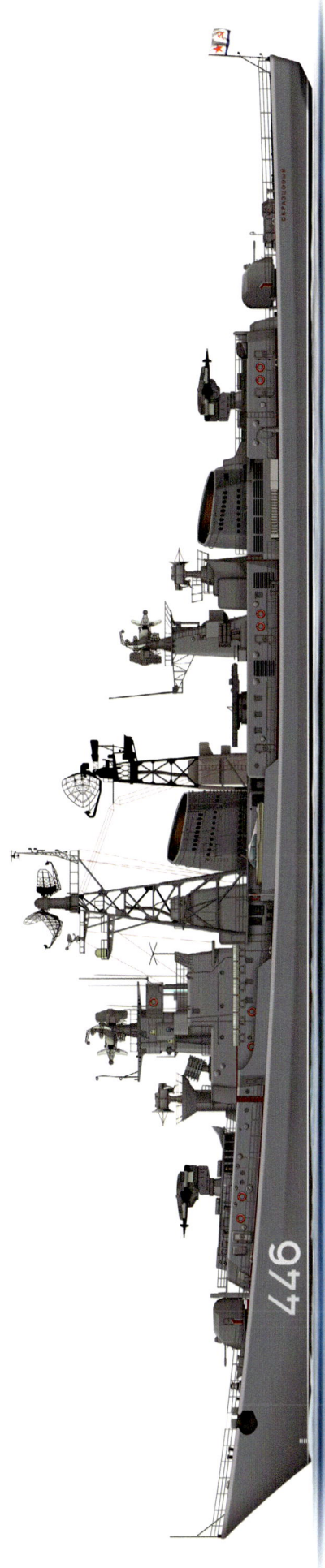

The *Obraztsovyy* ('Exemplary') was a large antisubmarine warfare ship of 128th Missile Ship Brigade in Baltiysk. She was 143.95m long. Her primary weapons consisted of antisubmarine rockets and 533mm torpedoes. The class (Project 61; NATO reporting name Kashin) entered service in 1962 and constituted the first Soviet warship class designed to be closed down for nuclear fallout. The *Obraztsovyy* was commissioned in 1965. During the crisis, Vice Admiral Aleksey Kalinin employed her as flagship. The *Obraztsovyy* had a crew of 266 including 32 officers. (Artwork by Anderson Subtil)

The *Prozorlivyy* ('Sharp-eyed') was 126.1m long. A large missile ship of the class known as Project 56U (NATO reporting name Kildin-Mod), she had entered into service in 1958 but been modernised in 1976–1977. Commanded by Captain Third Rank Viktor Lyakin, she carried anti-ship missiles of the type P-15 Termit, NATO reporting name SS-N-2 STYX, which made her a more dangerous adversary to surface vessels than Kalinin's flagship. Before her return to the Baltic Sea to participate in Zapad 81 and other exercises, Captain Lyakin and the *Prozorlivyy* had been on a combat mission to Angola with orders to support the MPLA government against the insurgent UNITA. The *Prozorlivyy* had a crew of 270 including 19 officers. (Artwork by Anderson Subtil)

In winter, Swedish Air Force flying officers wore standard flight suit model 1976, with warm underwear to preserve body temperature. To the flight suit was added a flight helmet, anti-G trousers which when connected to a valve in the aircraft automatically pressurised during high-G manoeuvring, and an inflatable life vest. The flight suit came with large transparent thigh pockets for flight maps, which enabled the pilot to consult them without changing his position. (Artwork by Renato Dalmaso)

Western navies tended to be traditional, and the Swedish Navy was no exception. In 1981, Swedish Navy officers dressed in uniforms model 1948 which looked very similar to those of their Soviet counterparts. Some uniform items were of even older origin, for instance the black shoes of model 1903. Navy officers did not carry sidearms under normal working conditions. (Artwork by Renato Dalmaso)

The Coastal Artillery was the Swedish Navy's ground forces. They were not marines. The organisation originated in the system of coastal fortresses that constituted the nineteenth-century Archipelago Artillery, which in 1902 was merged with the Marine Regiment. The result was the Coastal Artillery, an independent branch within the Navy. One of its two regiments was Karlskrona Coastal Artillery Regiment (KA 2), with headquarters in Karlskrona. The regiment manned a collection of fixed and mobile artillery units located in often elaborate bunkers on islands in the archipelago. Their task was to defend the coastline against naval raids and invasion fleets. At the time of the 1981 crisis, most Coastal Artillery soldiers in KA 2 were fresh conscripts who had only received a few days of training. The majority were about 19 years old. Most of those who now were called to man the defences had actually been called up as cooks, not artillerymen, but they quickly learned on the job how to man the heavy cannons of the Coastal Artillery. They wore the Army's green field uniform model 1959 and were armed with the old 9mm submachinegun Carl Gustaf model 45B, adopted in 1945. The weapon was old but reliable and far from obsolete. It was manufactured under, and sometimes without, license in many countries, not least the United States where U.S. Navy SEALs and CIA operatives used it extensively during the Vietnam War. In U.S. service, the gun was often known as the 'Swedish-K'. (Artwork by Renato Dalmaso)

The Coast Guard was the maritime arm of the Swedish Customs Authority. Customs and Coast Guard officers were civilians. They were issued uniforms for formal occasions, but in similarity to the police, they could serve in either uniform or plainclothes. Like police officers, they had the right to carry handguns. Most Coast Guard sailors, particularly at sea, wore a combination of civilian dress and service-issue garments. The heavy-duty work overall and, in cold weather, the fur hat, seem to have been particularly popular. This sailor primarily wears civilian dress, and he carries necessary supplies in a variety of civilian containers. (Artwork by Renato Dalmaso)

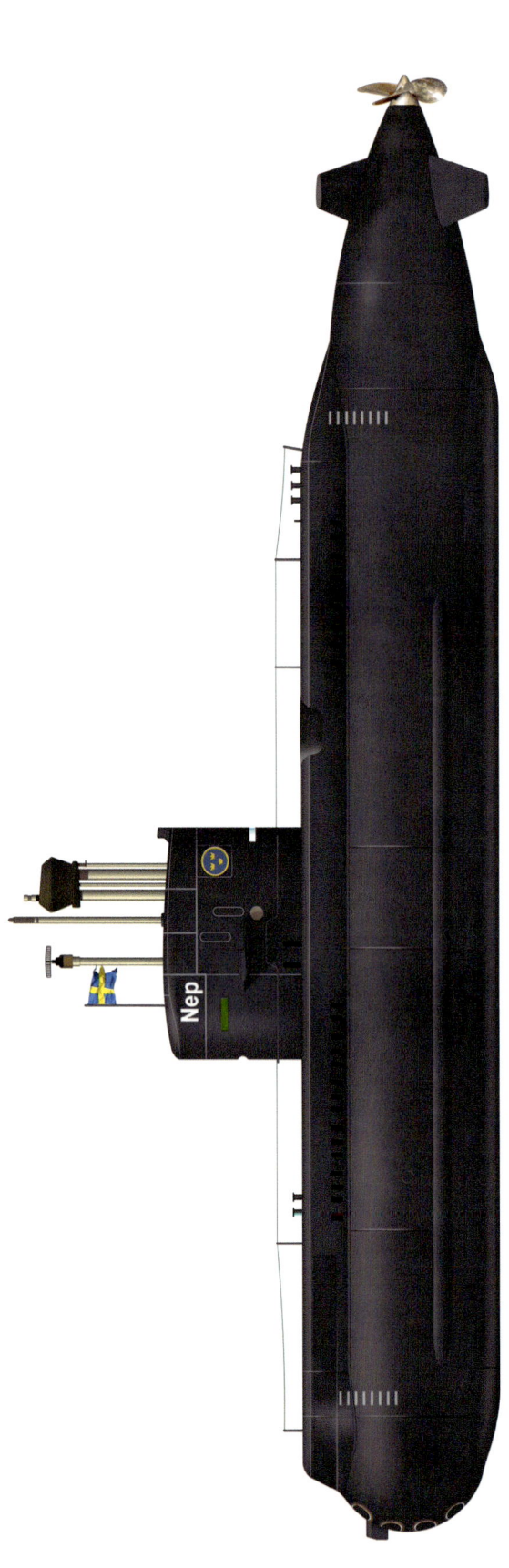

The submarine *Neptun*, built in 1979 as the *Neptun II* and one of the Swedish Navy's three modern Näcken-class submarines, had a length of 49.5m, a beam of 5.7m, and a draught of 5.5m. It carried a crew of only 19 men. The submarine was armed with eight 53cm torpedoes in six torpedo tubes and four 40cm torpedoes in two torpedo tubes. Surface displacement was 1,013 tons, with an underwater displacement of 1,125 tons. The submarine's maximum speed was 20kts on the surface, or 10kts submerged. Maximum regulation depth was 300m. During the crisis, Lieutenant Björn Hamilton was acting commander of the *Neptun*. (Artwork by Anderson Subtil)

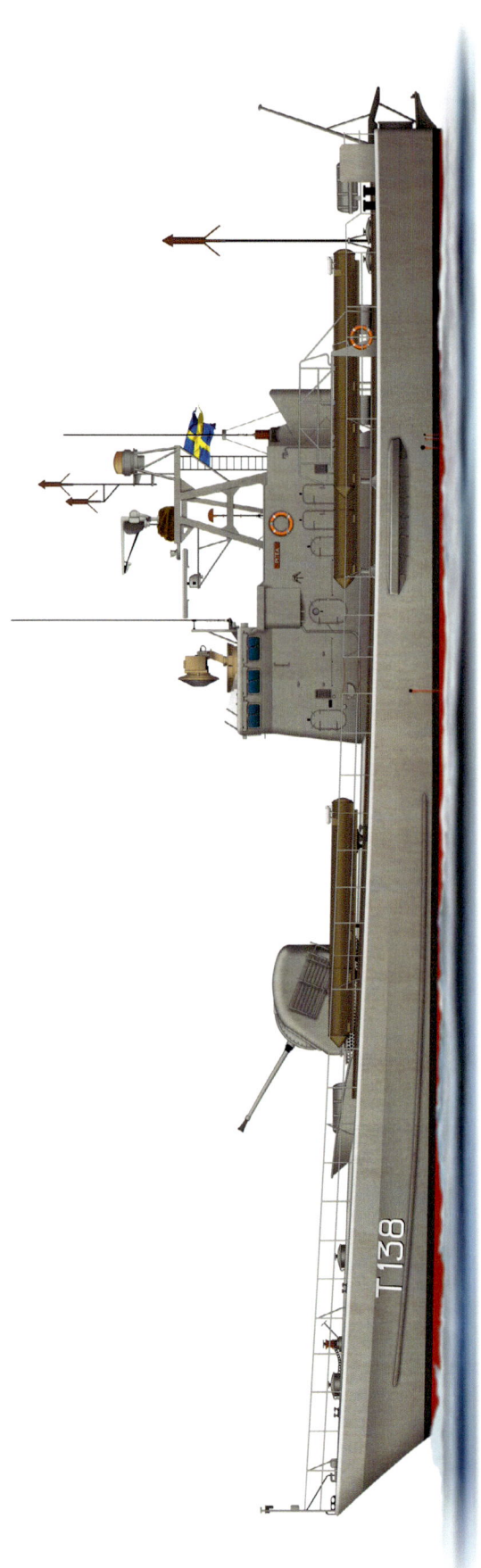

The T 138 *Piteå* (named after a town), under the command of Commander Bengt Törnwall who simultaneously also commanded the 13th Torpedo Boat Division, was the first Swedish torpedo boat that reached Gåsefjärden Bay during the crisis. She was 41.5m long. One of the 12 torpedo boats of the Norrköping class (named after another town) built between 1971 and 1974, she is depicted here with the full armament of a torpedo boat of her class. This means six 53cm torpedoes (one forward and two aft tubes on each side) and a single 57mm Bofors automatic cannon. However, in reality the *Piteå* was in the process of being converted into a missile boat and carried no torpedoes at the time. The *Piteå* had a regular crew of 14 officers and 16 conscripted sailors. (Artwork by Anderson Subtil)

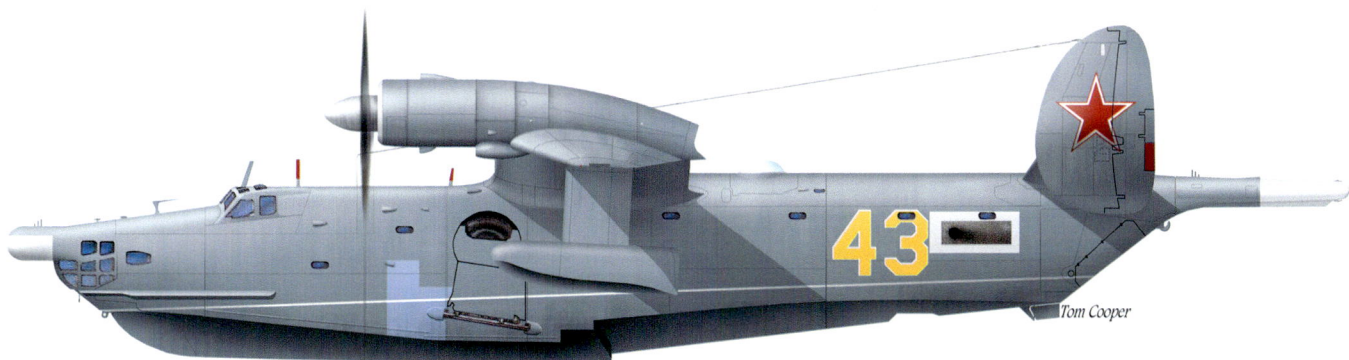

The Beriev Be-12 was a Soviet twin-engine turboprop-powered flying boat equipped to detect and combat submerged submarines. Known in the Soviet Union as *Chayka* ('seagull'), the Be-12 had retractable landing gear, which enabled it to land on normal land runways as well as water. It was taken into service in 1961, and production continued until 1973. The capacity to land on water made the Be-12 highly suitable for rescue operations at sea. The aircraft carried a maritime surveillance radar system housed in the nose cone, and an advanced magnetic anomaly detector (MAD) in the tail for detecting submerged submarines. In its antisubmarine warfare role, the aircraft could carry depth charges, mines, and antisubmarine torpedoes. A few were refitted to carry nuclear depth charges of the type 5F48, which was an unguided parachute bomb. The Be-12 carried a crew of five and was a very versatile aircraft. (Artwork by Tom Cooper)

The Antonov An-12 was a four-engine Soviet turboprop transport aircraft that existed in a large number of military and civilian variants, including dedicated versions for electronic intelligence collection, electronic countermeasures, and communications relay duties. Production began in 1958 and ended in 1973. There is some confusion over Soviet designations, because apparently the initial designation was sometimes retained even when the individual aircraft was modified for other tasks. The NATO reporting name for all ELINT versions was CUB B. Many An 12s, including the ELINT versions such as this one, carried two 23mm Afanas'yev Makarov AM-23 autocannons in a defensive tail gun turret. (Artwork by Tom Cooper)

The Ilyushin Il-20M (NATO reporting name 'COOT-A') was a Soviet signals intelligence (SIGINT) collection aircraft in production from 1968 to 1976. Based on the Il-18 passenger transport design, the Il-20M was an advanced reconnaissance aircraft capable of collecting a vast range of intelligence. The aircraft is equipped for electronic intelligence (ELINT) and communications intelligence (COMINT) with the Vishnya, Romb, and Kvadrat systems. The cigar-shaped case under the fuselage contains an Igla-1 side looking airborne radar (SLAR), employed for radar imaging and mapping purposes. Finally, the aircraft houses large A-87P camera equipment on the forward sides of the fuselage. There is a lounge with simple double passenger seats, a wardrobe, buffet, and a toilet in the tail of the aircraft. The Il-20M had a crew of 13: two pilots, navigator, engineer, radioman, and eight operators of reconnaissance equipment. (Artwork by Tom Cooper)

The Saab AJ 37 Viggen was the standard Swedish strike fighter aircraft. For operations against naval targets, the AJ 37 was typically armed with the powerful anti-ship missile RB 04E, two of which were carried below the delta wing. The aircraft also carries an auxiliary fuel tank. The number shows that this aircraft belonged to the Västgöta Air Wing (F 6). (Artwork by Tom Cooper)

The 37 Viggen also came in two reconnaissance versions. These were known, respectively, as SF 37 Viggen and SH 37 Viggen (F for photographic reconnaissance, H for maritime radar surveillance). Each reconnaissance squadron included both versions of the aircraft and one of each regularly flew together to complement each other during reconnaissance missions. The SF 37, intended for photo reconnaissance, had a characteristic nose cone that housed a set of advanced cameras. Additional camera pods were carried, too. This particular aircraft belonged to the Bråvalla Air Wing (F 13). (Artwork by Tom Cooper)

The closely related SH 37, intended for radar reconnaissance, could be recognised by its black nose cone that housed a radar. This particular aircraft, too, belonged to the Bråvalla Air Wing (F 13). Either reconnaissance version might also carry the auxiliary fuel tank and camera pods. (Artwork by Tom Cooper)

The stranded submarine *S-363*. (Naval Museum, Karlskrona)

that it would face difficulties in paying Swedish salvage fees in hard currency. The Soviet rouble was not easily convertible.

Andersson had noticed leaked oil around the submarine, the same oil that Sturkman had seen, too. Several days later (on Sunday 1 November), Avrukevich explained the presence of the oil to Andersson. Some of the submarine's tanks were combined diesel and ballast tanks. When the crew desperately had pumped water back and forth between the tanks in the attempt to get off the rock, some oil had leaked out.[35]

Since it was 12:30 p.m., Avrukevich invited Andersson to lunch. When first boarding the submarine, Andersson had already noted the seabed mud on the ladder outside the tower. Apparently, the Soviets had sent down divers. The Soviet officers gave him work gloves so that he would not soil his suede gloves when climbing the ladder. But to Andersson, the question of divers was of greater interest, since it was also not permitted for foreigners to dive within the restricted area. Andersson asked, by his own later admission in a perhaps overly sharp tone, whether they had sent down divers, which Avrukevich confirmed. He explained that they had checked the submarine hull and how the vessel was stuck.[36]

While waiting for the mess crew to prepare lunch, Andersson, Avrukevich, and Gushchin engaged in conversation. They told Andersson that they came from Baltiysk. Both Avrukevich and Gushchin mentioned that they lived there, and that both were married and had children.

Lunch consisted of bread, sardines in oil, tuna, and pastries. The Soviet officers served wine (which was allowed onboard in small quantities) and vodka (which formally was not). Andersson found the vodka highly dubious: it had a reddish colour and looked like the spirit used in a compass. When he tasted it, he discovered that it felt like drinking 96-percent-proof alcohol. He declined, at first politely but later in a sharp voice when the Soviets insisted that he toast, suspecting that it was some kind of trick to get him drunk.[37] Which indeed it was; Besedin much later related that Fleet Headquarters, in a desperate attempt to improve negotiations, had sent a telegram request that the submarine officers treat their Swedish counterparts with 'tea in the Russian manner'. This amused the submariners, since Soviet naval crews were not allowed to drink vodka during a mission. The vodka was accordingly prepared by the submarine's physician, Lieutenant Aleksey Starostenko, with the added expertise of chief engineer Arkhipov and chief navigator Korostov, who diluted pure medicinal spirit with water, and finally added cherry juice.[38]

5
THE SWEDES MOBILISE

When lunch was concluded, Andersson returned to deck. The *S-363*'s logbook gives the time as 12:57 p.m. Andersson later confirmed that it was just before 1:00 p.m. By then, the helicopter had returned to Kallinge, and the Swedish Navy torpedo boat T 138 *Piteå* had reached Gåsefjärden Bay (at 12:58 p.m. according to Swedish records, at 1:00 p.m. according to the *S-363*'s logbook), anchoring just beyond the *Smyge*. The *Piteå* had been on a trial run, and lacked much of its ordinary armament (she was in the process of being converted into a missile boat), but was diverted to Torumskär when Andersson reported in the submarine.

The two tugboats A 253 *Hermes* and A 322 *Heros* from Naval Base Karlskrona had arrived, too. This supports the suggestion that the Swedes at first intended to salvage and release the submarine, and that Karl Andersson's offer was not only made, as Besedin said, but also was supported by other officers at the naval base. Commanded by Commander Thor Widell, Master of Equipment (Swedish: *ekipagemästare*) at Karlskrona, the tugboats had set out already at 11:37 a.m. Their presence is the key evidence that not only Andersson but other base officers as well, including Widell, were ready to salvage and release the *S-363*. Why else bring two tugboats to the scene?

Andersson handed over command to Commander Bengt Törnwall, commanding officer on the *Piteå* and simultaneously commander of the 13th Torpedo Boat Division. He then boarded the *Smyge* to report to the Naval Base. At 2:00 p.m., Andersson returned to base with the *Smyge*. The two tugboats returned to base, too, but only at 4:45 p.m. The reason was likely either that the Soviets had refused to accept assistance or because of recent countermanding orders from Karlskrona. By then, the T 134 *Varberg*, a torpedo boat which belonged to the 13th Torpedo Boat Division, had joined the other vessels at Torumskär.[1]

It was difficult for Base Command to despatch more vessels. They lacked the men. Most crews of the 13th Torpedo Boat Division had just concluded a five-week mission to shadow the huge Warsaw Pact exercise Zapad 81 (which took place in July–September 1981 – officially, 4–12 September – and notably was the largest Soviet military exercise carried out in the Baltic region), so they had recently been sent home. Base Command recalled all those who lived in or near Karlskrona to Base. Andersson – who now had switched role from on-site incident commander to chief of staff (and from the next day again would switch role, to that of lead negotiator) – was acutely aware of the lack of armament during his own reconnaissance, so he ordered the torpedo boat crews to make sure that they brought live torpedoes and weapons fully loaded. Coastal Artillery Headquarters offered Base Command the loan of the artillery's minelayer, the *Mul 13*, and a picket boat.

Following a request for reinforcements from Lieutenant General Olson, commander of Military District South, the Defence Staff in Stockholm called up the 13th Patrol Boat Division at Gålö in the Stockholm archipelago, under Commander Anders Malmgren, ordering the patrol boats south to Karlskrona to reinforce the naval forces already in place. Olson also requested additional helicopters.[2] The Navy's underwater Explosive Ordnance Disposal (EOD) team with four small minesweepers, then deployed at Åhus to the southwest, were ordered to Karlskrona, too.[3]

Since the submarine had stranded between two permanent lines of mines, divers were sent out to investigate whether the mines remained in place and were intact.[4] Altogether, about 1,000 Swedish military personnel were called up in the Karlskrona area.[5]

Meanwhile, the *S-363* at 1:11 p.m. received acknowledgment of the previous message (sent at 11:46 a.m.). The actual response arrived at 1:24 p.m.[6]

The acknowledgment from Fleet Headquarters was the first telegram of the series of communications between the *S-363* and Kaliningrad that was intercepted by the Swedish national SIGINT service, FRA.[7] FRA had been slow to notice the Soviet transmissions from the Karlskrona area, but having been alerted to the situation, the SIGINT agency moved into action.

The Navy operated EW units, which henceforth were activated. Like the Osnaz section on the Soviet submarine, these primarily handled ELINT. Unfortunately, their interception systems were obsolete and, it was found later, had difficulties in distinguishing between, for instance, the surface surveillance radar Flag (NATO reporting name Snoop Plate) of Project 613 submarines and the similar radar systems used by civilian vessels including fishing boats.[8]

The Karlskrona police, too, had the submarine in their sights. The Swedish Constitution gave the police, not the Armed Forces, the mandate and duty to handle illegal border crossings and the

Coastal Artillery minelayer *Mul 13*, known as the *Kalmarsund*. Because of the abbreviation Mul (Swedish: *minutläggare*, 'minelayer'), these vessels were sometimes known as mules. Mul vessels were about 30m in length, carried rails and cranes for mines, and had a speed of about 10 knots. Each carried an anti-aircraft cannon for self-defence. Several classes of mostly similar minelayers formed part of the Coastal Artillery inventory at the time. Taken into service in 1953, the *Mul 13* was armed with a model 1936 (m/36) Bofors 40mm cannon, a well-known cannon widely used by multiple armies in the Second World War and later. The photo shows the *Mul 13* as a museum vessel, in 2010. (Photo: Bolstermage)

Coastal Artillery picket boat type 72, the type in common service in 1981. (Author's collection)

investigation of foreign nationals trespassing in restricted areas. In times of peace, it was always the police which was responsible for public order and security.

The police despatched two teams. The first consisted of two detectives, one of whom was Detective Inspector Sven Johansson, and two uniformed policemen onboard the Coast Guard vessel *Tv 012*. The Coast Guard vessel reached the submarine at 1:50 p.m.[9] They also brought a civilian interpreter, the 72-year-old Brian Olsson, a former sailor who in 1931 ran away from a Swedish ship in the Black Sea port of Poti and then lived for four years in Soviet Ukraine. Olsson served as interpreter for the first two days of the crisis.[10] The second team came in a small open boat, which brought acting county prosecutor Bengt Kviele and the policeman Bengt Abrahamsson. As acting county prosecutor, it was Kviele's duty to investigate whether the stranded submarine constituted a suspected case of espionage.[11]

Kviele boarded the Swedish torpedo boat, the T 138 *Piteå*, where he met Törnwall and Karl Andersson, who although he was in a hurry to get back to base told Kviele what he knew about the Soviet submarine. Realising that the situation was unusually sensitive, Kviele decided that the final decision on whether to carry out an investigation must be left to the national government.

Meanwhile, Detective Inspector Johansson first interviewed the crew of the *Piteå*, and then, at around 2:40 p.m., had the Coast Guard vessel *Tv 012* move up alongside the submarine. Johansson called out to the Soviet crew. The crewman in the tower confirmed to Johansson that this was indeed a Soviet submarine, but he then declined further questions. Seeing the Kalashnikov-armed sentry in the tower, Johansson decided to step back. He, too, concluded that the national government would have to decide how to proceed.[12] Henceforth, judicial considerations and the legislative framework would play a minimal role in how the Swedish government chose to handle the incident. Nonetheless, the police maintained a discrete presence in the area, including on the Coast Guard vessels, and remained in readiness to support an operation against the submarine, should one be required.

In the evening, the Coast Guard vessel *Tv 281* from Kalmar commanded by Arne Magnusson asked permission to moor next to the submarine. The submariners were only happy to have another vessel close. They also realised that this would ensure functioning communications with the Swedes.[13]

The Karlskrona Fire Brigade moved two powerful searchlights to Torumskär, from which they made sure that the submarine was fully illuminated from a distance of only 50m.[14] With soldiers, sailors, police, and firemen all present in the area, the Armed Forces established an operations headquarters on neighbouring Hästholmen Island.

Onboard the submarine, Besedin and Yakovlev made an inventory of supplies. They had food for 15 days, and a sufficient amount of diesel fuel. However, fresh water supplies were inadequate for a long-lasting wait. At sea, Soviet submariners on an old submarine such as the S-363 each usually received only one and a half litres of water per day, to be used for washing and for preparing soup and tea (modern Soviet submarines carried more water, which enabled the crew an allowance of six litres of drinking water per man per day[15]). Few drank the water, since canned fruit juice of various types usually was available. On the S-363, the water shortage meant that henceforth, for the duration of the crisis, each man received only half a litre of water per day, which only sufficed for soup and tea.[16] They also cancelled the regular shifts for use when at sea, and instead introduced a daily schedule of the same kind as the crew were used to when back home on the base. The sailors were set to work maintaining the submarine machinery, and carrying out regular training and study activities, again in imitation of conditions back at base.

Meanwhile, Gushchin spent most of his time in his cabin, attempting to understand what had gone wrong. Besedin worried that their commanding officer suffered from shock.[17]

Coast Guard vessel *Tv 281* from Kalmar anchored next to the submarine. (Photo: Medström)

General Ljung's Decision

Having been briefed by press officers Carlsson and Berg about the stranded submarine, Supreme Commander General Ljung immediately attempted to call Defence Minister Torsten Gustafsson (1920–1994). However, he was on an official visit to Norway together with his state secretary and deputy, the career diplomat Sven Hirdman (b. 1939). Both attended a meeting of the Nordic defence ministers. It took time before either could be reached. Hirdman got the call only around noon, after which he informed Gustafsson; they decided that Hirdman would return to Stockholm in the morning of the following day, while Gustafsson concluded the official visit as planned (a decision for which he later was criticised). Having failed immediately to get hold of Gustafsson or Hirdman, at 11:32 a.m. Ljung instead called the permanent cabinet secretary of foreign affairs, the career diplomat Leif Leifland (1925–2015).

The Cabinet Secretary was presiding over a Foreign Ministry meeting on the turmoil in Poland. Since the winter of 1979/1980, the government had regularly convened what was referred to as the crisis group. The group, which only dealt with foreign policy and security issues, usually consisted of Cabinet Secretary Leifland, who chaired the meetings; Lennart Eckerberg, the head of the Foreign Ministry's Political Department; Sven Hirdman, the state secretary of the Defence Ministry; Vice Admiral Bengt Schuback (1928–2015), the Chief of the Defence Staff; Colonel Bengt Wallroth, head of Operations Section 5 (Swedish: *Operationssektion* 5, Op 5) of the Defence Staff, that is, military intelligence and security; and Sven-Åke Hjalmroth, the

The Coast Guard vessel *Tv 281* from Kalmar in a more modern paint scheme. (Photo: Patrik Nylin, 2008)

head of the Security Department (Säk) of the National Police Board (*Rikspolisstyrelsen*, RPS) which was responsible for counterespionage and accordingly constituted Sweden's security service.[18] As noted, on this day Hirdman was in Oslo, while Schuback was in another meeting, the defence committee, from which he was recalled by General Ljung just before 11:30 a.m.[19] When General Ljung got hold of Leifland, he informed him about the submarine in Karlskrona. The crisis group meeting in the Foreign Ministry then immediately shifted focus from Poland to the submarine incident. The meeting concluded at 12:30 p.m. Henceforth, the crisis group would meet regularly while the submarine remained on Swedish territory.

After informing Leifland, Ljung called Prime Minister Thorbjörn Fälldin, who just had returned from the North-South Summit of 22–23 October in Cancún, Mexico. The call reached Fälldin just before 11:45 a.m.

Meanwhile, General Ljung ordered Naval Base Karlskrona not to allow the submarine to leave Swedish territory. The standing instruction IKFN did not apply in this particular situation, the General ruled, and the Whiskey must remain on the rock for the time being. Ljung issued this order already at 11:40 a.m.[20] It is clear that General Ljung already at some point between 11:30 and 11:40 a.m. made up his mind on the reason for the submarine's violation of Swedish waters: it was a deliberate intrusion, likely related to intelligence collection; and every alternative explanation was unthinkable. Henceforth, General Ljung's conclusion guided all government actions. General Ljung based his assessment solely on the encrypted teletype report from Karlskrona maritime surveillance centre, which included no more information than that Andersson had confirmed the presence of a Soviet submarine and identified it as of Whiskey class. Andersson had not yet established contact with the submarine crew when he radioed in the report. None of this uncertainty prevented General Ljung from reaching a decision based on gut feeling. He never documented his reasons for the verdict. Ljung kept a diary, but it offers no explanations.[21] The closest we come to a rationale was written in the diary several days later, on Wednesday 4 November, and this entry resembles nothing more than Ljung's attempt to persuade himself that his initial verdict was correct. We will return to this diary entry later. General Ljung's verdict must accordingly rate as one of the least fact-based decisions ever taken by a Swedish Supreme Commander.

As an initial assessment based on limited information, Ljung's verdict was understandable. With no more information available, most reasonable observers at the time would have agreed that a Soviet submarine stranded in a restricted military area likely had been involved in intelligence collection. The problem was that General Ljung never changed his initial conclusion as more information became available during, and after, the crisis. This was possibly a characteristic of General Ljung. Bengt Gustafsson, who eventually succeeded Ljung as Supreme Commander, found it disturbing that Ljung never explained the rationale behind any of his decisions. Incidentally, Ljung also failed to inform Gustafsson about Sweden's extensive cooperation with several NATO member-states.[22]

General Ljung may have developed ulterior motives for his assessment that went far beyond that of the then traditional Russophobia among Swedish military intellectuals. He needed a larger defence budget to maintain the state of the Armed Forces in the face of repeated government cuts in funding. On the previous occasions when the Navy had reported unidentified submarine

Foreign Minister Ola Ullsten, Prime Minister Thorbjörn Fälldin, and General Lennart Ljung during a press conference related to the *S-363* crisis. When it came to issues relating to military intelligence, the Cabinet members trusted General Ljung. They did not necessarily trust each other. Fälldin's agrarian-based Centre Party had formed a two-party coalition government with Ullsten's Liberal People's Party, which was based on urban voters, most of whom had completed a secondary education. Fälldin did not speak English, while Ullsten happily gave interviews to U.S. television crews. In the background, Defence Minister Torsten Gustafsson of the Centre Party. The limited role he played during the crisis is well illustrated by his position several steps behind his colleagues. (Photo: Medström)

intrusions, and asked for more money for antisubmarine warfare vessels and weapons, the media had often reacted harshly, insinuating that the reported intrusions were mere 'budget submarines' that the Navy invented to get the funding it wanted. But the other branches of the Armed Forces needed more money, too. On 14 October, only two weeks prior to the events in Karlskrona, General Ljung had delivered his official recommendation to the government to embark upon the JAS project, the introduction of a new advanced fighter aircraft. From a military and technical standpoint, the JAS project would bring many benefits. However, the project was an expensive undertaking, and General Ljung was determined that it must not impact negatively on existing Armed Forces budget, structures, and needs. Until his last day in office, the General continuously advocated for increases in the defence budget.[23] General Ljung must immediately have understood that the presence on Swedish soil of a Soviet submarine might make a reluctant Parliament more willing to allocate additional funding to defence. If it could be proven that the submarine carried intelligence officers engaged in war preparations, so much the better.

The government was unlikely to object to General Ljung's interpretation (and we will see that it did not). Neither Prime Minister Thorbjörn Fälldin nor Foreign Minister Ola Ullsten had much knowledge of, or interest in, military affairs and intelligence.[24] Both lacked the practical experience to assess intelligence. They trusted their professional consultants, and on military issues, General Ljung enjoyed the luxury of being their principal formal advisor. We will see that Ljung's initial assessment of the submarine intrusion for this reason became the corner stone of Swedish government policy, hence could not be questioned or overruled regardless of whatever new information might emerge.

General Ljung's personal assessment that the intrusion of the S-363 was deliberate and linked to Soviet intelligence collection and preparations for war against Sweden also became the corner stone of all subsequent Swedish assessments of all Soviet and, ultimately, Russian submarine activities. Without his assessment, Sweden's security policy might have taken a different path. General Ljung and

Lennart Ljung, here in the uniform of a major general, which he wore from 1972 to 1976. (Author's collection)

his officers had not heard of the S-178 disaster in the Far East a week previously, failed to recognise that Moscow viewed the S-363 as a submarine in distress instead of a pawn in a strategy of aggression against Swedish territory, and for reasons that will be explained assumed that Moscow inevitably would react with lies and violence.

SWEDISH RUSSOPHOBIA

Russophobia has a long history among Swedish intellectuals, but not quite as long as many are led to believe. While it is correct that Swedes and Russians frequently fought against each other up to and including the Napoleonic Wars, this caused no longer-enduring animosity than was usual between antagonists in European wars. However, Sweden's ultimate loss of Finland to Russia in 1809 caused an intellectual backlash against Russia among educated Swedes. Until then, Finland had been an integral part of the kingdom since the Middle Ages and its provinces enjoyed the same rights and obligations as those in central Sweden. The intellectual backlash was as open as it was obvious. The word Russophobia, defined as 'strong fear and dislike of anything Russian' first appeared in 1836. Five years later, Bishop Esaias Tegnér (1782–1846), a poet and professor of Greek who lacked personal experience from either Finland or Russia, in his poem *Kronbruden* (1841) exclaimed that '… ever since my childhood I hated the Russians and I will hate them as long as I breathe'. Unsurprisingly, Tegnér's poetry became a corner stone of Swedish nineteenth-century nationalism. Soon, Russophobic views spread from intellectual poets to military intellectuals. The Swedish military historian, soldier, and politician Julius Mankell (1828–1897) took a break from his research in 1863 to join the Polish uprising against Russian rule. In the so-called Cossack Election of 1928, a vicious election campaign primarily carried by posters depicting suitably evil-looking Russians selling Swedish women and children into slavery stridently proclaimed that 'anybody who votes for the so-called worker's party votes for Moscow' and that 'anybody who votes for the so-called worker's party votes for the dissolution of families, the demoralization of children, and the degradation of morals'. And so it continued until 1952 when U.S. President Harry Truman in a policy statement concluded that 'Swedes are traditionally anti-Russian and ideologically anti-communist' and embarked upon a series of secret agreements that put Sweden in parity with the NATO countries despite formally not joining the alliance.[25] Both General Ljung and Vice Admiral Schuback were deeply involved in the ongoing military and intelligence cooperation with the United States.[26]

Vice Admiral Bengt Schuback was equally, if not more, excited as his superior. When Schuback, having returned to the Defence Staff, heard the news about the stranded submarine, his first spontaneous comment was: 'At last!'[27] Schuback was a hawk who had long wished to see a Soviet submarine in distress in Swedish waters. He also, no doubt, hoped for the opportunity to hand over an intact submarine to Sweden's capable technical intelligence services. Perhaps the submarine even contained encryption devices and cyphers? Although in the final conclusion we must guess what was in Schuback's mind when he uttered this exclamation, the Vice Admiral certainly knew about the missed opportunity to gain Soviet military secrets during the ultimately failed mutiny onboard the Soviet warship *Storozhevoy* six years earlier.[28]

Because of the defence committee engagement, Schuback did not attend the crisis group meeting on this day. However, he called Leifland and the others from the Defence Staff while the crisis group meeting still was in session. Schuback informed them about General Ljung's decision. As a result, the crisis group ended the meeting at around 12:30 p.m. by following Ljung's lead in its conclusions: The submarine's intrusion was a deliberate violation of Swedish territory, the submarine had not been in distress, the submarine must be salvaged by Swedish personnel, and no Soviet representative must be permitted to go onboard the submarine.[29]

Immunity?

At 11:30 a.m., the Defence Staff summoned Bo Johnson Theutenberg, ambassador and advisor on international law to the Foreign Ministry. Theutenberg, an officer in the reserve, had for some time worked on the legal situation of submarine incursions after an extended but ultimately failed hunt for what was deemed a Polish or Soviet Whiskey-class submarine at Utö Island in September the previous year. When summoned, Theutenberg believed that the meeting would concern the ongoing crisis in Poland, which was the topic of the meeting chaired by Leifland from which he now was summoned. Instead, his task became to brief General Ljung on the legal aspects of the stranded submarine.

Vice Admiral Bengt Schuback, as promoted to Chief of the Navy. (Naval Museum, Karlskrona)

THE SUBMARINE INCIDENTS AT HUVUDSKÄR AND UTÖ ISLANDS, 1980

On 18 September 1980, the crew of the Swedish tugboat A 252 *Ajax* observed the characteristic masts and exhaust pipe of a Whiskey-class submarine south of Huvudskär Island in the outer southern Stockholm archipelago. Since both the Soviet Union and Poland operated submarines of this class in the Baltic, they could not determine its nationality. A helicopter followed by successively more antisubmarine warfare resources were deployed to locate the submarine. Later during the day, a helicopter made sonar contact with a submarine, leading a second helicopter to fire a depth charge at a safe distance to warn it off. It remains unknown if it was the same submarine. A similar observation of submarine masts was made in the area on 23 September, which resulted in a massive antisubmarine warfare operation over the following week. This involved sonar contacts on 24, 26, and 27 September. In response, the Swedish Navy fired depth charges to warn off the unidentified submarine or submarines. On 28 September, the Swedish destroyer *Halland* launched an antisubmarine rocket against a submarine near Utö Island, in the same general area. Yet another weapons launch took place on 30 September. Meanwhile, the Soviet Baltic Fleet engaged in an exercise on the other side of the Baltic Sea. FRA noted a significant spike in signals traffic to submarines from Baltic Fleet Headquarters, which may have been related to either, or both, events. On 5 October, Swedish aircraft discovered and took photographs of a Polish salvage ship, the ORP *Piast*, a variant of the Soviet Project 861, NATO reporting name Moma. The *Piast* was accompanied by two Polish Whiskey-class submarines, one of which the Swedes deemed to be damaged. Some Swedes accordingly believed that one of the Polish submarines was involved in the incident. Swedish naval intelligence later deemed this unlikely. Be that as it may, the second submarine at Utö Island was of a different type, which never was identified but some suspected to have been West German. Swedish naval intelligence later deemed this implausible. The submarine incidents at Huvudskär and Utö Islands were the first to gain the attention of the Swedish media. Because all available information derived from the Navy, the press department of the Defence Staff was able to control the information flow, which consisted of mostly pre-authorised comments by officers involved in the operation. Soon, everybody assumed that Soviet submarines were the culprits.[30] Eyewitness reports sometimes disagreed on what happened, and no independent body ever compiled a full report on the incidents at Huvudskär and Utö Islands. In addition, and perhaps surprisingly, it seems that the Polish Navy was never queried on its possible presence in the area, not even after the dissolution of the Warsaw Pact and Poland's entry into NATO.

The ORP *Piast*, with bort number 281 which was used in 1980. (U.S. Department of Defense)

Theutenberg was a hawk on Soviet affairs. His interpretation of relevant international law, which was highly innovative and accordingly controversial among his peers, was that a situation of innocent passage or distress could not be said to exist. Hence, the submarine and its crew were subject to Swedish authority and could not claim immunity as per international law and the IKFN General Order.

Having wrapped up the crisis group meeting, Leifland walked to the room next door to inform the Foreign Minister, Ola Ullsten (1931–2018). The foreign minister lacked foreign policy experience, and enjoyed little respect in this role. When it came to matters abroad, he was more interested in providing development aid to the Third World than negotiating the perilous relations between East and West. Even so, his Party colleagues criticised him for choosing the classy assignment at the Foreign Ministry over that of the Ministry of Health and Social Affairs, which would have carried more voters. The Foreign Ministry staff found his lack of knowledge of international affairs disturbing and preferred to consult Cabinet Secretary Leifland, who essentially ran the ministry as he pleased.[31] Ullsten was in the process of writing a political speech, and greeted the information about the Soviet submarine with disbelief. Ultimately, he instructed Leifland to draft a diplomatic protest note.

Meanwhile, the press officer of the Defence Staff, Jan-Åke Berg, and the press officer of the Navy Staff, Sven Carlsson, prepared a brief, joint statement, which Schuback then approved for dissemination. The press release stated:

A Soviet submarine of Whiskey class has during Wednesday morning gone aground in Swedish waters in Gåsefjärden Bay in the Karlskrona archipelago. Ships from the South Coast's Naval Base are currently next to the submarine which is on the surface, is damaged, and leaks oil. The submarine commander claims distress and has requested assistance. The reason why the submarine entered Swedish sea territory is currently unknown.[32]

Short as it was, the press release contained several errors of fact. First, the Defence Staff assumed that since the submarine was discovered on Wednesday morning, it must also have struck the rock on the same morning. The press release also mentioned 'ships' from the Naval Base, but at the time of writing, the only navy vessel there was the *Smyge*. The second Swedish vessel was the torpedo boat *Piteå* which only reached the submarine at 12:58 p.m. Nor did the submarine leak oil. The note that the submarine commander had claimed distress and requested assistance was soon dropped, since a claim of distress would have implied his right to immunity according to international law which we will see that General Ljung and most other Swedish policymakers clearly were unwilling to grant. In fact, the Defence Staff managed to call back to the Swedish wire service, Tidningarnas Telegrambyrå (TT) before the news flash was sent, ordering them to delete this sentence, since 'This is not how matters stand.'[33]

The urgent correction was perhaps misunderstood. The press release was transmitted by the TT at 12:28 p.m. It now stated:

Stockholm (TT). A Soviet submarine has gone aground in Gåsefjärden Bay in Karlskrona archipelago, reports the Defence Staff. The commander claims a distress situation.[34]

The news flash made it into the midday radio news at 12:30 p.m. on the news report *Dagens eko* ('Daily Echo').[35]

Having consulted General Ljung, Vice Admiral Schuback personally called Lieutenant General Olson in Military District South. We have seen that the official standing operating procedures for the Armed Forces in cases of peacetime violations of the territory, the IKFN, limited the Navy's freedom of manouvre by insisting that the submarine, upon discovery, merely should be salvaged and turned away from Swedish territory. Schuback now explained to Olson that the Soviet submarine had lost its right to immunity, so the IKFN instruction did not apply. In response, Olson suggested that Stockholm should inform the Soviet embassy about this. He also proposed that the Supreme Commander as soon as possible should order the salvage of the submarine so as take the psychological initiative.[36]

National and Local Planning

At around 12.30, Leifland constituted an ad hoc submarine crisis group. Among its participants were Bo Johnson Theutenberg, called back from the Defence Staff, and Lieutenant Commander Frank Rosenius from military intelligence, brought along by Theutenberg when he was recalled to Leifland's meeting.[37]

The crisis group early on reached consensus on two key points, both based on General Ljung's initial assessment. First, the Navy must prevent additional Soviet vessels from crossing the 12-nautical-mile (22km) line that delimited Sweden's territorial waters. Second, Soviet Embassy representatives must not be allowed to visit the submarine.[38] The crisis group then began drafting a protest note.

In the somewhat naive hope of catching the Soviet ambassador, Mikhail Yakovlev, off guard, the Foreign Ministry at 1:00 p.m. summoned him to see Leifland already at 1:15 p.m. This would necessitate the ambassador to drop whatever he was doing to jump into a car for a quick drive from the embassy to the ministry. The Swedish government at this point believed that the submarine had stranded earlier in the morning (incorrect), and that Yakovlev had not yet received any instructions from Moscow (correct). However, when Yakovlev arrived, he responded that he had already heard of the incident. Apparently, a journalist had called Naval Attaché Yuriy Prosvirnin and asked for a statement, after which Prosvirnin had informed Yakovlev. Considering that the story had broadcast in the radio news 45 minutes before the meeting, this should not have surprised the Foreign Ministry.[39] Ambassador Yakovlev then returned to the embassy.

Ullsten, inexperienced in international affairs, must have been briefed by Leifland on the consensus decision of the crisis group. He seems not to have added anything to it, or even questioned Leifland, who henceforth acted as if it was he, not the Foreign Minister, who made foreign policy. In the same way, the Defence Staff in Stockholm announced that the Swedish Armed Forces would salvage the submarine and that the timing for this was to be decided by the Supreme Commander. Again, Foreign Minister Ullsten added nothing.

Ambassador Yakovlev returned to the Foreign Ministry at 3:30 p.m. to receive the Swedish protest note from Foreign Minister Ullsten. Importantly, the note stated that the Soviet Union would not be allowed to salvage the submarine on its own.[40] Their meeting ended around 4:30 p.m.

At 6:00 p.m., Ambassador Yakovlev returned to Leifland with a response to the Swedish protest note (his third trip to the Foreign Ministry on this day). By then, the news had reached the Politburo and Soviet supreme leader Leonid Brezhnev in Moscow from both military and diplomatic channels. The Soviet response was that the intrusion was involuntary, and caused by malfunctioning navigation equipment, primarily a faulty gyrocompass. The Soviet government also requested permission to send four salvage vessels into Swedish waters and the restricted military area to salvage the submarine and bring it home.[41] Leifland immediately rejected the Soviet request. He also rejected Yakovlev's request to visit the submarine crew, on the grounds that it was stranded within a restricted military area to which foreign nationals could not be admitted. Instead, Leifland demanded that the Soviet government order the commander of the submarine to accept being questioned as part of the Swedish investigation into the cause of the violation of the Swedish border.

Later in the evening (at 7:30 p.m.), Foreign Minister Ullsten in a public statement during the television news broadcast *Rapport* ('Report') categorically ruled out Soviet access to the submarine.

A planning meeting was during the afternoon also held in the headquarters of Naval Base Karlskrona with participation of representatives of Military Region South. The meeting focused on practicalities and the local situation. What was the legal state of affairs? Should the Navy salvage the submarine? It was undamaged, so it could safely be pulled off the skerry on which it had stranded. On the other hand, the submarine could not get off on its own, so the participants agreed that it was better for the time being to leave it in a stranded position. The Soviets demanded the right to salvage the submarine with their own resources, but as we know, this was incompatible with the requirements of the restricted military area and Commander Karl Andersson had already refused this request. Furthermore, we have seen that General Ljung already at 11:40 a.m. decided that whatever happened, the submarine must be held for the time being. On this day, most of the orders from the Defence Staff to Commodore Lennart Forsman, commander of the Naval Base, were oral only. The first written order was only issued on the afternoon of the following day (29 October).

However, the Defence Staff left no instructions on what to do if the submarine by one means or another attempted to flee. The participants discussed a variety of ideas, including stopping it with artillery fire and blocking the exit route with ships.

Discussions also took place on whether to allow the crew to remain onboard, be interned ashore, or be prosecuted for espionage. In Karlskrona, local military commanders argued that they should use military force and storm the submarine.[42] They now drew up a detailed plan on how the submarine would be captured. A strike force of Coastal Ranger officers would take the crew prisoner and hand them over to the police.

They would then need an internment camp for the Soviet prisoners. At first, discussions were held over the use of a school for interning the sailors. However, they soon agreed that they needed a fenced and easily-secured area. Not only must the sailors be prevented from escaping, they must also be prevented from talking to journalists. Preparations were then begun to modify already-existing arrangements for the expected inflow of Polish refugees into a prisoner-of-war camp for the submarine crew in a local housing facility. Local police and the Armed Forces would cooperate in the arrangement, which was completed on the following day. Buses were prepared for moving the Soviet crew. Finally, the Coastal Artillery volunteered an abandoned barrack in a fenced area at Gräsvik, which would be sufficient to contain the expected number of crewmen. Soldiers from the Coastal Artillery would patrol the perimeter, while the police would maintain security inside the camp. The internment contingency was based on the premise that each Soviet national would be registered, identified, photographed, fingerprinted, and ultimately deported as an illegal alien.[43]

If any of the Soviet crew wished to defect, this would be handled by the police in accordance with standard procedures. Many Swedes were convinced that most any Soviet citizen was ready to defect as soon as an opportunity opened up.

Ultimately, the internment camp was never used. Stockholm overruled the local authorities. A solution of the type employed during the Second World War was no longer politically feasible.[44]

The local civil defence authorities prepared the nearby hospitals for emergency casualties. Together with the Armed Forces, they established a field hospital in barracks on Kille Mountain (Swedish: Killeberget), only a few hundred metres from the submarine, with capacity for a hundred wounded (although it reached full readiness only on the evening of Saturday 31 October) and evacuation capability by helicopter and ambulance, since a Swedish assault on the submarine was expected to result in casualties.[45]

When the Soviet crew had been disposed of, the Navy would pull the submarine off the rock and tow it to Karlskrona. Where would the submarine be anchored, after salvage? The initial plan was to tow the submarine into the naval port at Karlskrona, which was fenced and protected. One alternative was the commercial port of Karlskrona. Other choices were the dockyard, or in an easily guarded and defensible location in the archipelago. The last option was chosen as the one least likely to cause collateral damage. (On the following day, at 4:40 p.m., the Supreme Commander to the surprise of the local commanders ordered the submarine to be anchored deeper inside Gåsefjärden Bay after salvage instead of in any of the already-prepared locations.[46])

To retain the initiative versus the press, Commodore Forsman at an early stage decided to hold a press conference in a school in central Karlskrona. The idea was to keep the press away from the submarine. The officers realised that if the press approached the Soviets, there was a high risk that the press through its reporting effectively would take control over the situation and force decisions that would reduce the freedom of action of the responsible political and military authorities.[47]

At 5:10 p.m. Commodore Lennart Forsman and Commander Karl Andersson held the first press conference of the crisis. However, they had no message to give the media regarding their plans on how to deal with the submarine and its crew.

Technical Intelligence
During the afternoon, somebody raised the possibility that the submarine might carry nuclear weapons. Swedish government sources have suggested that the impetus came from an unnamed NATO member-state.[48] The suggestion apparently originated with the U.S. assistant naval attaché, Commander Edmond Pope, who later claimed that he was the one who recommended the Swedes to test the submarine for radiation.[49] By this time, most Swedes, including naval intelligence officers, could not believe that obsolete submarines such as those of the Whiskey-class would carry nuclear weapons. As mentioned, Soviet naval doctrine was little known in the West, and the intelligence that Pen'kovskiy had handed over two decades ago had apparently not been shared with Sweden. This was unsurprising, since as we have seen even most U.S. naval intelligence officers failed to understand the significance of Admiral Gorshkov's reforms. Besides, the entire issue of nuclear weapons was taboo in Sweden. The taint of nuclear weapons must be kept away from Swedish territory at all costs. The message to the public of all governments since the 1960s was that because Sweden formally was a non-aligned country which had eschewed the use of nuclear munitions, it would not, indeed could not be attacked with nuclear weapons. And for this reason, everybody was safe.

The question of whether the submarine carried nuclear weapons was also raised during the press conference in Karlskrona. The Navy then responded that an old vessel such as this submarine would not carry any such advanced weaponry.[50]

During the afternoon, a meeting took place at the Defence Research Establishment (FOA). As noted, FOA was, among other tasks, responsible for most of Sweden's technical intelligence analysis and collection with regard to platforms and weapon systems. At this point in time, FOA was carrying out a field exercise which involved the measurement of levels of radiation. During the meeting, somebody suggested that they should take advantage of the fact that both personnel and measuring equipment already was mobilised to investigate whether the submarine carried nuclear warheads onboard.[51]

The outcome of the meeting was that Nils-Henrik Lundquist (1919–1997), the Director General of FOA, contacted General Ljung who voiced his approval for a discrete external measurement of any radioactivity emitted from the submarine. State Secretary Hirdman later claimed that he personally authorised the mission on the following afternoon (29 October), without consulting or informing any cabinet minister.[52] However, according to another account, it was General Ljung who contacted Leifland at approximately the same time. Leifland, a diplomat, did not believe that an old Whiskey-class submarine might carry nuclear weapons, but nonetheless agreed that FOA could carry out a spot check. Leifland, too, apparently did not discuss the matter with any cabinet minister.[53]

In reality, neither the right personnel nor the right equipment was mobilised. In the evening, FOA summoned one of its foremost radiation expert, Lars-Erik De Geer (b. 1945), to a meeting. De Geer was then at the Stockholm University campus and prepared to go home. A minor problem was that De Geer did not at the time have any suitable radiation meter. During the evening, he contacted the Radiation Protection Institute, where he borrowed one. De Geer later recalled that the lady who was responsible for the meter primarily worried that the FOA men would scratch the surface of the delicate and expensive tool.[54]

6
THE SOVIET SALVAGE EXPEDITION

Having received Gushchin's message early in the morning, Fleet Headquarters ordered a task force under Vice Admiral Aleksey Kalinin to set out to assist the *S-363*. Kalinin had recently been promoted to First Deputy Commander of the Baltic Fleet, but until then he had served as the Fleet's chief of staff. Standard procedure within the Soviet Navy for disasters at sea was to give the responsibility to lead the ensuing salvage expedition to the Fleet's chief of staff. This was, as we have seen, the procedure employed during the recent *S-178* disaster in the Pacific Ocean, and likely also explains why Vice Admiral Kalinin received the task. Kalinin decided to bring along Captain First Rank Raimundas Baltuška, a Lithuanian naval officer who was the head of the Baltic Fleet's Navigation Directorate. Baltuška was the one who authorised the continuation of the *S-363*'s mission after the collision with the fishing trawl.

Fleet Headquarters found Gushchin's first telegram inexplicable. How could the submarine have gone aground, and where was it? When daylight conditions allowed, Fleet Headquarters sent out a Beriev Be-12, NATO reporting name MAIL, an antisubmarine warfare aircraft from 49th Independent Antisubmarine Squadron at Neutief, near Naval Base Baltiysk, to locate the submarine. The Be-12 was a twin-engine amphibious aircraft equipped to detect and combat submerged submarines. It was taken into service in 1961. Being amphibious, it was also highly suitable for rescue operations at sea. The Be-12 flew to the area east of Bornholm and north of the Polish coast where the submarine was thought to be in distress. From 8:37 a.m., it began to search for the submarine. When the Soviet antisubmarine aircraft returned home to refuel, it was replaced by another aircraft of the same type from the same unit. While the Be-12s remained at a great distance from Swedish territorial waters, parts of their missions were caught by Swedish air surveillance radar. However, the radar coverage did not capture their entire flight patterns, since part of the search took place at an altitude of 300m, which was below then-available Swedish radar coverage of the area (for more on which see below).[1] SIGINT intercepts from the Be-12 aircraft suggest that they searched for the *S-363* east of Bornholm, in short, where the *S-363* was supposed to be at the time. We know this, because a Be-12 pilot was asked if he had managed to establish radio contact with the submarine, whose last known position also was mentioned. The search continued even after Karl Andersson told the submarine crew where they had stranded and the submariners had reported the position to Fleet Headquarters. Captain First Rank Baltuška, who led the search, later told Sweden's General Bengt Gustafsson that he ordered the airmen to continue searching the Bornholm waters because he simply could not believe the coordinates that Gushchin finally had radioed in as their location.[2]

In addition, an Antonov An-12A communications relay aircraft, NATO reporting name CUB, was ordered into the air from the Khrabrovo Air Base outside Kaliningrad to relay radio communications between the *S-363* and Fleet Headquarters. The An-12 stayed in a holding pattern southeast of Blekinge, from which it maintained communications between the units involved by transiting radio traffic, something required because of the long distances within the operational area. The An-12, too, was caught by Swedish radar, since it flew at a higher altitude. Even so, the An-12 operated at the extreme range of Swedish radar coverage, so only the northernmost portions of the flight were recorded. During the course of the crisis, Fleet Headquarters continued to use the An-12 as a communications relay aircraft, and on 30 October Swedish fighter jets identified one such aircraft with the bort number 11364.[3] This particular aircraft appears to have been an Antonov An-12BK, which was a model that was only produced for military transports.[4]

Meanwhile, Vice Admiral Kalinin began to organise the salvage expedition. From around 2:00 p.m. the ships left port individually when they were ready to sail. Kalinin commanded the task force from the *Obraztsovyy* ('Exemplary'), a large antisubmarine warfare ship with bort number 446 of the type known as Project 61, NATO reporting name Kashin. For some obscure reason, NATO reporting names for Soviet warships – but not submarines or aircraft – were invariably made up to sound Russian even though many, including Kashin, were imaginary words with no meaning in any language. The Project 61 class entered service in 1962 and constituted the first Soviet warship class designed to be closed down for nuclear fallout. This particular ship was commissioned in 1965. At the time, U.S. intelligence found it hard to believe that they were intended for antisubmarine warfare and because of their size and armament incorrectly classified them as guided-missile destroyers.

Vice Admiral Kalinin's task force included a second warship. This was the *Prozorlivyy* ('Sharp-eyed'), a large missile ship with bort number 351 of the class that the Soviet Union called project 56U, NATO reporting name Kildin-Mod, the suffix short for Modified.[5] NATO navies referred to her as a destroyer. The *Prozorlivyy*, commanded by Captain Third Rank Viktor Lyakin, carried anti-ship missiles of the type P-15 Termit, NATO reporting name SS-N-2 STYX. The ship had entered into service in 1958. The *Prozorlivyy* already operated in the southern Baltic Sea. She was a more dangerous adversary to surface vessels than Kalinin's flagship. Before her return to the Baltic Sea to participate in Zapad 81 and other exercises, Captain Lyakin and the *Prozorlivyy* had been on a combat

Vice Admiral Aleksey Kalinin, First Deputy Commander of the Baltic Fleet. (Author's collection)

mission to Angola with orders to support the MPLA government against the insurgent UNITA. The Angolan insurgency was a proxy war of the kind typical of the Cold War. The Soviet Union and Cuba supported the national government, while the United States and South Africa supported the insurgent UNITA.

The Swedish Defence Staff thought it saw signs that one of the warships carried a regular unit of naval infantry.[6] For sure, the two warships were sufficiently large to hide a few infantrymen onboard, but under normal operations neither carried any naval infantry and there is no evidence that they did on this mission.

The Swedish Defence Staff believed that Kalinin's force primarily was an armed relief force, not a salvage force, and was tasked with the retrieval of the immobilised submarine by any means necessary. That its primary task was a salvage operation seems not to have registered.

However, except the two warships, the rest of the task force consisted of support vessels, most of which belonged to 54th Rescue Ship Brigade in Liepaja. These, importantly, included the submarine salvage ship *SS-30*, of the class known as Project 532, NATO reporting name Valdai, which carried no name beyond her numerical designation. With her sailed the ocean-going salvage tugboats MB 171 *Loksa*, MB 178 *Saturn*, and MB 165 *Serdityy*. The tugboats were of the class known as Project 733S, NATO reporting name Okhtenskiy. They were manned by combined crews consisting of both Navy and civilian sailors from the Soviet Emergency Rescue Group (*Avariyno-Spasatel'naya Partiya*, ASP). The salvage vessels were unarmed. At least the *Loksa* set out from Liepaja, and perhaps others as well. The Swedish Defence Staff later stated that the task force also included the hydrographic survey ship *Andromeda*, of a class known as Project 861, NATO

Beriev Be-12 (MAIL) antisubmarine warfare aircraft, photographed by the Swedish Air Force in the early 1980s. (Photo: Medström)

Antonov An-12 (CUB) communications relay aircraft. Overview of the aircraft, and close-up of an An-12 from Khrabrovo Air Base photographed by the Swedish Air Force in the early 1980s. The An-12 was produced from 1958 until 1972. Note the rear cannon for self-defence. (Photo: Medström)

reporting name Moma.⁷ In addition, the Swedish government claimed, two ELINT vessels joined the task force. One was the *Reduktor*, which already operated in the southern Baltic. The other was the *Khersones*, a small intelligence ship of the class known as Project 502, NATO reporting name Mayak-Mod. In total, the Swedes assessed the task force as consisting of nine vessels. Yet, the intelligence vessels, and possibly also the *Andromeda*, were in reality engaged in routine activities in the southern Baltic and merely happened to be in the area. Perhaps Moscow gave Vice Admiral Kalinin command of them. However, it seems equally likely that the Swedish Defence Staff mistakenly assessed them as included in the task force – perhaps because General Ljung already had decided that the *S-363* was on an intelligence-related mission into Swedish waters and it accordingly seemed plausible to bundle all existing Soviet intelligence assets of the Baltic Fleet into the task force.

The large antisubmarine warfare ship *Obraztsovyy* of 128th Missile Ship Brigade in Baltiysk, employed as flagship by Vice Admiral Kalinin. (Photo: Royal Netherlands Navy, provided by the U.S. Department of Defense)

The large missile ship *Prozorlivyy*, commanded by Captain Lyakin and with recent experience from two combat deployments to Angola. (Photo: Royal Netherlands Navy, provided by the U.S. Department of Defense)

The *SS-30* was the first submarine salvage ship of the class known as Project 532, NATO reporting name Valdai. Built in 1958 based on a minesweeper of Project 264, NATO reporting name T58, she entered service in 1960. Note the diving bell for rescuing submarine crews. (Photo: U.S. Department of Defense).

Ocean-going salvage tugboat of the class known as Project 733S, NATO reporting name Okhtenskiy. The MB 171 *Loksa*, MB 178 *Saturn*, and MB 165 *Serdityy* were of the same class. The abbreviation MB stood for *morskoy buksir*, 'sea-going tugboat'. This tugboat is painted in post-Soviet colours. (Photo: A. Brichevskiy)

The hydrographic survey ship *Andromeda*, of a class known as Project 861, NATO reporting name Moma. This class of ships was built in Gdańsk, Poland, between 1967 and 1973. The *Andromeda* was built in 1972 and belonged to the Baltic Fleet.

The small intelligence ship GS-47 *Khersones* of the class known as Project 502, NATO reporting name Mayak-Mod. Based on the hull for a common class of trawlers, the *Khersones* was taken into service as a SIGINT collection ship in 1969.

We have seen that the Soviet Navy contacted the Swedish government through Ambassador Yakovlev, asking for permission to send in four of these vessels to salvage the submarine. Although the Swedish government never released this request to the public, we can assume that the named vessels were the *SS-30*, *Loksa*, *Saturn*, and *Serdityy*, since these were the only vessels of the task force that were suitable for the task.

Welcoming the Soviets

The appearance of Vice Admiral Kalinin's task force made the Navy concentrate all available forces to the Karlskrona area. The guarding of the Swedish maritime border was tightened, and also on land surveillance increased. Intelligence collection against Soviet naval objects intensified.

Since the late 1960s, Sweden had made extensive cuts in its armed forces. General Ljung's budgetary concerns were genuine. As a result, Sweden had no real fleet with which to confront any Soviet incursion. Instead, Sweden activated several batteries of the Coastal Artillery. One, on Tjurkö Island, was a fixed coastal artillery battery with four model 1937 Bofors 15.2cm cannons from the 1940s. Only one cannon could be manned because of a shortage of personnel. Among the few available soldiers were some 20 conscripted cooks who had only spent three days in uniform.[8] They were sent to the battery on Tjurkö Island, where their first task became to clean away the thick layer of old grease and oil that for years had protected the gun barrels from rust, so that they could be readied for firing. Far worse, the fixed battery lacked fire guidance. The old, obsolete system from the 1950s had been removed, but the new, modern Arte 719 (the Swedish abbreviation for *Artillerieldledning 719*) fire control system was not yet installed. This was the first Swedish fire control with digital transmission of data to the firing units. One mobile Arte unit was available elsewhere, in a storage depot in Rosenholm, a suburb to Karlskrona. The artillerymen got it in order and rapidly drove towards Tjurkö Island.

Another cannon was a recently delivered, still untested self-propelled Coastal Artillery 12cm variant of the Army's howitzer model 1977 (*Haubits 77*). Deployed at the Torhamn Promontory, it in a hurry fired off a few rounds to conclude the initial trial protocol and then redeployed to protect the inlet to Gåsefjärden Bay. The 12cm cannon was finally operational at 10:00 a.m. on the following day (Thursday).[9] Except that it, too, lacked the Arte 719 fire control system, which was presently deployed for trials near Kalmar much further to the northeast.

The Coastal Artillery also activated several lines of fixed mines, controlled from four mine stations in underground bunkers. The right personnel had to be found, and this took time, too. The mine station most close to Torumskär became operational only on the following day, at 10:30 a.m.[10] It turned out that the submarine had stranded in-between two lines of mines. Having activated them, nobody could get in or out of the bay, unless the mine station permitted it. If the mine station was destroyed or disabled, the mines went into automatic mode and would explode as soon as any ship came within range.[11]

Karlskrona also had a coastal missile battery, established in 1968 for the launching of the anti-ship missile Saab Rb 08 (*Robot 08*), with a maximum range of about 250km. This missile battery would almost certainly have been activated as well, if personnel had been available – but none were.[12]

When fully manned, the Coastal Artillery alone was no pushover for an intruding naval task force. With the help of the strike fighters of the Air Force and the fixed mine lines, Sweden expected to be able to defend itself, despite the recent cuts in weapons and manpower.

Late in the day, General Ljung again called Prime Minister Fälldin. He asked for instructions on how to respond if additional

Mobile Arte 719 fire control unit. (Gotlands Försvarsmuseum)

Model 1937 Bofors 15.2cm cannon. The ordnance had a weight of almost 15 tons, and fired projectiles with a range of 23km. The photo shows a model 1937 on display at Fårösund, Gotland. (Photo: Mr Bullit)

The heavy model 1937 cannon were deployed in batteries in well-protected bunkers at strategic locations on islands in the archipelago. The photo shows a 15.2cm cannon deployed in a battery at Landsort. (Photo: Holger Ellgaard)

Saab Rb 08 (*Robot 08*) anti-ship missile. The almost six-metre-long missile, with a high-explosive warhead with a weight of 250kg, was based on Nord Aviation's CT20 target missile but further developed by Saab. Maximum range was about 250km. The missiles were deployed in a battery in a well-protected bunker in the archipelago. Unfortunately, the Coastal Artillery on this occasion lacked the men to man the battery.

Self-propelled Bofors coastal artillery howitzer model 1980, also known as KARIN. This was a 12cm variant produced for the Coastal Artillery based on the Army's FH77 self-propelled howitzer (model 1977). The ordnance had a maximum firing range of 32km and, for its time, an exceptionally high rate of fire (16 rounds per minute). The system included a computer that allowed remote targeting from radar stations and other sources. The Coastal Artillery guns were painted solid green. (Photo: Naval Museum, Karlskrona)

Soviet naval vessels crossed into Swedish territorial waters. Fälldin responded that the IKFN should be followed. This meant that the Armed Forces under certain conditions were authorised to take any appropriate action, up to and including the use of deadly force. One such condition was fulfilled if any Soviet warships crossed the border with hostile intent.

NATO member-states, too, took a keen interest in what went on. On the morning after the *S-363* stranded, West Germany and Britain sent three aircraft over the southern Baltic Sea. It is not known if their missions were connected to the events in Gåsefjärden Bay, since such aircraft often operated over the southern Baltic, but at least the last of the three is likely to have been. They were able to establish that the Soviet Union only used maritime rescue and transport aircraft. No Soviet fighter aircraft operated over the southern Baltic, nor would they do so during the coming dramatic days.

The first NATO aircraft was a West German Bréguet Br.1150 Atlantic which immediately headed for the area where the Soviet Union believed that the submarine might be located. The Atlantic was a long-range maritime reconnaissance aircraft. After flying for an hour or so along the normal route along the Baltic coast, the West German Atlantic returned to the initial search area.

The second was a British Hawker Siddeley Nimrod R1 SIGINT aircraft from RAF Wyton in eastern England.

At the same time as the Nimrod aircraft, another West German maritime reconnaissance aircraft of the Atlantic type was sent east

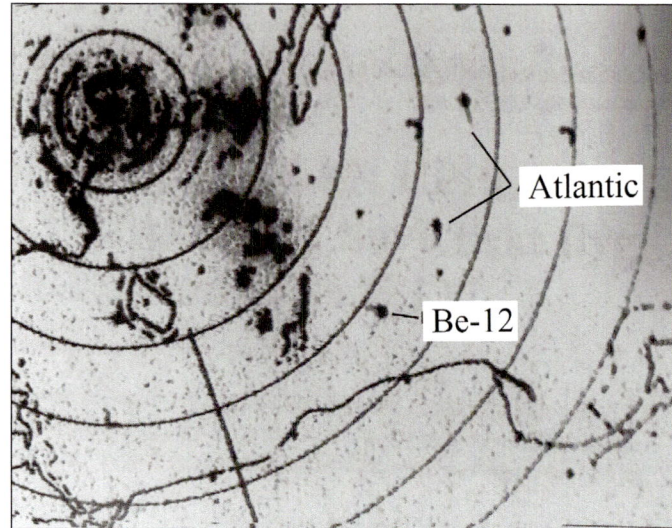

Radar image captured from a plan position indicator (PPI) radar display, showing the Be-12 and two West German aircraft, and the poor weather east of Bornholm. (Author's collection)

towards Bornholm where it remained in a holding pattern from which it could monitor the events.

At about 3:00 p.m., the three NATO aircraft returned home.

In addition, Denmark later sent the corvette F354 *Niels Juel* to monitor the Soviet task force and take photographs of it.[13]

West German Naval Aviation Bréguet Br.1150 Atlantic maritime reconnaissance and antisubmarine warfare aircraft. The Br.1150 Atlantic was the result of the collaboration of several European states under French leadership. This Atlantic is photographed at extremely close range by a Viggen pilot a few years after the events in Karlskrona. West Germany also operated a SIGINT version of the Atlantic. One such aircraft, with the number 6114 and obviously interested in the development around Karlskrona, was identified by Swedish fighter jets east of Bornholm on 3 November (Darwall, *Luftens dirigenter*, p.142). (Photo: Medström)

British Hawker Siddeley Nimrod R1 Mk1 SIGINT aircraft. (Ministry of Defence)

Danish corvette F354 *Niels Juel*, 1978. (Author's collection)

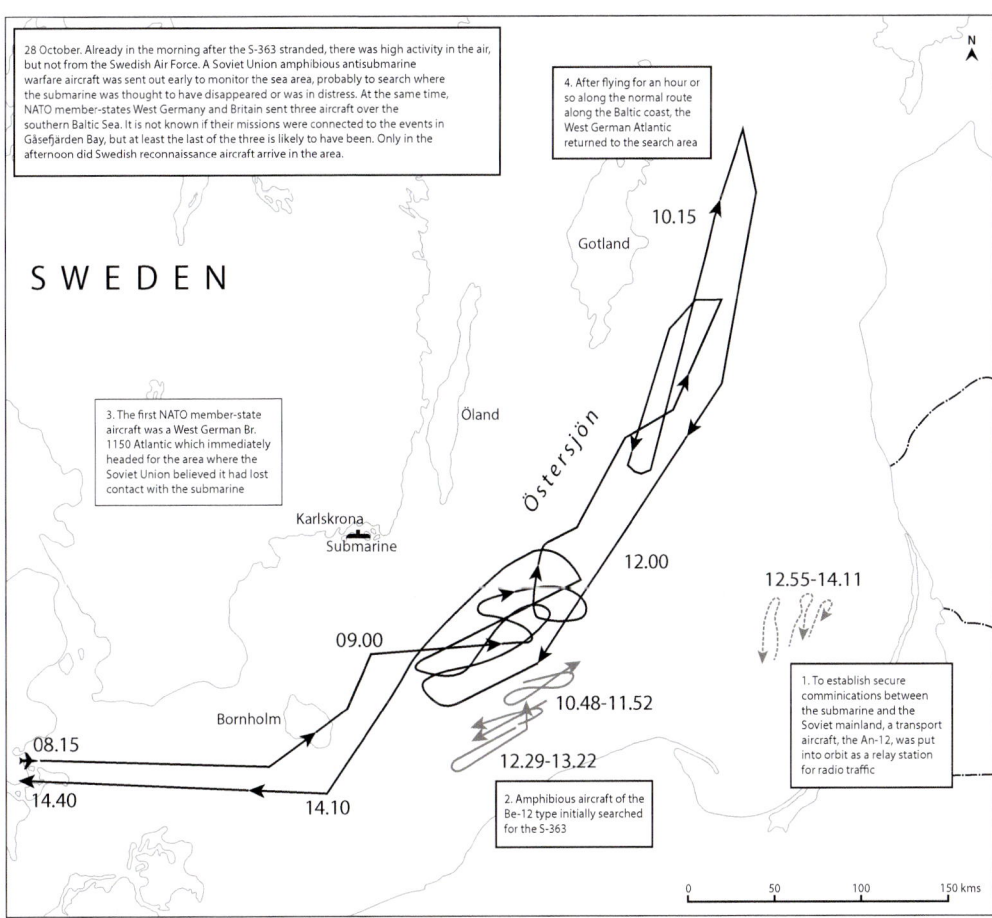

West German reconnaissance mission over the Baltic. (Map by George Anderson)

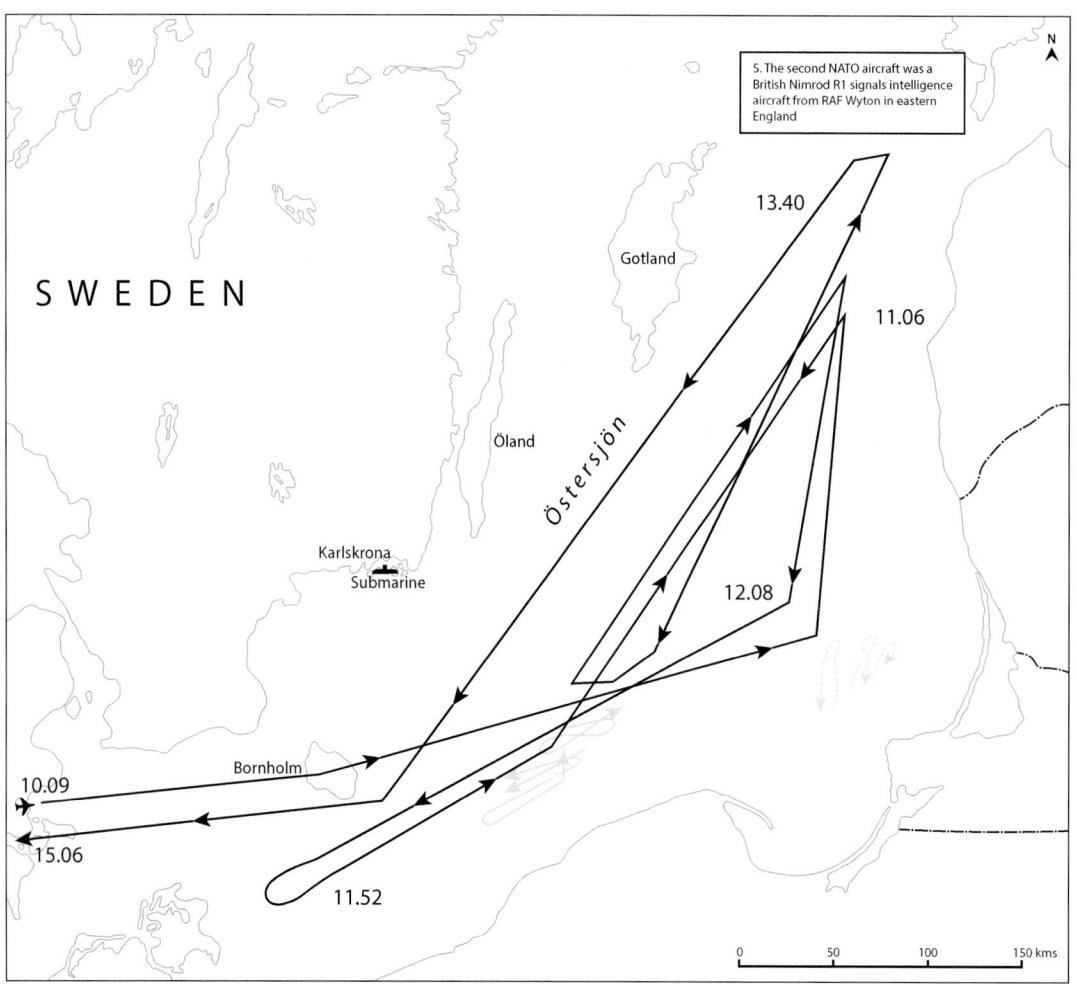

British SIGINT mission. (Map by George Anderson)

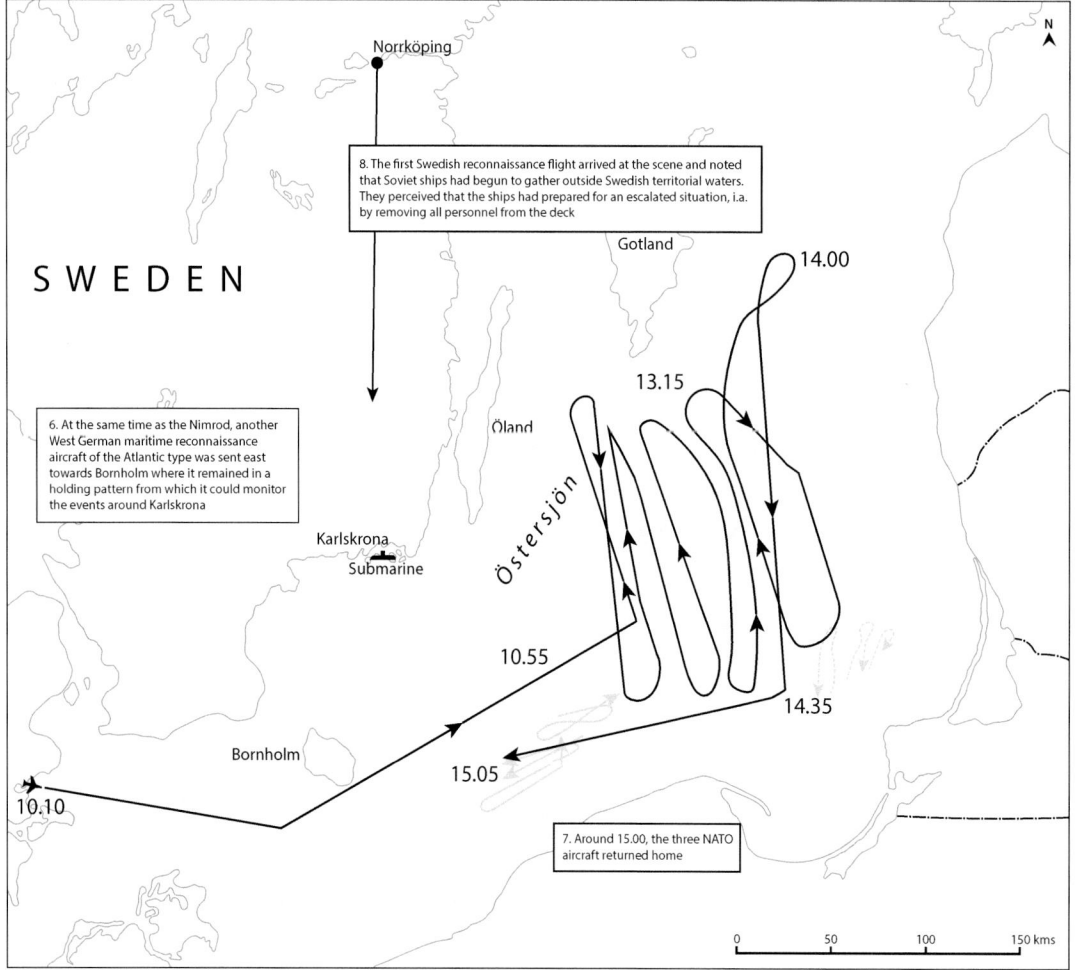

The second West German reconnaissance mission. (Map by George Anderson)

Swedish reconnaissance aircraft arrived in the area only in the afternoon. On this day, the Air Force's Bråvalla Air Wing (F 13) at Norrköping was on quick reaction alert and responsible for what NATO somewhat incongruously terms air policing. The duty had nothing to do with policing and really signified being on standby to defend Sweden's borders against external threats. Radar air surveillance was the responsibility of the large Air Defence Sector Centre W2 Svalan ('Swallow') in Mölndal outside Gothenburg. Svalan, located in a secret bunker hidden under a mountain, carried primary responsibility for daytime reporting. Data from the Karlskrona area was transmitted to Svalan from Low Altitude Filter Centre S2S Myran ('Ant') in Rödeby, located in another secret bunker buried under a mountain about 20km north of Gåsefjärden Bay.[14] Some of the staff in Myran were Navy conscripts. At night and during weekends, overall responsibility was instead assumed by the somewhat more modern Air Defence Sector Centre O5 Puman ('Puma') in Bålsta outside Stockholm. All participating centres were also linked to the FRA SIGINT stations.[15]

At this point, FRA reported that Soviet warships and salvage vessels were gathering south of Blekinge. The same intelligence also reached the Defence Staff in Stockholm and the commander of Military District South, Lieutenant General Sven-Olof Olson. The Lieutenant General understood that the situation was serious. Soviet forces had previously intervened with sharp weapons to prevent the loss of warships and aircraft to the West, including six years earlier in the Baltic Sea during the aforementioned mutiny onboard the warship *Storozhevoy*.

At 3:02 p.m., Olson accordingly ordered an increased level of combat readiness and the reinforcement of the reconnaissance aircraft at Blekinge Air Wing (F 17) at Kallinge in Ronneby Municipality with a unit from Bråvalla Air Wing (F 13) at Norrköping, further to the north, which he had been assigned from Military District East.[16]

He ordered the reconnaissance aircraft continuously to follow the Soviet task force that was heading towards the maritime border and to monitor the Blekinge archipelago and the waters beyond.[17]

Two reconnaissance aircraft from 1st Squadron of Bråvalla Air Wing (F 13) took off from Norrköping to monitor the situation at sea. The squadron commander, Captain Jan Andersson (b. 1955), flew a Saab SF 37 Viggen, intended for photo reconnaissance, while his wing man Captain Jan Gisselsson in a Saab SH 37 Viggen carried out radar reconnaissance. Each reconnaissance squadron included both versions of the aircraft (F for photo reconnaissance, H for maritime radar surveillance) and one of each regularly flew together to complement each other during reconnaissance missions.[18]

Soon the pilots discovered the task force of Soviet ships that was heading towards Sweden. Jan Andersson relates:

> I turned towards and flew parallel to the convoy from behind for low-altitude photos with the side cameras as per routine… I started to take photos, but when I passed the destroyer it wasn't like it used to be with personnel on deck waving and looking. I was struck by an unpleasant feeling when I saw that all the hatches were closed and that no one was visible on deck. I concluded that it was probably not very healthy to stay as close as I was.[19]

If Soviet military units crossed Sweden's border, it might be necessary to use armed force. To reinforce Military District South, the Supreme Commander, General Ljung, assigned Lieutenant General Olson the 1st Strike Wing (E 1), the air unit that reported directly to the Supreme Commander and for this reason was colloquially known as the 'Supreme Commander's bludgeon'. Olson himself had previously commanded the E 1 which would carry out the operation.

Lieutenant General Olson therefore ordered the commander of E 1, Major General Erik Nygren (1923–1999), to keep his assigned units ready to attack the Soviet task force, in the event that it attempted to carry out a relief operation. To this end, Olson personally called both Major General Nygren and Colonel Gunnar Hovgard (b. 1926), the commander of the Västgöta Air Wing (F 6) at Karlsborg. On Olson's order, Swedish strike aircraft now prepared for an attack with live weapons against the approaching Soviet ships.[20]

In the evening, Swedish surveillance radar observed the Soviet task force as it approached the 12-nautical-mile (22km) line that delimited Sweden's territorial waters. Tensions were then high within the Swedish Coastal Artillery, and many expected, possibly looked forward to, an artillery duel with the Soviet ships. Coastal Artillery radar stations prepared fire solutions when the task force seemingly reached the border, and were ready to open fire, if ordered. The Soviet warships were equipped with radar warning receivers, so Vice Admiral Kalinin knew that the Swedes were ready. It was not a friendly welcome.

The Operations Room, colloquially known as 'the Church', in Air Defence Sector Centre W 2 Svalan. (Author's collection)

Saab SF 37 Viggen, intended for photo reconnaissance and with a characteristic nose cone that housed a camera, 1977. (Photo: Medström)

The closely related SH 37 Viggen, intended for radar reconnaissance, could be recognised by its black nose cone that hid a radar. Either version might also carry auxiliary fuel tanks and a camera pod. (Photo: Medström)

The only problem was that the Coastal Artillery radar stations were not yet calibrated, so the cannon would probably not have hit, had they opened fire. Of course, the Soviets did not know this. Betting that Vice Admiral Kalinin would notice their high level of activity through his own ELINT capability, Major Rolf Lindén (b. 1943) who at the time headed the Operations Section at Blekinge Coastal Artillery and Karlskrona Defence District (Fo 15) gave the orders to turn on everything they had to bluff the Soviets into believing that Swedish defences were ready.[21]

By 8:00 p.m., Swedish military forces in the vicinity consisted of the squad from Karlskrona Coastal Artillery Regiment (KA 2), some vessels from the 13th Torpedo Boat Division for which crews had been found, a few minesweepers and picket boats of little combat value, and the two manned Coastal Artillery cannons. Commander Thor Widell, also in charge of the Swedish salvage unit, held command in Gåsefjärden Bay. Commander Bengt Törnwall on the torpedo boat *Piteå*, commander of the 13th Torpedo Boat Division, commanded at sea beyond the archipelago. The Coastal Artillery, technically under the command of Brigadier General Jean-Carlos Danckwardt (1922–2001), led all land forces in the operation. In reality, Danckwardt had been sent to Malmö in the province of Scania to supervise a pre-planned exercise in the straits between Denmark and Sweden on behalf of Military District South and as part of Sweden's liaison with BALTOPS already before the *S-363* stranded. As soon as the information of the *S-363* reached Military District South, the exercise was aborted and Danckwardt was recalled. Meanwhile, Major Lindén held effective command.

Although reinforcements were already on the way, the first patrol boats from the 13th Patrol Boat Division at Gålö were not expected before the next morning. The Army had ordered the infantry Kronoberg Regiment (I 11) in Växjö to be ready to send its duty squad to the area, to be reinforced with a full infantry company if need be, at 8:00 a.m. next day.[22]

At Västgöta Air Wing (F 6) at Karlsborg, Major Leif Åström (b. 1949) commanded 2nd Squadron, which was called Filip Blå. At about 7:30 p.m., he was called to the base to set up the strike group of four Saab AJ 37 Viggen that would intervene against what the Swedes then expected to be a full-scale Soviet relief attempt. He was given the task of choosing a weapon load in order to warn as well as fire limited or full effect fire, depending on the situation. The choice of weapon was not only based on tactical experience, but also on the peacetime regulation to first warn and only then, if necessary, launch effective fire. The IKFN instruction demanded that warning fire preceded limited or full effect fire in times of peace. Åström accordingly selected a weapons load as follows:

For warning purposes (one aircraft):

Sixteen 120kg high-explosive parachute bombs that could be dropped ahead of the Soviet ships. This would not damage an intruder but the detonations would be felt as a shock wave throughout the entire ship:

For limited effect fire (one aircraft):
Twenty-four 13.5cm attack rockets in four rocket pods and eight 80kg illumination bombs

For full effect fire (two aircraft):
Two RB 04E tactical naval air-to-ground missiles[23]

The RB 04E missiles were to be used only if the Soviets opened fire or did not heed the warning fire.

Having prepared the aircraft, Åström and two groups of AJ 37 Viggen pilots were put on alert in the evening.[24]

Then they waited.

An operation with combat-loaded aircraft could have quickly escalated into war between Sweden and the nuclear superpower that was the Soviet Union. And there certainly seemed to be growing cause for concern, as the Soviet ships consolidated their presence near Swedish waters. Would the Soviet task force attempt to free the submarine by force? This worry was at the time exaggerated but, which will be shown, not wholly unfounded.

Vice Admiral Kalinin's task force reached the Swedish territorial line around 9:00 p.m. and anchored just outside Swedish territorial waters. The *SS-30* apparently failed to stop in time and crossed the Swedish border at 8:14 p.m., if so ahead of the rest of the task force, continued almost 500m, but was turned back by a torpedo boat from the 13th Torpedo Boat Division under Commander Bengt Törnwall's command, and returned south at 8:32 p.m.[25] With the exception of this mishap in the darkness, there was nothing in the behaviour of Kalinin's task force that suggested hostile intentions.

During the night, the Filip Blå squadron led by Leif Åström carried out two missions with the group of four combat-loaded AJ 37 Viggen. The first mission already started at 12:20 a.m, but was ordered to abort when the weather deteriorated and visibility dropped below the minimum permitted for landing at all air bases in Sweden. Åström wanted to continue, despite the risk. The serious situation justified the risk of having problems on landing, he argued.[26]

The second mission was planned with take-off at 6:40 a.m., so that the flight would take place in darkness, but the approach to the target would occur exactly at dawn. That way, the ships would be visible as clear silhouettes against the first light of dawn in the east, while the Swedish aircraft could be spotted by their switched-on navigation lights and thus not surprise the Soviets. A surprise might escalate the situation.

Having reached the Soviet task force, Åström carried out the flyby at a fairly moderate speed and at a sufficient altitude for the ships to be able to detect the Viggen aircraft early. The aircraft with air-to-ground missiles did not participate in the flyby, but were kept out of range of the ships' surface-to-air missiles. Åström noted during the passage that the ships were stationary, right on the 12-nautical-mile (22km) line, without any fire control radar in operation and without any visible activity onboard. The Soviet task force showed no hostile intent. After passing the Soviet ships, the Viggen aircraft returned to Karlsborg. The squadron then handed over the task as well as the loaded aircraft to 1st Squadron, known as Filip Röd, of Västgöta Air Wing (F 6).[27]

Then it became time for the next flight. Major Kjell Öfverberg, who commanded Filip Röd, related:

> Filip Röd was then ordered to carry rockets on the aircraft to mark our readiness and our determination not to allow any further violation of Swedish territory. We set off with a combat-loaded group down towards the so-called relief force. The weather was quite bad, but we got down under clouds to the south of Öland and looked for the group of ships that were lying still, completely silent, without either radar emission or any other signaling. We, on the other hand, had everything on (radar, IFF, navigation lights, anti-collision lights, and so on) to avoid our arrival being a surprise.
>
> We flew in among the ships calmly and gracefully and showed off our rocket load. The hope was that it would be noted that the Swedish strike aircraft were prepared to act if required. Our load was also chosen to allow both warning and full-effect fire. (This far in hindsight one can allow oneself to wonder what would have happened to us if we had attacked these modern warships with rockets.) We noted no reaction whatsoever from the relief force. After a few flybys among the ships, we left towards the north and flew home to F 6.[28]

If the Soviet task force had chosen to enter Swedish waters without permission in a rescue attempt, the Soviets would have risked being

Saab AJ 37 Viggen, armed with the anti-ship missile RB 04E. (Photo: Medström)

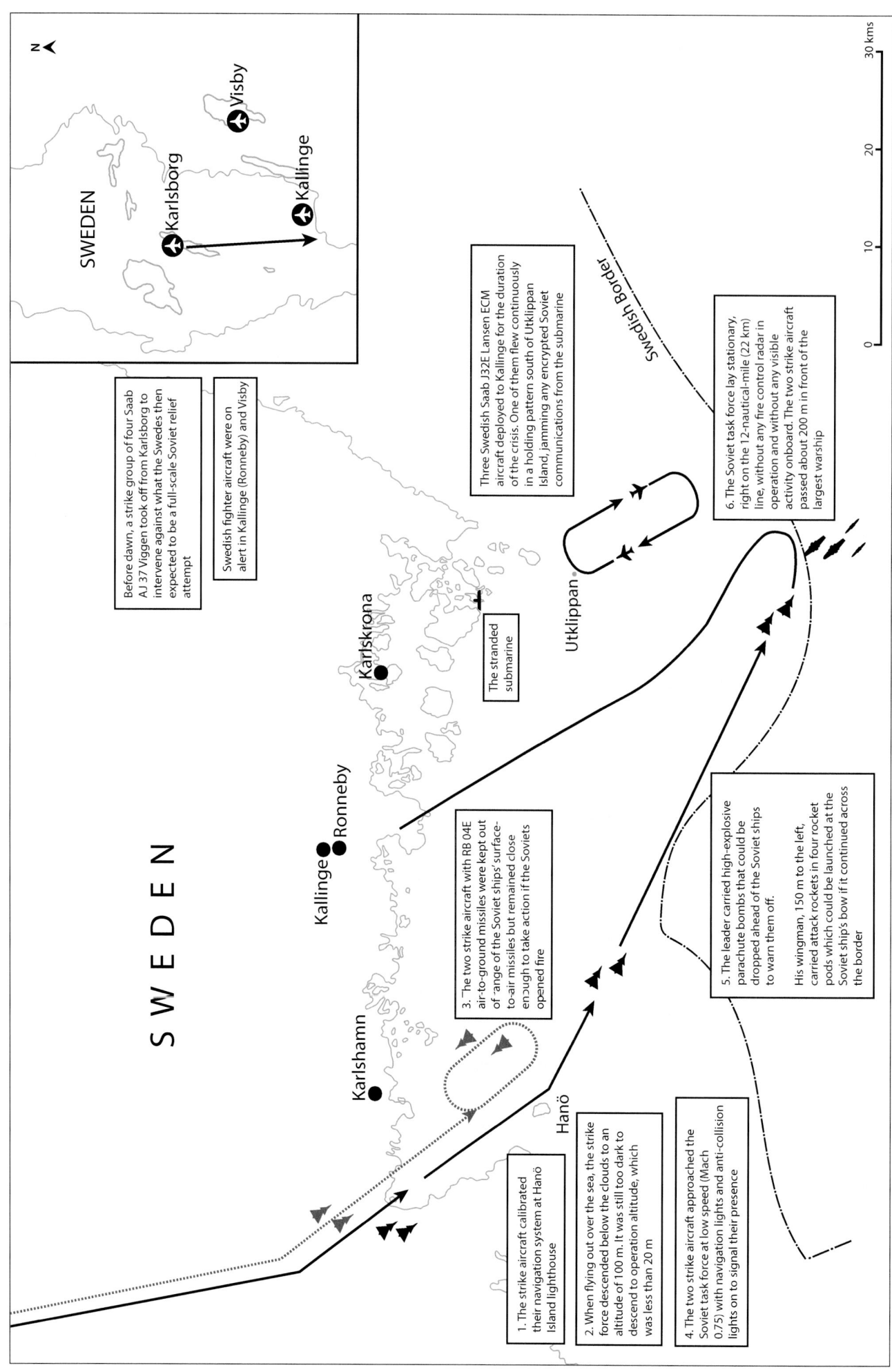

Missions by Swedish ground attack aircraft. (Map by George Anderson)

attacked by aircraft, coastal artillery, and mines. The tugboats needed almost an hour from the maritime border to reach the stranded submarine. Along the way, they would also have encountered the Swedish torpedo boats. Would a Soviet armed intrusion have been feasible, had Vice Admiral Kalinin received orders to push on? He could possibly have used his two warships to break through the Swedish defences. However, the rest of the task force would have been vulnerable to attack at least from the air and, from the following day, the fixed mine lines and coastal batteries. Moreover, it was really only during the first evening and the ensuing night that a Soviet intrusion would have had a reasonable chance of success. On the next day, we will see that additional Swedish reinforcements arrived, and that the Swedes did their best to cut off access to Gåsefjärden Bay.

The Swedish military aircraft were on the following day followed by Swedish civilian helicopters. These were manned by television crews, eager to film the action. Knowing that they were in range of Western television broadcasts, the personnel of the Soviet salvage task force, still at anchor, set up television sets. Soon they could watch their own ships from the air in the news broadcasts that they tuned in to.[29]

A Night at the Opera
In Stockholm, the Swedish government also had a visit of state to deal with. The President of Iceland, Vigdís Finnbogadottír, visited Stockholm. The parliament had rented the Royal Dramatic Theatre to perform a play, August Strindberg's 'Playing with Fire' (*Leka med elden*), in honour of the Icelandic President. In the evening she would attend a gala performance there in the presence of King Charles XVI Gustavus of Sweden. Other attendees were Prime Minister Fälldin, Foreign Minister Ullsten, General Ljung – and the Soviet Ambassador, Yakovlev, in his role as doyen and representative of the diplomatic corps. More than one within the audience reflected on the play's title, which seemed highly appropriate for the present confrontation outside Karlskrona. Except politicians and civil servants, the audience consisted of what was referred to as 'busloads' of Security Service personnel. The reason was that somebody had telephoned in a hoax bomb threat. The anonymous potential terrorist had not specified where he would strike, but the Security Service preferred not to take any chances. Fälldin sneaked out to give a radio interview so that he could avoid shaking hands with Yakovlev when the doyen arrived. During the intermission, Fälldin, Ullsten, and Ljung informed King Charles about the ongoing developments.

Fälldin also approved Ljung's urgent proposal to cancel the latter's upcoming official visit to the Soviet Union, previously scheduled for 19 November.[30] Ljung did not wish to visit Moscow.

At some point during the evening, Ullsten and Fälldin discussed the issue of whether the submarine enjoyed immunity. Based on their later testimonies, they 'possibly' already during this meeting decided 'in principle' not to grant the submarine the traditional full immunity enjoyed by foreign warships not engaged in hostile activities. Nor did they claim that the submarine had no immunity whatsoever. Instead, in the words of State Secretary Sven Hirdman, the government chose 'neither full immunity nor no immunity, but a state in-between'.[31] But neither Fälldin nor Ullsten informed the military commanders in Karlskrona who spent the evening planning how to storm the submarine by military force.

Meanwhile, on Torumskär the squad on guard duty prepared to be relieved. On the nearby Coast Guard vessel, the crew already rested. On the *S-363*, most of the crew rested, too, although some still manned duty stations. Besedin was still awake and in the tower. He relates how the signals rating Aleksandr Morozov came to report that they had observed a motor launch 100m ahead. The Soviets may not have noticed, but the launch had set out from the Coastal Artillery minelayer *Mul 13*. The launch carried a squad – six conscripts under Captain Lennart Lindquist from Karlskrona Coastal Artillery Regiment (KA 2) – to relieve the one hitherto on guard duty. Executive officer Viktor Yakovlev ordered his men to turn on a search light to illuminate the shore, since he realised that the motor launch otherwise might hit the same rocks that the *S-363* had struck. However, the waves were too rough for the launch, so about 100m from the shore, the launch capsized. Besedin, Yakovlev, and Morozov saw the men in the water in the light of the search light. The situation was serious; the Baltic Sea is cold in late October, waves were strong, and it was pitch dark.

Besedin whistled loudly to attract the attention of the Coast Guard crew. This was the Coast Guard vessel *Tv 281* from Kalmar under Arne Magnusson. When a Coast Guard man stepped out on deck in response to Besedin's whistle, Besedin indicated the soldiers in the water. The Coast Guard officer understood, raised the alarm, and turned on the vessel's siren and search light. Seconds later, the Coast Guard crew emerged on deck, launching a dinghy. Fortunately, they managed to rescue all soldiers in the water. The event was logged at 7:48 p.m., and the conscripts lost several submachineguns in the water.[32]

Coastal Artillery gun crews still carried the old Carl Gustaf model 45B submachinegun, adopted in 1945, as sidearms. The weapon was manufactured under, and sometimes without, license in various countries. U.S. Navy SEALs and CIA operatives and advisors used the model 45 extensively during the Vietnam War. One of the gun's qualities that appealed to the U.S. Navy was that the model 45 can fire almost immediately when out of the water. In U.S. service, the gun was often known as the 'Swedish-K'. The Swedish police used a variant of the gun to fire tear gas canisters. In the Swedish Armed Forces, the model remained in service until 2007. (Photo: Swedish Railway Museum)

7
THURSDAY 29 OCTOBER

At 10:00 a.m. on Thursday 29 October, General Ljung and State Secretary Hirdman, who had just flown in from Norway's capital Oslo, attended a crisis group meeting with Cabinet Secretary Leifland at the Ministry of Foreign Affairs. The Defence Minister remained in Oslo until late in the evening, among other events inspecting the Norwegian Armed Forces' dog training school and hobnobbing with defence ministers from NATO countries. Nor did the Prime Minister or Foreign Minister attend, since the crisis group primarily was an assembly of the heads of security-related agencies. Theutenberg, the advisor on international law, played a prominent role in the meeting. The discussion dealt with the question of whether they would send men to storm the submarine, in case Captain Gushchin refused to follow Swedish instructions. The usually so belligerent General Ljung and Schuback now responded that such an operation was tactically difficult, and required anti-tank weapons and armour-piercing explosives to breach the hull if the submariners closed the hatches and resisted. There would be casualties. The Soviet Union might treat the assault, and the associated loss of life, as an act of war. Based on later interviews, the option of armed force was therefore quickly dismissed.[1] Leifland and the others also discussed whether they should expel a few Soviet diplomats to show Sweden's displeasure. However, since the obvious candidates were Ambassador Yakovlev and the Naval Attaché, Prosvirnin, who both were needed in Stockholm to handle the ongoing negotiations, this idea, too, was quickly dismissed.[2] Besides, the expulsion of Soviet diplomats would only result in tit-for-tat expulsions of Swedish diplomats in Moscow, which was inconvenient since the Foreign Ministry then must find other assignments for them. As for the issue of international law, Theutenberg's interpretation of the legal situation, which also became Sweden's official position, was that a situation of innocent passage or distress could not be said to exist. Hence, the submarine and its crew were subject to Swedish authority and could not claim immunity.

Leifland's crisis group also reached consensus that the submarine at least must be subjected to a seaworthiness inspection before it was allowed to leave Swedish jurisdiction.[3] We will see that this decision apparently originated in an initiative from General Ljung.

At 11:15 a.m., Leifland, Hirdman, Theutenberg, General Ljung, and Schuback walked the short distance to the Cabinet Office, where they informed the participants about the conclusions of the crisis group meeting. The Cabinet approved the conclusions and issued formal instructions for the Swedish negotiating position:

1. The submarine must remain in the custody of the Armed Forces.
2. The submarine must remain in place for the time being.
3. The Supreme Commander will be responsible for the investigation that must take place.
4. The Supreme Commander will be responsible for the salvage operation.
5. The government will demand an apology from the Soviet Union.

It seems that the crisis group and the Cabinet also reached a consensus about not resorting to violence against the submarine crew. This is, at least, the conclusion to be drawn from Defence Minister Gustafsson's comment in the television news show *Rapport* in the evening of Sunday 1 November that he could 'see no circumstances' under which Sweden would resort to armed force.[4] If a consensus was reached, General Ljung did not know this. Upset over Defence Minister Gustafsson's message, General Ljung wrote in his diary that the Defence Minister's message was really peculiar 'since first, we have an IKFN that gives us this right in certain situations and moreover, we have mobilized our military in the area'. General Ljung noted with satisfaction that the press was upset, too, and most media outlets demanded the Defence Minister's immediate resignation because of his unwelcome comment.[5]

According to what Fälldin and Ullsten later related, the Cabinet took the formal decision not to grant the submarine full immunity at 11:00 a.m., even though we have seen that they both admitted that the decision in principle 'possibly' was taken already the previous evening.[6]

After the Cabinet meeting, representatives of the Ministry of Justice met with Magnus Sjöberg, the National Prosecutor. On the previous day, the Acting County Prosecutor in Karlskrona, Kviele, had asked Sjöberg about the legal implication of the option of prosecuting the submarine crew for espionage. Sjöberg told him not to do anything for the moment, then pondered the situation. Legally, the government could decide on abolition, to close the case, and this seemed the most likely outcome if the County Prosecutor proceeded with legal action. Sjöberg gave a public statement, which ultimately was reported on the evening television news (*Rapport*, at 7:30 p.m., 29 October), that suggested that the Soviet crew could claim immunity, as long as they stayed in the submarine. This was also the decision that Sjöberg communicated to Kviele. This legal decision at first upset the political and military leadership, which argued that it tied their hands and prevented them from dealing with the crisis as they liked. However, they soon concluded that Sjöberg's legal decision brought something good, because it immediately removed the entire justice system from the equation. If it had not, it seems likely that the local police would have been compelled to act against the crew of the submarine. Moreover, soon afterwards, taking the advice of the Foreign Ministry, Sjöberg changed his interpretation of international law to conform with that of Theutenberg. Later, representatives of the Swedish government including Prime Minister Fälldin and Foreign Minister Ullsten concluded that it was highly beneficial to remove the justice system entirely from the decision-making process, since this gave the government the desired freedom to frame the situation in political, not legal terms.[7] Prime Minister Fälldin explained that when told that the international legal interpretation of whether the submarine and its crew enjoyed immunity or not remained unclear, he regarded this not as a challenge but an opportunity. The uncertainty permitted the government to act according to what seemed politically most advantageous at the time.[8]

By then, General Ljung had already requested the Ministry of Communications to endorse the use of a recently introduced law on seaworthiness as the legal basis on which to demand a thorough inspection of the submarine. The idea was to make the claim that an on-site inspection was a non-negotiable condition demanded by law before the government could release the submarine. The

Cabinet eagerly, and hastily, decided to apply the relevant law to the Soviet submarine. During the afternoon, officials at the Ministry of Communications discussed the ramifications of this decision. Their lawyers then discovered that the new law included a codetermination clause on democracy in the workplace which, quite contrary to the Cabinet's wishes, meant that the Soviet crew must be involved in any assessment of the working conditions onboard the vessel. Under normal circumstances, the law was never implemented with regard to warships. Should the Swedish law be applied to Soviet, but not Swedish, warships? Soon, the lawyers also realised that in case the Ministry of Communications inspector assigned to the case found the submarine unseaworthy, his verdict would tie the government's hands if a political decision by then already had been made to release the submarine to the Soviets. Nobody wanted an over-zealous Ministry of Communications inspector to decide a national security issue. Worse, unsubstantiated rumours began to circulate within the Defence Staff and the Foreign Ministry that the appointed inspector, Gunnar Mattsson, was an overzealous nitpicker who surely would cause problems. Foreign Minister Ullsten went so far as to tell Claes Elmstedt, Minister of Communications, that the inspector was a problem who must be dealt with, that is, removed from authority. From a legal point of view, Ullsten's order was unconstitutional, but Ullsten probably regarded such trivialities as irrelevant in a moment of national crisis. Ultimately, the Cabinet had to reformulate the legal interpretation of the law on seaworthiness so that the Cabinet would have the final say on the issue. The re-interpretation meant that only the two articles of the law that supported the government's position would be implemented.[9]

At 2:00 p.m., Ambassador Yakovlev arrived to learn the Swedish position. Foreign Minister Ullsten set forth the Cabinet's demands. First, Swedish representatives must investigate the submarine and question its commander. Second, salvage must be carried out by the Swedish authorities, without involvement by the Soviet Navy. Third, Sweden demanded a formal Soviet apology for the intrusion. Ullsten also explained the legal requirement for an on-site inspection of the submarine's seaworthiness and informed the Ambassador that the Supreme Commander of the Swedish Armed Forces had been ordered to salvage the submarine.

Yakovlev forwarded the Soviet government's formal request for the assistance of the Swedish government with the salvage operation. On this issue the two sides agreed. The Swedish side interpreted this as a confirmation that the Soviets would not free the submarine by force. Yakovlev also stated the Soviet position that the submarine after salvage would be towed to international water and there handed over to the waiting Soviet task force. Yakovlev again requested that his representatives be allowed to visit the submarine crew. Ullsten rejected this demand, again arguing that the submarine had stranded in a restricted military area to which foreign nationals could not be admitted.

When Ambassador Yakovlev returned to the embassy, Ullsten joined Prime Minister Fälldin in a press conference. Friday was the day before a public holiday. Having recently returned from Cancún, Fälldin wanted to spend both Friday and the entire weekend in his remote country home in northern Sweden. However, Fälldin also felt the need to appear on the evening television news. Since this prevented him from taking the last flight home, he instead boarded the 11:25 p.m. overnight train to the north. In a world without mobile telecommunications, this placed him incommunicado for the entire train ride of eight and a half hours. Ullsten was away, too, spending the evening in a political meeting in Uppsala, a town north of Stockholm. Of the senior political policymakers, it was only Leifland who remained in Stockholm.

Swedish Reinforcements

But let us return to the Armed Forces and its preparations during the day. Early in the morning of Thursday 29 October, Jan Erik Walter (b. 1937), Assistant Master of the Armed Forces School of Interpreters in Uppsala, north of Stockholm, received a phone call at home just before he would go to work. Walter was an expert linguist who among other achievements had reformed and modernised the traditional teaching of Russian grammar, which in most institutions of higher learning remained tied to obsolete rules primarily applicable to the nineteenth-century Russian literary classics. If Walter had been employed by a university in an English-speaking country, he would have achieved worldwide renown for his new approach to the teaching of Russian. But Walter was Swedish, so he ended up at the Armed Forces School of Interpreters, where he spent his working life. Academe's loss was the Armed Forces' gain. Many Swedish males of military age benefited from his system of teaching (including the author of this book). Walter was a quiet scholarly man. He was perhaps not what one might call a charismatic teacher, but everybody who studied under him agreed that he was an extraordinarily competent educator.

But on this occasion, Walter's linguistic skills were better needed elsewhere than in the classroom. Asked if he could fly to Karlskrona already on the same day, Walter was picked up by a military car which drove him to Bromma Airport in Stockholm, where he boarded a military Lockheed C-130 Hercules transport, in the Swedish Air Force known as Tp 84, together with two platoons of altogether 60 Parachute Rangers (conscripts like most Swedish soldiers, but well-trained and already experienced in field operations) and 16 Coastal Ranger officers from Vaxholm Coastal Artillery Regiment (KA 1) in the archipelago east of Stockholm. The soldiers were armed to the teeth, with assault rifles, machine guns, and grenade launchers.

Upon arrival in Karlskrona, Walter was taken to the naval base to acquaint himself with those for whom he would interpret in the coming days. His arrival also relieved the hard-working old Brian Olsson, who by then was growing exhausted from his work as the sole available interpreter. In addition to Walter, the Armed Forces in the coming days sent four regular interpreters to Karlskrona: Thomas Tjäder, Per Jansson, Klas Helmerson and Tadeusz Wieloch.

The soldiers who had flown down in the same aircraft as Walter were met by policemen experienced in the handling and use of tear gas. The policemen gave the soldiers a crash course in gas operations. The use of so-called Riot Control Agents (RCAs) is permissible in the military for training purposes and for forcing combatants out of concealed or covered positions so that they can be engaged with conventional weapons. They were accordingly not prohibited under international humanitarian law by the 1925 Geneva Protocol. While all Swedish soldiers were trained to protect themselves against chemical warfare, they were not trained to use gas in offensive operations. Now they would have to learn this as well. The police and military had made a joint plan for how to storm the submarine. The Swedes would use gas against the submarine crew. There were also plans to employ artillery, if necessary.[10] The operation would be carried out in conjunction with the police under Police Commissioner Dag Felin. Meanwhile, tear gas, together with submachineguns and all available police-issue body armour and helmets, was brought to Karlskrona.[11] The Armed Forces at this time did not generally employ body armour. Buses then took the soldiers to the operations area. At 2:30 p.m., the Parachute Rangers disembarked at Kille Mountain, from which they could see the submarine below.[12] An hour later, Brigadier General Danckwardt could report that the men were deployed within sight of the submarine and ready for action.[13]

Lockheed C-130 Hercules transport, in the Swedish Air Force known as Tp 84. (Photo: Towpilot, 1975)

Parachute Rangers with the submarine in their sights. (Naval Museum, Karlskrona; Photo: Sören Ljungek)

To block sea access to the submarine, Naval Base Karlskrona rented a civilian tugboat, the *Karlshamn*, belonging to the municipality of Karlshamn. It would block the passage until the icebreaker *Thule* could arrive on the following day. The *Karlshamn*, under Ulf Jansson, arrived before noon. Jansson and the tugboat crew thought that they were contracted to salvage the submarine, so began fastening a tow cable to it. However, they soon received countermanding orders from the Navy.[14] Instead, they were ordered to cast anchor in the narrow strait that marked the exit to the sea of Gåsefjärden Bay. On the following day, when the *Thule* arrived to block the strait, the *Karlshamn* was sent into Karlskrona, with orders to wait there until needed.

But let us return to Thursday. From 10:30 a.m., when the Coastal Artillery manned the mine station off Gåsefjärden Bay and put it in operation, there was really no practical way for the submarine to exit the bay, even had it been able, unless the Swedes so allowed. The mines would also prevent any Soviet relief force from entering the bay.[15] In addition, more Coastal Artillery cannons were manned. Already in the morning, enough conscripts had been found to man the Coastal Artillery cannons, which Sweden still had aplenty. However, because of the shortage of trained men, most soldiers were unprepared for their duties. The Swedish system of conscription worked well if time was available for mobilisation, training, and preparations, but a sudden and unforeseen military emergency was not something that the numerically strong Armed Forces really practiced for. Swedish governments assumed that any war only would begin after a long period of easily-detected mobilisation of enemy forces which would give the Swedish Armed Forces time to mobilise its own considerable reserves.

Already at about 9:00 a.m., the Navy sent a press vessel (a landing craft from the Coastal Artillery) with journalists to see and record the submarine. Since foreign journalists were not allowed into the restricted military area, the Navy would from this day onwards arrange daily press tours as a means to broadcast the incident without formally breaking its own restrictions which included a prohibition to take photographs without special permit. The journalists began to refer to the daily tour as 'the tram'. Officially, foreign nationals were not supposed to join, but some did.[16] It was usually enough to say a sentence or two in Swedish to be admitted onboard. The Naval Base also transformed part of its headquarters into a press centre. This was an unusual measure since the building was inside a restricted area but one that facilitated contacts between the press and the Navy. The Armed Forces put up quite a show for the media. The press tours usually got really close to the submarine. Then, a Viggen fighter suddenly came flying towards them. It passed at an altitude of perhaps 300m, and then descended to only 25 or 30m for a second flyby. The manoeuvre was repeated a couple of times as a display of strength. Fighter pilots flew from as far away as Luleå in northern Sweden to participate in the flybys in what was labelled air navigation exercises. From initially ignoring the press boat, the submarine officers eventually lost patience and made it clear that they did not want it there. Neither did Colonel Danckwardt, who was in command on land. On one occasion, he even called Air Defence Sector Centre W2 Svalan outside Gothenburg, angrily telling them that the aircraft flew so low over the submarine that the Soviet crewmen in the tower almost had to duck.[17]

Saab Viggen fighter on a flyby over the *S-363*. (Photo: Medström)

Landing craft L 55, equally useful for landing soldiers as for press tours. This type of landing craft served the Coastal Artillery from the 1950s to the 1980s. Other vessels, too, may have been used for the press tours. (Photo: Medström)

At around 9:40 a.m. one of the navy's antisubmarine helicopters, the Y 69, spotted what was deemed to be the periscope of a foreign submarine at a position five nautical miles south of Utklippan Island, quite a distance from the *S-363* at Torumskär but well inside Swedish territorial waters. The helicopter was one of those which had been ordered to the area to reinforce existing units. Unfortunately, the helicopter was out of fuel, so had to abandon the hunt and return to Kallinge in Ronneby Municipality. At 11:35 a.m., the foreign submarine was located again, but this time by sonar. However, this was the last of the possible contacts, and despite a major search effort, the submarine was never found or identified.[18]

The 1st Submarine Flotilla in Karlskrona was ordered to send the submarine *Neptun* under Lieutenant Björn Hamilton to the 12-nautical-mile (22km) line that delimited Sweden's territorial waters on a reconnaissance mission to monitor the Soviet task force there. Having borrowed sailors from other submarines to make up a full crew, the *Neptun* set out about 9:30 a.m. Following the aforementioned torpedo trials, Hamilton's crew had not yet been called out, except for a few men who on the previous afternoon had embarked upon the T 138 *Piteå* or T 134 *Varberg* to observe the *S-363* in the capacity of submarine experts.

Soon, the *Neptun* received orders not to dive east of Utklippan Island. Hamilton's order remains classified, but the reason was likely the ongoing submarine hunt in the area. Hamilton accordingly remained in a position between the islands Utlängan and Utklippan, awaiting new instructions. While waiting, the *Neptun* crew just before noon visually observed what looked like a tugboat approaching from the east in Swedish waters. They identified it as a Soviet vessel by visual observation. Based on what Hamilton later reported, it was perhaps the salvage tugboat MB 171 *Loksa*. She was painted as a civilian vessel, with the name *Loksa* and, in even greater letters, the word RESCUE (Russian: SPASATEL') prominently displayed, so was easy to identify. Moreover, the identification of the vessel with the *Loksa* would make sense, since the *Loksa* sailed independently from Liepaja with orders to join Vice Admiral Kalinin's salvage task force.

The *Neptun* first flashed a stop signal and also attempted to contact the Soviet vessel by radio. Hamilton wanted to fire a warning shot, but the submarine had no weapons suitable for this, with not even a personal weapon onboard, Hamilton later related. Not receiving any response, Hamilton then tried to get in the way, but the vessel swerved and continued its journey. The *Neptun* chased after but could not catch the faster tugboat. Visibility was poor because of mist, but Hamilton saw a vessel veering west towards the port Karlshamn and concluded that this was the Soviet tugboat. The *Neptun* followed, but soon lost visual contact because of the thickening mist. The time was then around 1:50 p.m.

Hamilton also called for assistance, but no surface vessels were available. He later related that the only other Swedish unit in the area was an aged Saab Sk 50 propeller-driven trainer aircraft, still occasionally used as a liaison aircraft, which apparently monitored the situation. In the end, the *Neptun* received orders to turn back to its patrol area. Hamilton was later told that the tugboat ultimately returned unimpeded to the Soviet force, intercepted and turned back to international waters by a Swedish surface vessel (more on which below). He was also told that the 13th Patrol Boat Division had attempted to assist, but received wrong coordinates and searched for the Soviet vessel east of Utklippan Island.[19]

It was possibly this incident that persuaded the Swedes to order the icebreaker *Thule* to anchor in the entrance to Gåsefjärden Bay instead of the civilian tugboat *Karlshamn* to make extrication attempts more difficult. We will return to the *Thule* later.

The *Neptun* located the Soviet task force at about 10:30 p.m. It lay at anchor, in international waters and with lit anchor lights and personnel on deck. The Soviets did not use active sonar. Hamilton approached the largest Soviet ship, which must have been Vice Admiral Kalinin's *Obraztsovyy*, until he reached a distance of about 75 to 100m. He then, while remaining submerged, ordered his crew to light up the tower searchlight, still aimed upwards. The effect was that the Soviet crew could see a large greenish light progress under the water next to their ship. Hamilton could see through the periscope that the Soviet crew noticed the green light, but they did not respond to the provocation. Still no active sonar, nor any other signs of hostile intent. Hamilton continued to cruise in submerged mode with a lit searchlight between the anchored ships until about

The *Loksa*, as photographed by the pilot of the Saab Sk 50 trainer. The exact place and time of the photograph is unknown, as is the identity of the pilot. (Author's collection)

Saab Sk 50 trainer aircraft, abroad better known as the Saab 91 Safir. (Photo: Towpilot)

3:00 a.m. His action was highly provocative. In comparison to the Air Force pilots who when they approached the Soviet ships were careful to display their presence in a manner that the Soviets would not believe constituted an attack, and then withdrew after a flyby, Hamilton continued what seemed to be a blatant provocation for several hours. Finally, having elicited no response, he gave up and returned to Karlskrona. Hamilton entered the port at about 4:30 a.m., and was back in his bed at home at 5:00 a.m., or shortly thereafter.[20]

It is hard to assess the purpose, and impact, of Hamilton's stunt. We also do not know whether he acted upon orders or a personal initiative. The submarine arm's orders remain classified. It was an audacious action, in the grand tradition of the Swedish Navy in its heyday centuries earlier, but was it sound tactics? Hamilton certainly demonstrated the *Neptun*'s presence to the Soviets.

Did Vice Admiral Kalinin have hostile intentions? He had orders to tow the submarine home, but was he expected to employ force? The commander of the Baltic Fleet, Vice Admiral Ivan Kapitanets, much later recalled: 'We understood that an intrusion into Sweden's territorial waters was a world-class scandal, but nevertheless the [Baltic] Fleet was prepared for such an action.'[21] Yet, for the time being the Soviet task force remained outside the 12-nautical-mile (22km) line that delimited Sweden's territorial waters.

It is possible that Vice Admiral Kalinin began planning for the contingency to rescue the submarine and its crew by force, if the Swedes refused to release them. This was at least the situation if we can believe Gaidis Andrejs Zeibots (b. 1945), a Latvian who then was deputy chief of staff of 128th Missile Ship Brigade in Baltiysk and accordingly a member of Vice Admiral Kalinin's staff on the *Obraztsovyy*. More than a decade later, after the dissolution of the Soviet Union, Zeibots became commander of the Latvian Navy. Aiming to increase Latvian-Swedish naval cooperation and elicit additional Swedish development aid, he then told Hamilton about the Vice Admiral's 'devilish plot'.

According to Zeibots, Vice Admiral Kalinin on the evening of Thursday 29 October informed his men that they must prepare to go in to rescue the *S-363* in the early hours of Friday 30 October. The operation was scheduled to begin at 3:00 a.m. The tugboat *Loksa*, which was discovered in Swedish waters by the submarine *Neptun* in the morning of 29 October, was supposedly involved in the initial part of the operation. Zeibots said that the crew on the tugboat received orders to salvage the submarine and make sure that it was afloat in open water. But as we have seen, the tugboat never reached the stranded submarine. If the *Loksa* formed part of an operations plan of this kind, she failed to carry out her mission. Zeibots never explained exactly what the Soviet task force was expected to do at 3:00 a.m., or what kind of violent action was contemplated. According to Zeibots, the entire operation was finally aborted at 2:30 a.m. because Swedish military mobilisation then had gone so far that the operation seemed unlikely to succeed.[22]

There probably was no such operations plan. If Vice Admiral Kalinin actually contemplated the use of military force at an early stage, one may wonder why he did not strike immediately, before the Swedes had activated their defences. Instead, he anchored outside the 12-nautical-mile line and waited there while the Soviet Union formally requested permission from Sweden to send in his salvage vessels to Torumskär. Assuredly, Kalinin and his men would have carried out contingency planning for all sorts of situations, but this does not mean that he really expected that he would have to carry them out. There was certainly nothing in the behaviour of his task force that suggested hostile intentions.

In case there actually is some truth in the story about Vice Admiral Kalinin planning an operation of the kind that Zeibots described, and if the said operation was aborted at 2:30 a.m., this was half an hour before the *Neptun* set out for home. If so, then Hamilton's demonstration of the vulnerability of the Soviet task force may have been a contributing factor to the decision to abort the operation.

Yet, if Kalinin truly had planned an armed raid, he could easily have destroyed the self-illuminated *Neptun* with the weapons available on the large antisubmarine warfare ship *Obraztsovyy*, and then proceeded with the plan. Besides, Hamilton could not have known of Kalinin's operations plan, or that the operation was planned to take place at 3:00 a.m. The most likely explanation seems to be that Zeibots remembered the provocative behaviour of the Swedish submarine and much later linked this with some discussion about an aborted operations plan. The apparent link in time between the two events may well have been a mere coincidence. Besides, under the circumstances of the meeting between Zeibots and Hamilton, it was in the Latvian's interest to give the Swedes a story that highlighted the 'devilish' maliciousness of the common enemy.

Even though there accordingly is no real evidence that Vice Admiral Kalinin even prepared to carry out a raid to free the submarine, it is entirely plausible that others within the Baltic Fleet planned for this contingency. Decades later, the former GRU Special Forces (Spetsnaz) commander Gennadiy Zakharov (1940–2012) claimed that he and his men prepared for the operation, in case the Swedes refused to release the *S-363*. Captain First Rank Zakharov was then the commander of the Baltic Fleet's 561st Independent Maritime Intelligence Post (Russian: *561-y otdel'nyy morskoy razvedyvatel'nyy punkt, OMRP*), a brigade-sized special forces unit. Some of his men might have been present on the *Obraztsovyy* or, perhaps more likely, the *Prozorlivyy*, which had carried a Spetsnaz contingent already during the mission to Angola. However, the Spetsnaz team never received the go-ahead for the mission.[23]

Based on much later press revelations, Zakharov formulated a plan to storm the Swedish ship that from 29 October blocked the submarine's exit route and then force the crew of this ship to salvage the submarine and tow it into international waters.[24] If so, this meant either the civilian tugboat *Karlshamn*, which arrived before noon on this date and accordingly would seem the most likely target, or the icebreaker *Thule*, which we will see moved into position at about 11:55 a.m. on 30 October.

If the *Karlshamn* was the target, it was a good plan. The *Karlshamn* was at this time manned by a reinforced crew, but still no more than eight civilians – the harbour master John Törneryd, the commander Ulf Jansson, a deputy commander, two engineers, two sailors, and a pilot – who all were unarmed. Assuming that Zakharov's men could reach the tugboat, they would almost certainly have gained control of it. However, it seems unlikely that they would have succeeded in bringing out the *S-363*, since both tugboat and submarine then would have to cross at least one active line of mines under the eyes and guns of the Coastal Artillery, which itched for a fight and at this time was ready. Most likely, Zakharov's mission would have ended in a bloodbath with numerous civilian and military casualties. One day we may learn if Zakharov's plan was for real, or a paper product produced later. Even if Zakharov's plan was contemporary and genuine, we will never know if he could have carried it out, and as Zakharov himself said, Vice Admiral Kalinin never gave him the go-ahead to try.

As noted by Hamilton, a Soviet vessel, which he believed was the *Loksa*, was intercepted and turned back to international waters by a Swedish surface vessel at some point during the evening. The surface vessel was the torpedo boat T 134 *Varberg*, under Christer Bjurman of the 13th Torpedo Boat Division. Bjurman has related that the Soviet vessel only turned back when he threatened to open fire.[25] Some reports make this a second Soviet attempt to enter Swedish waters.[26] This would imply that two Soviet vessels were entering Swedish waters on this day. The prevalent thick mist confused identification. The official military report to the public did not mention the action carried out by the *Neptun* under Hamilton, presumably so as not to divulge any information about the sensitive submarine arm.

The vessel which the *Neptun* observed veering towards Karlshamn, a commercial port significantly further to the west, was later determined to be a civilian Soviet ship, the *Leninets*, on its way to Karlshamn on legitimate business, to pick up a dredger in this port.[27] As we have seen, the submarine crew lost visual contact with the *Loksa* during the chase, while the crew of the *Varberg* only observed the unknown vessel through a searchlight in the dark of night. It was probably the *Leninets*. Both the *Loksa* and *Leninets* were civilian vessels, and the torpedo boat crew had never seen either of them.

Blow Up the Submarine!
During the day, 16 Coastal Ranger officers and some 25 Parachute Rangers deployed in the vicinity of the *S-363*. Commanded by

The Swedish submarine *Neptun*, being towed to Karlskrona for maintenance, 2011. By then, it was already decommissioned. The *Neptun* had a length of 49.5m, a beam of 5.7m, and a draught of 5.5m. It carried a crew of only 19 men. The submarine was armed with eight 53cm torpedoes in six torpedo tubes and four 40cm torpedoes in two torpedo tubes. Surface displacement was 1,013 tons, with an underwater displacement of 1,125 tons. The submarine's maximum speed was 20kts on the surface, or 10kts submerged. Maximum regulation depth was 300m. Built in 1979, the *Neptun* was significantly more advanced than the old *S-363* which was based on Second World War technology. (Photo: EKS)

Lieutenant Colonel Torbjörn Elming, head of the Swedish Parachute Ranger School at Karlsborg, they deployed on Torumskär itself, at a distance of only some 60 to 100m from the stranded submarine, where they dug in and deployed machine guns, aimed at the submarine tower. A sniper was positioned only 78m from the *S-363*'s tower.[28] The Soviets had compared the previous soldiers, regular conscripts in green uniforms from the Coastal Artillery, to border guards and generally regarded them in a favourable light, essentially as security to protect the perimeter around the submarine. The soldiers who now replaced the conscripts from the Coastal Artillery were quite different in character. They wore camouflage, painted their faces for camouflage purposes, and were more aggressive. It was obvious that they watched the submariners through their weapon sights and maintained constant readiness. The men in the tower felt that snipers constantly had them in their sights and were ready to fire – a very unpleasant and disturbing realisation.

Although Coastal Rangers and Parachute Rangers, too, mostly consisted of conscripts, they were soldiers of a quite different calibre than their infantry and artillery counterparts. Physically fit, well-trained, and with a no-nonsense attitude to combat, many made of point of displaying a high level of aggressiveness towards any enemy – which in this case meant the Soviet submarine crew.

Besedin relates that the threat from the newly-arrived soldiers felt very real. He and his colleagues drew the conclusion that had the Swedes intended to pull the submarine from the skerry and release them, they would not have reinforced the military presence in this manner. Did the Swedes actually plan to storm the submarine? Had the diplomatic talks between Moscow and Stockholm broken down?

Coastal Rangers deploy near the *S-363*, with Captain Leif 'Ecka' Eriksson (right) in command. (Author's collection)

Parachute Rangers disembark. The general-issue service rifle of the Swedish Armed Forces from 1965 to 1986 was the license-built Swedish version of the 7.62 x 51mm NATO Heckler & Koch G3 battle rifle, in Sweden known as the Ak 4 (*Automatkarbin* 4) assault rifle. Swedish paratroopers carried a variant of the Ak 4 with insertable stock, specially developed for airborne operations. (Author's collection)

Thoroughly out of the loop of decision-making, neither submarine crew nor officers had any idea of what went on through diplomatic channels.[29]

Meanwhile, rumours began to spread among the Swedish military and civilian personnel that Besedin was a fanatic communist politruk, the term for a Soviet political officer during the Second World War, whose only duty was to sit in the tower at all times, armed with an assault rifle and a box of hand grenades, to gun down any crew members who tried to defect. The story probably derived from a series of popular novels by the controversial Danish author Sven Hassel which purported to describe events on the eastern front during the Second World War. These novels were widely read by young men at the time, including those in the Swedish Armed Forces. Incidentally, the novels remain in print and continue to sell well.

At 3:20 p.m., Avrukevich called Gushchin and Besedin to a meeting. Minutes before, an encrypted telegram with new orders from Fleet Headquarters had arrived. Besedin relates that the contents of the order alarmed and amazed them. They were ordered to reinforce the guard. If the Swedes attempted to storm the submarine, they must destroy all confidential documents and equipment (radios, encryption devices, torpedo guidance instruments) and also blow up the submarine itself.[30]

The three officers realised that if the Swedes stormed the submarine with full military force, the crew could not possibly defend the submarine for more than 15 to 20 minutes, that is, the time they expected the Swedes needed to break through the hull with shaped charge explosives and artillery fire. Hence, they must prepare confidential documents and equipment for destruction already now, and also make preparations for blowing up the vessel. But what would they do with the torpedoes with nuclear warheads?

Acting upon the orders of the two senior officers, Besedin instructed Senior Lieutenant Vladimir Pershin, head of the department for mines and torpedoes, to prepare blowing up the torpedo section. Pershin said that he needed two hours, and he was ordered to commence preparations immediately.[31]

If an order to blow up came, there were two options, according to Besedin. Either they could detonate the nuclear torpedoes where they were in the congested forward torpedo compartment or deactivate and launch them and then blow up the submarine itself. Blowing up the torpedoes in the launch tube might result in a nuclear explosion, he believed. The order from Fleet Headquarters had not specified what to do with the nuclear warheads. If the explosion turned nuclear, this would probably result in a war between the Soviet Union and Sweden, Besedin and his colleagues argued. They certainly had no wish for such an outcome. Accordingly, the latter option was chosen. The torpedoes would end up at some distance from the boat, but there would be no risk for a nuclear explosion.[32]

At 6:10 p.m., Pershin reported to Gushchin that preparations for blowing up the torpedo compartment were concluded. Soon afterwards, Pershin told Besedin that the sailors had carried out the preparations in silence, without commenting on the situation. They were apparently ready to follow orders, even if this would result in the death of them all.[33]

We do not know exactly what other preparations were made to carry out the order to blow up the *S-363*. Karl Andersson later said that 'the explosion is a misunderstanding' and that they would not sacrifice the crew to make the submarine unusable, but instead destroy the propeller shaft and valves.[34] Likewise, Captain First Rank Boris Shkanov, first officer of the operations command within the Central Staff of the Naval Forces who was responsible for the communications with the *S-363* at the time, later said that no order to blow up the submarine was sent.[35] Yet, Besedin's story contains numerous details and sounds credible. Moreover, Besedin sensed, but did not know, that Lieutenant Colonel Elming had deployed his best sniper, a man only identified by the personal name Lage but according to other information was Steve Jacobsson, near the submarine. The sniper had orders immediately to kill Besedin if it ever seemed that the Soviet officer might give the order to destroy the submarine.[36]

Soon before 8:00 p.m., the Swedish Coast Guard vessel *Tv 281*, hitherto moored next to the submarine, cast off and departed, without offering any explanation to the Soviet officer on duty. Besedin interpreted the situation such that the Swedes might storm the vessel already during the night. On sentry duty, Besedin and the signals rating Savchenko prepared for a night during which anything might happen. Since it was a real chance that both Besedin and Savchenko would be shot by snipers, they arranged for a third sentry inside the tower, who if the worst happened could raise the alarm.

Fortunately, soon after the submariners had taken these precautions, another Coast Guard vessel, the *Tv 253* from Karlshamn under Conrad Söderholm, arrived to replace the vessel *Tv 281* which previously had departed. Söderholm moored the *Tv 253* next to the submarine. Söderholm, the chief of Blekinge Coast Guard District, was a cheerful fellow. With him in charge, the submariners and Coast Guard crew quickly established a modus vivendi. Both crews realised that if anything bad happened, both would be caught in the crossfire. Soon, they visited each other's vessel. Söderholm naturally got on particularly well with Avrukevich, who could speak some German and also understood a little English.[37]

Moreover, the *S-363* had during the day been allowed to contact Fleet Headquarters in Kaliningrad via shortwave radio, a communication that was carefully monitored by the Swedish authorities. The *S-363* used the call sign '*Fasad-140*', while Fleet Headquarters used '*Fermer-204*'. Commander Thor Widell assigned a radio channel (which remained in use until 1 November, when Karl Andersson assigned the *S-363* the High Frequency (HF) channel 3198 Khz for these communications).[38] The *S-363* crew was instructed to use only this radio frequency and not to use encrypted communications. The Soviets mostly followed the instruction, and when they did not, their communications were jammed, following guidance by FRA, by a Swedish Air Force Saab J32E Lansen, equipped for Electronic Countermeasures (ECM).[39] Three J32Es deployed to Kallinge for the duration of the crisis. One of them flew continuously in a holding pattern south of Utklippan Island but over Swedish water, since they were not permitted to cross the border into international airspace.[40] Nonetheless, we will see that the occasional encrypted telegram slipped through.

At 9:00 p.m., Karl Andersson again visited the submarine. He explained that the Swedish government had decided that Gushchin must be questioned before the submarine could be released. Avrukevich replied that they were willing to comply but first must receive orders to proceed from Fleet Headquarters.

Besedin later related that during the first three days of the crisis quite a few Swedish civilian vessels, sailing yachts and motor boats, sailed past and openly studied the submarine, albeit at some distance. None came closer than 50 to 100m. They did not approach, either because of the Swedish naval vessels nearby or because they could see the armed sentries in the tower.

Moreover, the radar operators in Air Defence Sector Centre W2 Svalan complained that so many small, private aircraft circled the submarine that it was almost impossible to monitor the airspace. Some private pilots did so out of curiosity, but others were hired by Swedish and foreign journalists who wanted close-up photos or videos of the submarine.[41]

The presence of civilians bothered Lennart Forsman, the commander of Naval Base Karlskrona. He accordingly asked

Iosif Avrukevich (centre), with Swedish Navy, Police, Coast Guard, and Coastal Artillery officers. (Author's collection)

Swedish Saab J 32E Lansen ECM aircraft at the time of the *S-363* incident, with the author. (Author's collection)

Brigadier General Danckwardt to contact the County Administrative Board. Danckwardt was commander of Blekinge Coastal Artillery and Karlskrona Defence District (Fo 15). As commander of all land forces in the operation, his duties included liaison with the local civilian authorities. Just before 9:00 p.m., Danckwardt asked the County to ban access to the area around the submarine also for Swedish nationals. Too many journalists were arriving, with boats, helicopters, and aircraft, and it was difficult to preserve order. Moreover, if combat took place between Coastal Rangers and submariners, Forsman and Danckwardt wanted all civilians out of the way. At 10:30 p.m., the County officials called in a secretary, Gun-Britt Wickström, to draft a formal decision that would apply effective immediately. By midnight, the decision was formally signed and gained legal force. At 3:00 a.m., County found somebody at the local newspaper who promised to announce the decree in the first print edition next (Friday) morning.[42]

While Besedin pondered these conflicting positive and negative signals, and if there were any other precautions they could take to ensure their safety and that of the submarine, Savchenko in the middle of the night suddenly reported the silent approach of a small boat on the port side of the submarine. The little wooden boat that now approached the *S-363* was surely not an innocent civilian.[43]

8
RADIATION READINGS

Earlier in the day, Lars Beckman (1920–2005) and Lars-Erik De Geer (b. 1945), two experts from the Defence Research Establishment (FOA) boarded the regular morning flight from Stockholm to Ronneby, the airport next to Karlskrona, with a Scintrex BGS-41 reader with which to measure gamma radiation. Beckman and De Geer then had to wait all day until the Navy arranged an open, small wooden boat to take them to the submarine. A third man from FOA joined them: the veteran engineer Olle Nord from the FOA office in Linköping. He had considerable experience with Soviet military technology, particularly in the field of aerospace. In 1957, he carried out a field investigation of a MiG-15 fighter aircraft flown to Sweden by a defector. In the next two years, he was called in to examine the on-site remains of what some, incorrectly, thought were UFOs from outer space. And he would continue to study Warsaw Pact military technology in the field until the end of the Cold War and beyond.

Under the cover of darkness, the FOA men approached the submarine in the small boat, steered by a Navy skipper. With the submarine stranded on the skerry, the forward torpedo tubes were sufficiently high above the water to enable a clear reading. De Geer sat in the bow of the boat with the gamma radiation reader hidden under his raincoat. He read the instrument with a hand torch.

Suddenly, they were briefly exposed by a searchlight, not from the submarine but from a Swedish vessel nearby. The FOA men did not know it at the time, but it was the searchlight from a vessel chartered by a Swedish television crew that briefly spotted the team.[1]

But the television searchlight also enabled Senior Sailor Savchenko, on duty in the tower, to spot the wooden boat moving towards the submarine bow. Besedin relates how they saw four men in the boat, all dressed in what looked like black diving wet suits (but which in reality, were standard Navy raincoats and life jackets). The boat was almost touching the submarine.

Besedin's first thought was that the men in the boat were commandos coming to assault the submarine. He pulled out his Makarov pistol, released the safety, and shouted to Savchenko to turn on the searchlight, aiming it at the intruders.

When the searchlight came on, the two submariners could see that the men in the boat reached out with their hands towards the submarine. Were they attaching explosives to breach the hull? Besedin raised his pistol to shoot at the intruders. What he did not know was that the men in the boat reached out, not to attach anything to the submarine hull but to reduce the boat's speed to avoid bumping into it. Besedin was an accomplished marksman and expected to hit one of the intruders, if he fired. The distance between Besedin and the men in the boat was only about 20m.

At this point, Conrad Söderholm on the Coast Guard vessel *Tv 253* noticed that the Soviets in the submarine tower had aimed a searchlight at some point ahead of the submarine. Three submariners shouted, and the duty officer aimed what Söderholm in the darkness took to be an assault rifle in the direction of the searchlight. Looking in the same direction, Söderholm saw a small wooden boat with an outboard motor, manned by three or four men, close to the submarine.

Then there was the Parachute Ranger sniper. We do not know what he saw or did. At least no shot was fired.

It suddenly struck Besedin that the men in the boat, who no doubt belonged to the Parachute Rangers who had taken up positions on Torumskär, must be a provocation. If he fired, the Swedes could argue that the Soviets had fired first and commence the planned assault on the submarine.

At this point, the men in the Coast Guard vessel, too, had been alerted to the danger. Söderholm, together with his crew, angrily shouted to the FOA men to leave the area. Nobody had informed them about what was to take place and they did not wish to be caught in crossfire.

For a while, it seemed that the Soviets would open fire at the approaching boat, but then the men onboard realised the gravity of the situation. Besedin related that the men in the boat, having noticed that they were spotted, threw themselves to the floor. The boat then turned sharply to port and moved away from the submarine. The Soviet searchlight followed the boat as it withdrew. Besedin kept his handgun trained on it.

Needing more light, Besedin ordered Savchenko to launch an illumination rocket. They could see the boat in the distance, moving towards the shore. In reality, the boat headed back to the M 63 *Aspö*, the minesweeper on which the Navy had established a forward command post.[2]

In hindsight, Besedin realised that his initial impression had been wrong. Surely, a boarding attempt would not take place at the bow, where the hull side was almost vertical. A boarding attempt was more likely at the stern, where it was easier to reach the deck. Had the men in the boat attached something to the outer side of the hull at the torpedo tubes? Besedin called the bosun, Warrant Officer Pyotr Dolgov, to bring a hand torch to investigate. Dolgov searched the hull for a considerable time, but found nothing suspicious.

Meanwhile, everything was quiet on the shore, and among the Swedish soldiers. Avrukevich joined Besedin in the tower. They discussed the situation, and agreed that whatever the men in the boat had been up to, their actions had not been an attempt to storm the *S-363*. Nonetheless, the Soviet officers and crew spent the rest of the night at full alert. Besedin relates that they nervously awaited all sorts of outcomes, and only calmed down by dawn.

The FOA team was not dissatisfied. Beckman's men were only spotted by the television crew's searchlight on their second approach to the submarine. They had already carried out a radiation measurement during the first approach. The second had been intended to confirm the initial, positive instrument reading. The FOA men even contemplated going in a third time. The veteran Nord advocated a third run, but Beckman, who was in charge of the mission, decided that two readings were sufficient for their needs.[3]

It was a busy night for everybody. At 3:30 a.m., Karl Andersson again visited the submarine, asking if Captain Gushchin had

Lars Beckman. (Author's collection)

received orders from Fleet Headquarters to take part in the questioning that Stockholm desired to hold on 30 October (that is, later in the day).[4] The submarine officers told him that the vessel's commander was not permitted to leave the submarine except when in port. They had not received any orders to take part in any kind of questioning. But the submariners also told Andersson about the events during the night. Besedin was sure that Andersson already knew everything, but the Swedish officer reassured them that he would make inquiries. On a more positive note, Andersson informed them that some progress was taking place in the negotiations, and that Swedish tugboats fairly soon would salvage the submarine and assist it in returning to sea. Andersson also asked if the Soviets needed any assistance, and if they had anybody onboard who needed medical attention. The Soviet officers appreciated the offer, which they, correctly, interpreted as genuine.[5]

In daytime, the submariners again searched the hull, but found nothing suspicious.

By then, the FOA team had already watched themselves on television, with a commentary by the journalist Christer Åström whose studio claimed that he broadcast live from the submarine. Åström had no idea of what his cameraman had caught on film during the night, but he knew it must mean something, which made it headline news.[6]

To be continued.

BIBLIOGRAPHY

Agrell, Wilhelm. *Bakom ubåtskrisen: Militär verksamhet, krigsplanläggning och diplomati i Östersjöområdet* (Stockholm: Liber, 1986)

Agrell, Wilhelm. *Fred och fruktan: Sveriges säkerhetspolitiska historia 1918-2000* (Lund: Historiska Media, 2000)

Andersson, Karl. 'Ubåt på grund!'. *Rapport från Medborgargruppen i Ubåtsfrågan: Seminarium på Tekniska Högskolan i Stockholm 29-20-10.1994* (Stockholm: Medborgargruppen, 1994): pp.10–13.

Andersson, Lennart. *Flygvapnets spaningsflyg: Sveriges ögon och öron under kalla kriget* (Stockholm: SMB, 2013)

Andersson, Per. 'U 137: Verkligheten är aldrig som den ser ut att vara'. *Tidskrift i Sjöväsendet* 4, 2021: pp.493–511.

Andersson, Per. 'Vad gjorde de här? Personliga reflexioner om den främmande undervattensverksamheten'. *Tidskrift i Sjöväsendet* 3, 2010: pp.211–124.

Andrew, Christopher; and Oleg Gordievsky. *Instructions from the Centre: Top Secret Files on KGB Foreign Operations 1975-1985* (London: Sceptre, 1993)

Andrew, Christopher; and Vasili Mitrokhin. *The Mitrokhin Archive: The KGB in Europe and the West* (London: Allen Lane The Penguin Press, 1999)

Andrew, Christopher; and Vasili Mitrokhin. *Mitrokhin Archive II: The KGB and the World* (London. Allen Lane, 2005)

Åström, Leif. 'AJ 37 och AJS 37 i tjänst'. Ulf Edlund and Hans Kampf (eds). *System 37 Viggen* (Stockholm: SFF, 2009): pp.85–102.

Åström, Leif. 'Förhindra fritagning av grundstött sovjetisk ubåt U-137!' (Ikaros: Flygvapenmusei årsbok, 2010): pp.45–60.

Bergström, Lars; and Klas Åmark (eds). *Ubåtsfrågan: En kritisk granskning av den svenska nutidshistoriens viktigaste säkerhetspolitisk dilemma* (Uppsala: Verdandi Debatt, 1999)

Besedin, Vasilij. *Inifrån U 137: Min egen berättelse* (Karlskrona: Albinsson & Sjöberg, 2009)

Besedin, Vasilij. *Ubåden der ramte Sverige. Den sovjetiske ubåd U 137s grundstødning i 1981 – set indefra* (np: Hovedland, 2021). Translated by Hans Christian Bjerg.

Björeman, Carl. *Sex överbefälhavare söker en roll: Tvekampen mellan det territoriella och det teknologiska försvaret under kalla kriget och i nutid* (Stockholm: Försvarshögskolan, Försvaret och det kalla kriget (FoKK) 53, 2017).

Borg, Lennart. 'Wendisten som besökte U 137'. *Wendisten*, 13 September 2020. Republished online in Wendistföreningen web site, https://wendisten.se/sida-9.

Darwall, Bjarne. *Myran: En hemlig anläggning går ur tiden* (Kallinge: Blekinge Flygflottilj, 2000)

Darwall, Bjarne. *Luftens dirigenter.* (Nässjö: Air Historic Research, 2004)

De Geer, Lars-Erik. *Kärnvapen på svensk mark!* (Karlskrona: Ranunkel, 2024)

Fältström, Herman. 'U 137-incidenten: En fallstudie'. Gunnar Artéus and Kent Zetterberg (eds). *Högsta ledningen: Förhållandet mellan regeringen och överbefälhavaren under det kalla kriget* (Stockholm: Försvarshögskolan, Försvaret och det kalla kriget (FoKK) 26, 2011): pp.113–128.

Fältström, Herman (ed.). *Ytspänning: Ett seminarium om kalla krigets verklighet.* (Stockholm: Försvarshögskolan, Försvaret och det kalla kriget (FoKK) 30, 2011).

FOA Tidningen 19: 4 (December 1981): 1-9. FOA's account of the radiation measurements next to the *S-363*.

Forsberg, Tore; and Boris Grigorjev [Grigor'yev]. *Spioner emellan* (Saltsjo-Duvnas: Efron & Dotter, 2006)

Försvarsstaben. *Ubåt 137 på svenskt vatten* (Stockholm: Försvarsstabens informationsavdelning, 18 December 1981). The public version of the Supreme Commander's report on the incident.

Fredholm von Essen, Michael. 'Redo för strid: Flyget och ubåt 137'. *Svenskt flyg under kalla kriget.* (Stockholm: Medström, 2016): pp.212–227.

Fredholm von Essen, Michael. *Afghanistan Beyond the Fog of War: Persistent Failure of a Rentier State* (Copenhagen: NIAS Press, 2018)

Fredholm von Essen, Michael. 'When Intelligence Made a Difference: How Sweden Chose Sides'. *Intelligencer Journal* (AFIO, 2019): pp.41–43.

Fredholm von Essen, Michael. 'The Power of Fear: Soviet Intelligence, the Politburo, and the 1979 Threat from Afghanistan'. *Journal for Intelligence, Propaganda and Security Studies* (JIPSS) 13: 2 (2019): pp.104–122.

Fredholm von Essen, Michael. *Hemligstämplat: Svensk underrättelsetjänst från Erlander till Bildt* (Stockholm: Medström, 2020)

Fredholm von Essen, Michael. *U 137 inifrån* (Stockholm: Medström, 2025)

Frithiofson, Ola. 'Ett amerikanskt hydrofonsystem etableras i svenska vatten'. *Historisk Tidskrift* 141: 2 (2021): pp.284–303.

Godin, Oleg A., and Palmer, David R. *History of Russian Underwater Acoustics* (Singapore: World Scientific Publishing Co. Pte. Ltd., 2008)

Grahn, Jan-Olof. *Om svensk signalspaning: Kalla kriget* (Stockholm: Medström, 2019)

Grigor'yev, Boris Nikolayevich. *Shvetsiya pod udarom: Iz istorii sovremennoy skandinavskoy mifologii* (St. Petersburg: Morskoye naslediye, 2012)

Gustafsson, Bengt. *Det sovjetiska hotet mot Sverige under det kalla kriget* (Stockholm: Försvarshögskolan, Försvaret och det kalla kriget (FoKK) 12, 2007)

Gustafsson, Bengt. *Sanningen om ubåtsfrågan: Ett försök till analys* (Stockholm: Santérus, Försvaret och det kalla kriget (FoKK) 23, 2010)

Gustafsson, Bengt. *Ubåtsfrågan: Sanningen finns i betraktarens öga* (Stockholm: Försvarshögskolan, Försvaret och det kalla kriget (FoKK) 4, 2005)

Hamilton, Björn. '1981: Ett särdeles händelserikt år på ubåten Neptun'. *Årsbok för Marinmusei vänner 2010* (Karlskrona: Marinmuseum, 2010): pp.56–76.

Hasselbohm, Anders. *Ubåtshotet: En kritisk granskning av Hårsfjärdenincidenten och Ubåtsskyddskommissionens rapport* (Stockholm: Prisma, 1984)

Hellberg, Anders; and Anders Jörle. *Ubåt 137: Tio dagar som skakade Sverige* (Stockholm: Atlantis, 1984)

Hellborg, Ragnar. 'Foreign Submarine'. Bengt Forkman and Kristina Holmin Verdozzi (eds). *Physics in Lund: In Time and Space* (Lund: Department of Physics, Lund University, 2016): pp.426–438.

Hellborg, Ragnar. *Sovjetisk ubåt U-137 med kärnvapen* (np: Nomen, 2020)

Hofsten, Hans von. *I kamp mot överheten: Örlog och debatt* (np: SMB, 2017). First published in 1993.

Hultgren, Roland. 'Hävdande av rikets integritet'. Erling Johansson (ed.). *Minnesbok Södra militärområdet* (Kristianstad: Södra militärområdet, 2000): pp.143–154.

Hultgren, Roland. 'KA 2 och händelsen med ubåt 137'. Olle Melin (ed.). *Kungliga Karlskrona Kustartilleriregemente 1/1 1902 – 31/10 2000* (Karlskrona: Marinmuseum Årsbok 2002): pp.91–104.

Jansson, Nils-Ove. *Omöjlig ubåt: Stridsberättelser från ubåtsjakten och det säkerhetspolitiska läget under 1980-talet*. np: Forum navale 52, 3rd edn 2016. First published in 2014.

Jansson, Nils-Ove. 'Submarine Intrusions in Swedish Waters: Past and Present'. *Kungliga Krigsvetenskapsakademien Handlingar och Tidskrift* 1, 2016: pp.52–59.

Jörle, Anders (ed,). *U137: Vi som höll gränsen – kustartillerister berättar om sin del av insatsen och sina upplevelser de dramatiska dagarna 1981 då en kärnvapenbestyckad sovjetisk ubåt står på grund i Karlskrona skärgård* (np: Page One Publishing, 2021)

Kapitanets, Ivan Matveyevich. *Na sluzhbe okeanskomu flotu 1946-1992*. Moscow: Andreyevskiy flag, 2000.

Kocherov, Vyacheslav; and Aleksandr Mozgovoy. 'Dolgiye posledstviya odnogo intsidenta'. *Morskoy sbornik* 1, 1993: pp.9–16.

Kormilitsin, Yury N.; and Oleg A. Khalizev. *Theory of Submarine Design* (St. Petersburg: St. Petersburg State Maritime Technical University, 2001)

Lindén, Rolf. 'I sista minuten: Fem timmar vid en arbetsplats i Kalla krigets skugga'. *Årsbok för Marinmusei vänner 2010* (Karlskrona: Marinmuseum, 2010): pp.77–95.

Lindén, Rolf. 'I sista minuten: Fem timmar vid en arbetsplats i Kalla krigets skugga'. Republished online, 17 April 2016 (https://navyskipper.blogspot.com/2016/04/i-sista-minuten-fem-timmar-pa-en.html).

Lindén, Rolf. 'U-137: Dagen då ryssen kom till Karlskrona'. *Wendisten*, 13 September 2020. Expanded version of the above, republished online in Wendistföreningen web site, https://wendisten.se/sida-9.

Ljung, Lennart. *Överbefälhavare Lennart Ljungs tjänstedagböcker 1978-1983* (Stockholm: Samfundet för utgivande av handskrifter rörande Skandinaviens historia, 2010). Edited by Evabritta Wallberg.

Lundin, Lars-Erik; Carl-Johan Groth; Rutger Lindahl; and Lennart Myrsten. *Den främmande undervattensverksamheten på svenskt territorium under perioden 1980-1995 sedd ur ett säkerhetspolitiskt perspektiv* (Stockholm: Utrikesdepartementet, 1996). Declassified on 30 March 2000.

Magnusson, Thomas; and Simon Olsson. 'Konsten att sälja underrättelser: De polska tavelförsäljarna'. *Svenskt flyg under kalla kriget* (Stockholm: Medström, 2016): pp.228–243.

McCormick, Gordon H. *Stranger than Fiction: Soviet Submarine Operations in Swedish Waters* (Santa Monica, California: RAND/Project Air Force, 1990)

Medborgargruppen. *Rapport från Medborgargruppen i Ubåtsfrågan: Seminarium på Tekniska Högskolan i Stockholm 29-20-10.1994* (Stockholm: Medborgargruppen, 1994). Swedish National Archives (RA), Ubåtskommissionen, YK 4541, Vol. 2 (mag. 4266). Also published in an edited volume by Lars Bergström and Klas Åmark (see above).

Mossberg, Mathias. *I mörka vatten: Hur svenska folket fördes bakom ljuset i ubåtsfrågan* (Stockholm: Karneval, 2nd rev. edn 2016)

Myasnikov, Valeriy Fyodorovich. *Posledniy pokhod S-137: Khronika avtonomnogo plavaniya sovetskoy podvodnoy lodki* (Moscow: LitPres, 2021)

Myhrberg, Ingemar. *Ubåtsvalsen: En motbok till rapporterna från ÖB och Ubåtsskyddskommissionen* (Gothenburg: Haga, 1985)

Nilsen, Fred O. *Sovjetisk ubåtvirksomhed i nord: Behov og tradisjoner*. Oslo: Institutt for Forsvarsstudier (IFS), IFS info 1/1995.

Öfverberg, Kjell. 'Filip Röd och U137…'. Göran Jacobsson (ed.). *Fältflygare: Från dröm till verklighet* (np: Norlén & Slottner, 2009): pp.144–145.

Olson, Sven-Olof. 'MB 1980-1982'. Erling Johansson (ed.). *Minnesbok Södra militärområdet* (Kristianstad: Södra militärområdet, 2000): pp.193–200.

Ottosson, Kurt. 'Spaningsviggen: SF/SH 37'. Ulf Edlund and Hans Kampf (eds). *System 37 Viggen* (Stockholm: SFF, 2009): pp.103–110.

Pope, Edmond D. *Cold War Warriors: Whiskey on the Rocks – A Window on the 1981 Cold War Era* (Emmitsburg News-Journal, 2011) (www.emmitsburg.net/archive_list/articles/misc/cww/2011/whiskey.htm).

Prosvirov, Viktor. 'Ryska marinens utredning om U 137'. *Rapport från Medborgargruppen i Ubåtsfrågan: Seminarium på Tekniska Högskolan i Stockholm 29-20-10.1994* (Stockholm: Medborgargruppen, 1994): pp.14–18.

Rozin, Aleksandr. *Deystviya Baltiyskogo flota po okazaniyu pomoshchi sevshey na mel' v shvedskikh vodakh PL 'S-363' (U-137) osen'yu 1981g*. Published online, http://alerozin.narod.ru/U137.htm.

Säkerhetspolitiska utredningen. *Fred och säkerhet* (Stockholm: SOU 2002): p.108.

Stefenson, Bror (ed.). *Krishantering: U 137-krisen* (Stockholm: Kungl. Krigsvetenskapsakademien, 1992)

Stenfeldt, Bert. 'Svenska flygstridskrafter under U 137-krisen 1981'. *Svensk Flyghistorisk Tidskrift* 3, 2007: pp.20–21.

Svensson, Emil. *Under den fridfulla ytan* (Stockholm: Marinlitteraturföreningen, No. 90 [91], 2005)

Theutenberg, Bo J. *Dagbok från UD*. (Skara: Stockholm Institute of International Law, Arbitration and Conciliation, 5 vols, 2012–2020)

Tunander, Ola. *Det svenska ubåtskriget* (Stockholm: Medström, 2019)

Tunander, Ola. *Navigationsexperten: Hur Sverige lät sig bedras av U 137* (Stockholm: Karneval, 2021)

Tunander, Ola. *The Secret War against Sweden: US and British Submarine Deception in the 1980s* (London: Frank Cass, 2004)

Ubåtskommissionen. *Ubåtsfrågan 1981-1994* (Stockholm: SOU 1995): p.135.

Ubåtsskyddskommissionen. *Att möta ubåtshotet: Ubåtskränkningarna och svensk säkerhetspolitik* (Stockholm: SOU 1983): p.13.

Ubåtsutredningen. *Perspektiv på ubåtsfrågan: Hanteringen av ubåtsfrågan politiskt och militärt* (Stockholm: SOU 2001): p.85.

Wallén, Göran. Commentary in *Tidskrift i Sjöväsendet* 4, 2009: pp.316–322.

Zakharov, Gennadiy Ivanovich. 'Rutskogo v "Lefortovo" ya soprovozhdal sam'. *Vlast'* 14, 16 April 2002.

ENDNOTES

Chapter 1

1. CIA, *Soviet Naval Strategy and Its Effect on the Development of Naval Forces 1953-1963*, report dated 22 October 1963 (TOP SECRET; declassified).
2. CIA, *Soviet Naval Strategy*, pp.66, 68–69.
3. For more on Gorshkov's Naval Aviation, see Michael Fredholm von Essen, *The Hunt for the Storozhevoy: The 1975 Soviet Navy Mutiny in the Baltic* (Warwick: Helion, 2022).
4. Robert B. Bathurst, *Understanding the Soviet Navy: A Hand Book* (Newport, Rhode Island: Naval War College Press, 1979), p.127.
5. V. G. Yefremenko, 'Razvitiye i sovershenstvovaniye protivolodochnykh sil i ikh taktiki', *Morskoy sbornik* 10, 1970, pp.16–23.
6. Sergey G. Gorshkov, *Morskaya moshch' gosudarstva* (Moscow: Voyenizdat, 1976, 2nd edn 1979), p.359. Gorshkov's book was published in the West as *The Sea Power of the State* (Oxford: Pergamon Press, 1979). The Foreign Broadcast Information Service, an open-source intelligence component of the CIA, published a pirated edition for official use only, known as JPRS L/9439, 12 December 1980 (FOUO). Declassified and available from the CIA.
7. Bathurst, *Understanding the Soviet Navy*, pp. xiv–xv.
8. Bathurst, *Understanding the Soviet Navy*, p.39.
9. Gorshkov, *Morskaya moshch' gosudarstva*, p.315.
10. Central Intelligence Agency (CIA), *Soviet Naval Strategy: Concepts and Forces for Theater War Against NATO* (Intelligence Report, January 1975, TOP SECRET; declassified), p.5.
11. Excerpts from Warsaw Pact lectures on strategy for war in Europe delivered in 1969–1970; cited in Central Intelligence Agency (CIA), *Soviet Naval Strategy: Concepts and Forces for Theater War Against NATO* (Intelligence Report, January 1975, TOP SECRET; declassified), p.7.
12. Bathurst, *Understanding the Soviet Navy*, pp.xv–xvi.
13. See, e.g., John Jordan, *An Illustrated Guide to the Modern Soviet Navy* (London: Salamander Books, 1982), p.8, which otherwise gives a for its time authoritative description of the Soviet Navy.
14. Michael Fredholm von Essen, 'When Intelligence Made a Difference: How Sweden Chose Sides', *Intelligencer Journal* (AFIO, 2019), pp.41–43. For full details (in Swedish), see Michael Fredholm von Essen, *Hemligstämplat: Svensk underrättelsetjänst från Erlander till Bildt* (Stockholm: Medström, 2020).
15. For further details, see Michael Fredholm von Essen, *Afghanistan Beyond the Fog of War. Persistent Failure of a Rentier State* (Copenhagen: NIAS Press, 2018); Michael Fredholm von Essen, 'The Power of Fear: Soviet Intelligence, the Politburo, and the 1979 Threat from Afghanistan', *Journal for Intelligence, Propaganda and Security Studies* (JIPSS) 13: 2 (2019), pp.104–122.
16. Christopher Andrew and Oleg Gordievsky, *Instructions from the Centre: Top Secret Files on KGB Foreign Operations 1975-1985* (London: Sceptre, 1993), pp.111–140; Christopher Andrew and Vasili Mitrokhin, *The Mitrokhin Archive: The KGB in Europe and the West* (London: Allen Lane, 1999), pp.316, 512–513, 565–566; Christopher Andrew and Vasili Mitrokhin, *Mitrokhin Archive II: The KGB and the World* (London. Allen Lane, 2005), pp.131–133. Both Oleg Gordiyevskiy and Vasiliy Mitrokhin were employed by the KGB. Gordiyevskiy defected in 1985, Mitrokhin in 1992. RYaN continued until 1989: Bernd Schaefer, "RYAN: The Soviet warning system before a 'surprise nuclear missile attack' in the 1980s", *Need to Know IV. What We Know about Secret Services in the Cold War: A State of Affairs 25 Years after 1989* (international conference at Leuven university, 23–24 October 2014); based on Stasi documents.
17. Bengt Gustafsson, *Sanningen om ubåtsfrågan: Ett försök till analys* (Stockholm: Santérus, Försvaret och det kalla kriget (FoKK) 23, 2010), p.334.

Chapter 2

1. CIA, *Soviet Naval Strategy*, pp.66, 68–69.
2. CIA, *Soviet Naval Strategy*, p.81.
3. Yuriy Panteleyev, 'The Submarine Operation of the Navy: The Naval Operation of the Future', *Voyennaya Mysl'*, Special Collection 3, July 1961; as translated by CIA, *Soviet Naval Strategy*, p.85, and in associated document, CIA, CSDB 3/649,281, 21 February 1962, p.7. Declassified.
4. Panteleyev, 'Submarine Operation of the Navy'; as translated by CIA, CSDB 3/649,281, 21 February 1962, p.9. Declassified.
5. Nils-Ove Jansson, *Omöjlig ubåt: Stridsberättelser från ubåtsjakten och det säkerhetspolitiska läget under 1980-talet* (np: Forum navale 52, 3rd edn 2016), pp.146–147.
6. Vasilij Besedin, *Inifrån U 137: Min egen berättelse* (Karlskrona: Albinsson & Sjöberg, 2009), pp.15–16.
7. Translated and reprinted in Central Intelligence Agency (CIA), *Combat Regulations of the Soviet Navy* (Memorandum, 14 November 1986, TOP SECRET; declassified). While this is the 1983 edition of the Combat Regulations, there is no reason to believe that the edition employed by the S-363's command crew in 1981 was very different.
8. CIA, Combat Regulations of the Soviet Navy (Memorandum), p.13.
9. CIA, Combat Regulations of the Soviet Navy (Memorandum), p.15.
10. CIA, Combat Regulations of the Soviet Navy (Memorandum), p.16.
11. CIA, Combat Regulations of the Soviet Navy (Memorandum), p.21.
12. CIA, Combat Regulations of the Soviet Navy (Memorandum), p.28–29.
13. Details provided in Fredholm von Essen, *Hemligstämplat*, pp.118–121.
14. Per Andersson, 'Vad gjorde de här? Personliga reflexioner om den främmande undervattensverksamheten', *Tidskrift i Sjöväsendet* 3, 2010, pp.211–224, on p.222.
15. *Svenska Dagbladet*, 26 October 2006.
16. Rolf Lindén, 'I sista minuten: Fem timmar vid en arbetsplats i Kalla krigets skugga', *Årsbok för Marinmusei vänner 2010* (Karlskrona: Marinmuseum, 2010), pp.77–95, on p.94.
17. Captain First Rank was in the Soviet Navy the approximate equivalent rank of a Royal Navy or U.S. Navy captain.
18. Captain Third Rank was in the Soviet Navy the approximate equivalent rank of a Royal Navy or U.S. Navy lieutenant commander. The different national systems of military rank did not fully correspond, and official translations shifted over the years, so different sources may use conflicting translations into English of Soviet as well as Swedish military ranks.
19. Captain-Lieutenant was the rank above Senior Lieutenant and below Captain Third Rank, and the approximate equivalent rank of a Royal Navy or U.S. Navy lieutenant.
20. In Soviet terminology, the deputy to the commander in political matters (Russian: *zamestitel' komandira po politicheskoy chasti*, abbreviated *zampolit*).
21. In Soviet terminology, the senior aide to the commanding officer (Russian: *starshiy pomoshchnik komandira korablya*, abbreviated *starpom*), a title selected to mark that he was not the second in command.
22. In Soviet terminology, the commander of the electromechanical combat unit (Russian: *komandir elektromekhanicheskoy boyevoy chasti*).
23. We strictly speaking do not know if Arkhipov was his real name, although this seems likely. With the exception of the other officers mentioned in this chapter, whose names have been confirmed by logbooks and similar documents, the names of all known crew members of the S-363 derive from Besedin's interviews and memoirs. He may have altered names to protect his colleagues. If so, he made this choice already during his first interview (more on which below). What speaks in favour of this hypothesis is that the crewman whom Besedin consistently refers to as Kovalchuk in reality was named Savchenko. When under pressure, the sailor gave his name as Savchenko, and the name is also confirmed by logbooks.
24. Besedin, *Inifrån U 137*, 9.
25. Commander Thor Widell; cited in Anders Hellberg and Anders Jörle, *Ubåt 137: Tio dagar som skakade Sverige* (Stockholm: Atlantis, 1984), p.175. Widell was in charge of the salvage operation and

became friends with Avrukevich to the extent that they addressed each other with their personal names or, for Widell, his nickname Tosse.
26 The head of the navigation department, or in Soviet terminology, the commander of the navigator's combat unit (Russian: *komandir shturmanskoy boyevoy chasti*).
27 Karl Andersson, 'Ubåt på grund!', *Rapport från Medborgargruppen i Ubåtsfrågan: Seminarium på Tekniska Högskolan i Stockholm 29-20-10.1994* (Stockholm: Medborgargruppen, 1994), pp.10–13, on p.12.

Chapter 3

1 Besedin, *Inifrån U 137*, p.6.
2 Besedin, *Inifrån U 137*, p.13; interview with Gushchin, *Exxet* 40, 5 March 1995. Gushchin describes his mission orders as (1) the monitoring of passing ships and (2) maintaining combat readiness. These general combat tasks are also referred to in the mission order (which follows later in this chapter) and the Soviet commission of inquiry report (see Appendix 1).
3 The *S-363*'s mission order, Vyacheslav Kocherov and Aleksandr Mozgovoy, 'Dolgiye posledstviya odnogo intsidenta', *Morskoy sbornik* 1, 1993, pp.9–16, on p.11.
4 Combat Regulations of the Soviet Navy for Division, Brigade, Regiment, and Ship: Chapters 6–8; translated in a CIA/Directorate of Operations (DO) Intelligence Information Special Report, 11 November 1986. Declassified.
5 OP: *operativnyy prikaz*, operations order.
6 KP: *komandnyy punkt*, command post.
7 The abbreviation may signify the current specific regulations for the submarine division (that is, from the year 1975). The Swedish Armed Forces interpreted the abbreviation as the commander of the 75th submarine division. The full abbreviation is KDPL-75g, and 'g' usually signifies 'year'.
8 Encrypted high-speed radio was known as ZAS (*zasekrechennaya apparatura svyazi*; apparatus for secret communications) and at close range maintained with a radio station type R-811, a VHF radio transceiver in common use. The underwater telephone system was known as ZPS (*zvukovaya podvodnaya svyaz'*; sound-ranging underwater communications).
9 The abbreviation *yadernyye boyepripasy* (YaBP; nuclear munitions) seems to be redacted in the Soviet mission order, but the meaning is obvious.
10 *Boyevoy sekret* (BS), combat secret.
11 *Spasatelnyy otryad* (SO), rescue department.
12 *Rabochiye listy* (r/l), working paper.
13 Andrey A. Grechko, *The Armed Forces of the Soviet State: A Soviet View* (Washington, DC: United States Government Printing Office, 1978), p.86. Grechko's book was first published in Russian in 1975. The English translation is, unexpectedly, the final edition of Grechko's work, because it was based on revisions which Grechko made shortly before his death in 1976. The revised edition was apparently never published in Russian.
14 Besedin, *Inifrån U 137*, p.17.
15 Besedin, *Inifrån U 137*, p.15–16.
16 The *S-363*'s logbook.
17 Besedin, *Inifrån U 137*, pp.18, 37–38.
18 The date as given by Besedin, *Inifrån U 137*, p.19. Oddly, the logbook excerpt appended to the commission of inquiry report gives the date and time of the incident as 18 October at 5:53 p.m., at a depth of 42m. The logbook excerpt accordingly describes the incident as taking place after, not before, the *S-363*'s stay in Świnoujście. It will be shown that Besedin's narrative includes discussions with Fleet Headquarters about the damages. Besedin's date would accordingly transfer some, but certainly not all, responsibility for setting out with damaged navigation systems to Fleet Headquarters. The date in the logbook excerpt appended to the commission of inquiry report instead assigns full blame for not returning to port immediately to Gushchin's command crew and, ultimately, Gushchin himself. The commission of inquiry version may accordingly have been doctored to show Fleet Headquarters in a better light. This is also supported by the section of the logbook declassified later. While not covering 2 October, the declassified section of the logbook certainly does not mention any collision on 18 October. Oddly, the commission of inquiry's version may have been based on Gushchin's own testimony. Already when interrogated in Karlskrona, he said that the subsequent antenna problem appeared 'on approximately 18 October' (interrogation protocol 1, p.14). Besedin said in Karlskrona that the 'radio direction finder error' had appeared 'approximately a week' before the submarine stranded (interrogation protocol, p.8). They accordingly seem to have discussed the time when the error was noted, not when the collision took place. Ultimately, it was still Gushchin's responsibility to assess the seaworthiness of his vessel. Besedin's narrative does not change this. There accordingly seems to be little reason to discredit his version.
19 Besedin names the head as Warrant Officer 'Volodya' Grishin in his memoirs. Elsewhere, he mentions a warrant officer named Aleksandr Volodin as the man in charge of this section. Possibly, his memory was at fault, confusing the two names.
20 Besedin, *Inifrån U 137*, p.20.
21 Besedin, *Inifrån U 137*, p.23.
22 This, too, supports Besedin's account over that of the official commission of inquiry. If the commission's date for the collision had been correct, more extensive damages would have been visible when the submarine stranded on the Swedish coast. There would also have been no opportunity to repaint the scratch marks.
23 Besedin, *Inifrån U 137*, p.23.
24 Besedin, *Inifrån U 137*, pp.24–25. Swedish naval officer Karl Andersson, who later tested the radio direction finder, agreed. Andersson's comment in Viktor Prosvirov, 'Ryska marinens utredning om U 137', *Rapport från Medborgargruppen i Ubåtsfrågan: Seminarium på Tekniska Högskolan i Stockholm 29-20-10.1994* (Stockholm: Medborgargruppen, 1994), pp.14–18, on p.16.
25 Besedin, *Inifrån U 137*, p.25.
26 Interview with Admiral Bobby Ray Inman, U.S. Navy, published online by Caltech Heritage Project, 4 August 2022 (https://heritageproject.caltech.edu/interviews-updates/adm-bobby-ray-inman#the-cold-war-framework).
27 Later, Soviet Navy representatives noted that the onboard Decca system did not function properly. Prosvirov, 'Ryska marinens utredning om U 137', p.15. Karl Andersson, the Swedish naval officer, found that the crew of the *S-363* were poorly trained in the use of the Decca Navigator System. Andersson's comment, Ibid., pp.16–17.
28 Besedin, *Inifrån U 137*, p.27.
29 Besedin, *Inifrån U 137*, p.27.
30 Besedin, *Inifrån U 137*, pp.28–29.
31 Later, Soviet Navy representatives reported that the crew discovered that the NEL-5 echo sounder was failing on 18 October (due to the collision with the trawl which the official account put on this date), and that it broke down on 23 October. Prosvirov, 'Ryska marinens utredning om U 137', p.15. Karl Andersson tested the echo sounder, finding that the amplifier had been turned to maximum and the switch was missing. Andersson suspected that this had been done on purpose to have evidence that the system did not function. Andersson's comment in Ibid., p.17.
32 Besedin, *Inifrån U 137*, pp.29–30.
33 Besedin, *Inifrån U 137*, p.31.
34 The *S-363*'s logbook; Besedin, *Inifrån U 137*, p.32.
35 The *S-363*'s logbook.
36 Personal communication from the retired Danish naval officer Hans Christian Bjerg, 23 May 2024.
37 Besedin, *Inifrån U 137*, p.32.
38 Besedin, *Inifrån U 137*, pp.32–33. Later, Soviet Navy representatives noted that one of the sextants onboard was incorrectly calibrated. Prosvirov, 'Ryska marinens utredning om U 137', p.15.
39 Interview with Besedin in 1990 published in *Sovetskaya Molodyozh'* ('Soviet Youth'), and then translated into Swedish and republished in *Dagens Nyheter*, 11 November 1990, p.A4.
40 Besedin, *Inifrån U 137*, p.33.
41 Besedin, *Inifrån U 137*, p.34.
42 Besedin, *Inifrån U 137*, p.34; *S-363*'s logbook.
43 Besedin, *Inifrån U 137*, pp.34–35. The descent to the seabed was not noted in the *S-363*'s logbook, possibly because it was regarded as too risky.
44 Interview with Gushchin, *Exxet* 40, 5 March 1995.
45 *S-363*'s logbook.
46 This ascent to periscope depth was apparently not entered into the vessel's logbook, which because of the difficulties seems to have been added to only occasionally.

47 Besedin, *Inifrån U 137*, p.36.
48 *S-363*'s logbook.
49 Besedin, *Inifrån U 137*, p.37.
50 *S-363*'s logbook.
51 Besedin, *Inifrån U 137*, p.38–39.
52 *S-363*'s logbook.
53 Besedin, *Inifrån U 137*, p.39.
54 Interview with Besedin in 1990 published in *Sovetskaya Molodyozh'* and republished in *Dagens Nyheter*, 11 November 1990, p.A4.
55 Besedin, *Inifrån U 137*, p.41.
56 *S-363*'s logbook. The reference to Christiansø is not visible in the available photocopy of the handwritten logbook but is found in the typed logbook excerpt which was presented later.
57 Besedin, *Inifrån U 137*, p.40.
58 Besedin, *Inifrån U 137*, p.42.
59 *S-363*'s logbook. The coordinates are written where the reference to Christiansø is in the typed logbook excerpt.
60 Interview with Besedin in 1990 published in *Sovetskaya Molodyozh'* and republished in *Dagens Nyheter*, 11 November 1990, p.A4.
61 Besedin, *Inifrån U 137*, p.43. The controversy about the position possibly explains what might be a correction in the *S-363*'s logbook.
62 Interview with Besedin in 1990 published in *Sovetskaya Molodyozh'* and republished in *Dagens Nyheter*, 11 November 1990, p.A4.
63 Hellberg and Jörle, *Ubåt 137*, pp.40, 93. See also Karl Andersson, 'Ubåt på grund!', *Rapport från Medborgargruppen i Ubåtsfrågan: Seminarium på Tekniska Högskolan i Stockholm 29-20-10.1994* (Stockholm: Medborgargruppen, 1994), pp.10–13, on p.13.
64 Försvarsstaben, *Ubåt 137 på svenskt vatten* (Stockholm: Försvarsstabens informationsavdelning, 18 December 1981), p.6.
65 Interview with Björn Hamilton, *BLT* (*Blekinge Läns Tidning*), 29 October 2001.
66 Försvarsstaben, *Ubåt 137 på svenskt vatten*, p.2.
67 Fredholm von Essen, *Hemligstämplat*, p.179.
68 Instytut Pamięci Narodowej (IPN), BU 2602/23403, BU 003179/556, Raport o zmianach sytuacji wywiadowczej w Szwecji, March 1982. Declassified.
69 Indirectly confirmed by Tore Forsberg, former head of the Soviet Section of the Security Service, in Tore Forsberg and Boris Grigorjev [Grigor'yev], *Spioner emellan* (Saltsjö-Duvnäs: Efron & Dotter, 2006), pp.245, 264.
70 Ola Tunander, *Navigationsexperten: Hur Sverige lät sig bedras av U 137* (Stockholm: Karneval, 2021), p.61.
71 Dirk Pohlmann's interview with Karl Andersson for the television documentary *Täuschung: Die Methode Reagan*, Arte, 5 May 2015. Transcript reprinted in Tunander, *Navigationsexperten*, pp.168–186, on p.169. See also ibid., pp.61–62.
72 Tunander, *Navigationsexperten*, p.98.
73 On Swedish clandestine activities in this field, see Fredholm von Essen, *Hemligstämplat*, pp.335–340.
74 Edmond D. Pope and Tom Shachtman, *Torpedoed: An American Businessman's True Story of Secrets, Betrayal, Imprisonment in Russia, and the Battle to Set Him Free* (Boston: Little, Brown, 2001).

Chapter 4

1 Besedin, *Inifrån U 137*, p.43; *S-363*'s logbook. Besedin mentions the position 56°04'4"N 15°44'0"E, but the submariners had not yet identified it correctly. Later in his memoirs, Besedin talks about telegrams exchanged already the evening before, which cannot be reconciled with this statement or, for that matter, the *S-363*'s logbook. Besedin, *Inifrån U 137*, p.49. He presumably means the regular communication just before the *S-363* hit the rock.
2 All telegrams from the *S-363*'s logbook.
3 Besedin, *Inifrån U 137*, p.43.
4 Admiral Vladimir Yegorov, in Herman Fältström (ed.), *Ytspänning: Ett seminarium om kalla krigets verklighet* (Stockholm: Försvarshögskolan, Försvaret och det kalla kriget (FoKK) 30, 2011), p.121. From 1991 to 2000, Yegorov was the last commanding officer of the Soviet Baltic Fleet and the first commanding officer of the Russian Federation's Baltic Fleet. From 2000 to 2005, Yegorov served as Governor of Kaliningrad.
5 Michael Fredholm von Essen, 'Redo för strid: Flyget och ubåt 137', Lennart Andersson et al. (eds), *Svenskt flyg under kalla kriget* (Stockholm: Medström, 2016), pp.212–227, on p.222.
6 Captain Second Rank was in the Soviet Navy the approximate equivalent rank of a Royal Navy or U.S. Navy commander.
7 Ivan Matveyevich Kapitanets, *Na sluzhbe okeanskomu flotu 1946-1992* (Moscow: Andreyevskiy flag, 2000), pp.509–512; cited by Aleksandr Rozin, *Deystviya Baltiyskogo flota po okazaniyu pomoshchi sevshey na mel' v shvedskikh vodakh PL 'S-363' (U-137) osen'yu 1981g.* (web site, http://alerozin.narod.ru/U137.htm).
8 Most Swedish accounts of Vice Admiral Kalinin's task force claim that it consisted of a large number of Navy vessels and left port in the early morning. Both claims are incorrect. Swedish intelligence reports, both the real-time SIGINT reporting and the post-incident Armed Forces reports that relied on the SIGINT reporting, give incorrect times, positions, and sometimes identities for Kalinin's vessels. The mistake derived from an unfortunate analytical error that went unrecognised at the time. It is fair to say that Swedish intelligence underperformed both when the *S-363* entered Swedish waters and when Kalinin's salvage vessels assembled.
9 Andersson, 'Ubåt på grund!', p.10.
10 The maritime surveillance centre on the island of Gotland was already in 1979 equipped with an electronic surveillance and presentation system known as STINA (the Swedish abbreviation for maritime and customs information system, *Sjö- och Tull Informations Anläggning*). STINA was produced by Philips Elektronikindustrier, a Swedish electronics company, and was later exported to Yugoslavia. A STINA system was ordered to Karlskrona maritime surveillance centre in October 1981. However, it was delivered and put in operation only in 1982.
11 Hellberg and Jörle, *Ubåt 137*, pp.59–65; war diaries Headquarters Military District South and Naval Base Karlskrona.
12 Hellberg and Jörle, *Ubåt 137*, p.66.
13 Hellberg and Jörle, *Ubåt 137*, p.75.
14 Hellberg and Jörle, *Ubåt 137*, p.72–74; war diaries Headquarters Military District South and Naval Base Karlskrona.
15 War diaries Headquarters Military District South and Naval Base Karlskrona; the *S-363*'s logbook. The helicopter returned to Kallinge at 11:50 a.m. Besedin, *Inifrån U 137*, p.44, suggests that the aircraft was a Saab 37 Viggen fighter and that it arrived about 40 minutes after Sturkman's boat and 15 minutes before the *Smyge*. However, Besedin's memory fails him. The Saab 37 Viggen flew over the *S-363* at a later time. Incidentally, no aircraft is mentioned at around this time in the *S-363*'s logbook; another omission that shows the tension on this day.
16 Hellberg and Jörle, *Ubåt 137*, pp.77–80.
17 Roland Hultgren, 'Hävdande av rikets integritet', Erling Johansson (ed.), *Minnesbok Södra militärområdet* (Kristianstad: Södra militärområdet, 2000), pp.143–154, on p.150.
18 Hellberg and Jörle, *Ubåt 137*, p.92.
19 Sven-Olof Olson, 'MB 1980-1982', Erling Johansson (ed.), *Minnesbok Södra militärområdet* (Kristianstad: Södra militärområdet, 2000), pp.193–200, on p.196; war diaries Headquarters Military District South and Naval Base Karlskrona.
20 Hellberg and Jörle, *Ubåt 137*, pp.80–85.
21 Interview with Karl Andersson in *Dagens Nyheter*, 7 November 1981, p.7; Hellberg and Jörle, *Ubåt 137*, p.98; Pohlmann's interview with Karl Andersson, May 2014, for the television documentary *Täuschung*. Transcript reprinted in Tunander, *Navigationsexperten*, pp.168–186.
22 Karl Andersson, interviewed in Ingemar Myhrberg, *Ubåtsvalsen: En motbok till rapporterna från ÖB och Ubåtsskyddskommissionen* (Gothenburg: Haga, 1985), p.54.
23 According to interviews cited in Hellberg and Jörle, *Ubåt 137*, pp.99–100, Andersson informed the Soviets about their actual position during his second visit to the *S-363* on this day. However, the *S-363*'s logbook noted the information under Andersson's first visit, at 11:10 a.m., which also seems more likely.
24 Hellberg and Jörle, *Ubåt 137*, pp.86–89; Naval Base Karlskrona war diary.
25 Besedin, *Inifrån U 137*, p.45.
26 Besedin, *Inifrån U 137*, p.49.
27 Hellberg and Jörle, *Ubåt 137*, p.116; Roland Hultgren, 'KA 2 och händelsen med ubåt 137', Olle Melin (ed.), *Kungliga Karlskrona Kustartilleriregemente 1/1 1902-31/10 2000* (Karlskrona: Marinmuseum Årsbok 2002), pp.91–104, on p.93.
28 *S-363*'s logbook.
29 Karl Andersson, handwritten memoir, dated 18 November 1981.

30. Hellberg and Jörle, *Ubåt 137*, p.100.
31. Hellberg and Jörle, *Ubåt 137*, p.102.
32. Besedin, *Inifrån U 137*, p.45. Since Besedin was unfamiliar with foreign languages and wrote down Andersson's offer from memory, we cannot be certain that these were his exact words.
33. Besedin, *Inifrån U 137*, p.45.
34. Överbefälhavaren, *Instruktion för krigsmakten vid hävdande av rikets oberoende under allmänt fredstillstånd samt under krig mellan främmande makter varunder Sverige är neutralt: IKFN* (1967). Based on General Order No. 48, of 24 January 1967, with corresponding instructions.
35. Hellberg and Jörle, *Ubåt 137*, p.99.
36. Hellberg and Jörle, *Ubåt 137*, p.102.
37. Hellberg and Jörle, *Ubåt 137*, p.103.
38. Besedin, *Inifrån U 137*, 56. Andersson dates the episode to 28 October, Besedin to 29 October (in his memoirs written later), but otherwise their respective narratives correspond in every detail, down to the cherry juice.

Chapter 5

1. Hellberg and Jörle, *Ubåt 137*, pp.105, 111; Besedin, *Inifrån U 137*, p.46.
2. Hultgren, 'Hävdande av rikets integritet', p.145.
3. Hellberg and Jörle, *Ubåt 137*, pp.111, 117.
4. Hellberg and Jörle, *Ubåt 137*, p.133.
5. Försvarsstaben, *Ubåt 137 på svenskt vatten*, p.3.
6. *S-363*'s logbook.
7. Tunander, *Navigationsexperten*, p.37; citing FRA SIGINT reporting made available to the 2001 Submarine Inquiry under Ambassador Rolf Ekéus assisted by Ambassador Mathias Mossberg.
8. Jan-Olof Grahn, *Om svensk signalspaning: Kalla kriget* (Stockholm: Medström, 2019), pp.68, 104.
9. Hellberg and Jörle, *Ubåt 137*, p.119.
10. *Sydöstran*, 9 November 1981, pp.1, 5.
11. Hellberg and Jörle, *Ubåt 137*, pp.117–118, 120.
12. Hellberg and Jörle, *Ubåt 137*, p.121; Bror Stefenson (ed.), *Krishantering: U 137-krisen* (Stockholm: Kungl. Krigsvetenskapsakademien, 1992), p.7.
13. Besedin, *Inifrån U 137*, p.53.
14. Hellberg and Jörle, *Ubåt 137*, pp.132–133.
15. Yury N. Kormilitsin and Oleg A. Khalizev, *Theory of Submarine Design* (Saint-Petersburg: Saint-Petersburg State Maritime Technical University, 2001), p.93.
16. Besedin, *Inifrån U 137*, p.55.
17. Besedin, *Inifrån U 137*, p.50.
18. Stefenson, *Krishantering: U 137-krisen*, pp.8–9.
19. Hellberg and Jörle, *Ubåt 137*, p.96.
20. Stefenson, *Krishantering: U 137-krisen*, p.8; war diaries Headquarters Military District South and Naval Base Karlskrona.
21. Lennart Ljung, *Överbefälhavare Lennart Ljungs tjänstedagböcker 1978-1983* (Stockholm: Samfundet för utgivande av handskrifter rörande Skandinaviens historia, 2010).
22. Fredholm von Essen, *Hemligstämplat*, p.207.
23. See, e.g., Carl Björeman, *Sex överbefälhavare söker en roll: Tvekampen mellan det territoriella och det teknologiska försvaret under kalla kriget och i nutid* (Stockholm: Försvarshögskolan, Försvaret och det kalla kriget (FoKK) 53, 2017), pp.101–102.
24. Fredholm von Essen, *Hemligstämpat*, pp.21–22, 327, 352.
25. U.S. National Security Council, Statement of Policy Proposed by the National Security Council on the Position of the United States with Respect to Scandinavia and Finland, NSC 121 (TOP SECRET), 8 January 1952. Approved by President Truman on 17 January 1952. Declassified in its entirety and available from the National Archives and, with parts excised, from the Office of the Historian, Department of State.
26. Fredholm von Essen, *Hemligstämplat*, 207. See also Fredholm von Essen, 'When Intelligence Made a Difference: How Sweden Chose Sides', pp.41–43.
27. Hellberg and Jörle, *Ubåt 137*, p.96.
28. Fredholm von Essen, *Hunt for the Storozhevoy*.
29. Stefenson, *Krishantering: U 137-krisen*, p.9.
30. Hans von Hofsten, *I kamp mot överheten: Örlog och debatt* (np: SMB, 2017), pp.66–68; Ubåtsutredningen, *Perspektiv på ubåtsfrågan*, SOU 2001:85 (Stockholm: Försvarsdepartementet, 2001), pp.49–57; Jansson, *Omöjlig ubåt*, pp.14–18, 145.
31. Hellberg and Jörle, *Ubåt 137*, p.106.
32. Defence Staff press release, 28 October 1981; cited by Hellberg and Jörle, *Ubåt 137*, pp.92–93.
33. Hellberg and Jörle, *Ubåt 137*, p.94.
34. TT, 28 October 1981; cited by Hellberg and Jörle, *Ubåt 137*, p.94.
35. Hellberg and Jörle, *Ubåt 137*, p.94.
36. Hultgren, 'Hävdande av rikets integritet', p.145; war diary Headquarters Military District South.
37. Bo J. Theutenberg, *Dagbok från UD 1: Högdramatik i UD, ubåtar, protestnoter och annat (1981-1983)* (Skara: Stockholm Institute of International Law, Arbitration and Conciliation, 2012), p.36. The book contains Theutenberg's diary during the incident. Ibid., pp.36–50.
38. Stefenson, *Krishantering: U 137-krisen*, pp.52–53.
39. Stefenson, *Krishantering: U 137-krisen*, p.53; Hellberg and Jörle, *Ubåt 137*, p.109.
40. Stefenson, *Krishantering: U 137-krisen*, p.53.
41. Prime Minister Thorbjörn Fälldin to Björn Hamilton, 18 October 2001, cited in interview with Björn Hamilton, *BLT*, 29 October 2001; war diaries Headquarters Military District South and Naval Base Karlskrona. The specific salvage vessels (more on which below) were apparently named in the request, which the Swedish government has not yet declassified.
42. Stefenson, *Krishantering: U 137-krisen*, p.37.
43. Stefenson, *Krishantering: U 137-krisen*, p.6–7.
44. Hellberg and Jörle, *Ubåt 137*, pp.143–145.
45. Hellberg and Jörle, *Ubåt 137*, pp.148–149.
46. Hultgren, 'Hävdande av rikets integritet', p.147.
47. Stefenson, *Krishantering: U 137-krisen*, p.8.
48. Stefenson, *Krishantering: U 137-krisen*, p.56; citing television news broadcast *Rapport*, 7:30 p.m., 6 November 1981.
49. Edmond D. Pope, *Cold War Warriors: Whiskey on the Rocks – A Window on the 1981 Cold War Era* (Emmitsburg News-Journal, 2011; presently found at www.emmitsburg.net/archive_list/articles/misc/cww/2011/whiskey.htm).
50. Stefenson, *Krishantering: U 137-krisen*, p.56.
51. Stefenson, *Krishantering: U 137-krisen*, p.38.
52. Stefenson, *Krishantering: U 137-krisen*, pp.56–57.
53. Hellberg and Jörle, *Ubåt 137*, p.278.
54. Stefenson, *Krishantering: U 137-krisen*, p.38.

Chapter 6

1. Fredholm von Essen, 'Redo för strid', pp.212–227; Grahn, *Om svensk signalspaning: Kalla kriget*, p.103.
2. Rear Admiral Baltuška, then the commander of independent Lithuania's navy, to General Bengt Gustafsson, former Swedish supreme commander. Bengt Gustafsson, *Ubåtsfrågan: Sanningen finns i betraktarens öga* (Stockholm: Försvarshögskolan, Försvaret och det kalla kriget (FoKK) 4, 2005), p.30; Bengt Gustafsson, *Det sovjetiska hotet mot Sverige under det kalla kriget* (Stockholm: Försvarshögskolan, Försvaret och det kalla kriget (FoKK) 12, 2007), pp.97, 99.
3. Bjarne Darwall, *Luftens dirigenter* (Nässjö: Air Historic Research, 2004), p.142.
4. After the dissolution of the Soviet Union 10 years later, this particular An-12BK was probably transferred to the state-owned Russian airline Sakhalinskiye Aviatrassy (SAT Airlines), which was founded in 1992. After passing on the Baltic Navy's most sensitive secrets, the aircraft was thereby demoted to transporting goods around the Sea of Okhotsk in the Russian Far East. When SAT Airlines in 2013 was acquired by Aurora, a subsidiary of Aeroflot, the aircraft appears to have been taken out of service.
5. War diaries Headquarters Military District South and Naval Base Karlskrona.
6. Försvarsstaben, *Ubåt 137 på svenskt vatten*, pp.5, 13.
7. Försvarsstaben, *Ubåt 137 på svenskt vatten*, pp.3, 13; Hellberg and Jörle, *Ubåt 137*, p.136.
8. Hellberg and Jörle, *Ubåt 137*, p.149; Hultgren, 'Hävdande av rikets integritet', p.147.
9. Hultgren, 'KA 2 och händelsen med ubåt 137', p.95.
10. Hultgren, 'KA 2 och händelsen med ubåt 137', p.95.
11. Lindén, 'I sista minuten', p.84.

12. Rolf Lindén, comment in web site, https://försvarsbloggare.se/category/i-sista-minuten/, which also republishes his narrative from 2010. Last accessed on 22 August 2024.
13. Personal communication from the retired Danish naval officer Hans Christian Bjerg, 23 May 2024.
14. Fredholm von Essen, 'Redo för strid', pp.212–27.
15. Darwall, *Luftens dirigenter*, p.141.
16. War Diary, Naval Base Karlskrona; Hultgren, "Hävdande av rikets integritet", Erling Johansson (ed.), *Minnesbok: Södra militärområdet* (Kristianstad: Södra militärområdet, [2000]), pp.143–154, on p.145.
17. Bert Stenfeldt, "Svenska flygstridskrafter under U 137-krisen 1981", *Svensk Flyghistorisk Tidskrift* 3, 2007, sid. 20–21; Lennart Andersson, *ÖB:s klubba: Flygvapnets attackeskader under kalla kriget* (SMB, 2010), sid. 143–144, in part based on the same source.
18. Fredholm von Essen, 'Redo för strid', p.213.
19. Jan Andersson, in Kurt Ottosson, 'Spaningsviggen: SF/SH 37', Ulf Edlund and Hans Kampf (eds), *System 37 Viggen* (Stockholm: SFF, 2009), pp.103–110, on p.109.
20. Bert Stenfeldt, 'Svenska flygstridskrafter under U 137-krisen 1981', *Svensk Flyghistorisk Tidskrift* 3, 2007, pp.20–21, on p.20.
21. Lindén, 'I sista minuten', pp.87–91.
22. Hellberg and Jörle, *Ubåt 137*, p.133.
23. Leif Åström, 'AJ 37 och AJS 37 i tjänst', Ulf Edlund and Hans Kampf (eds), *System 37 Viggen* (Stockholm: SFF, 2009), pp.85–102, on p.95.
24. Bert Stenfeldt, "Svenska flygstridskrafter under U 137-krisen 1981", *Svensk Flyghistorisk Tidskrift* 3, 2007, sid. 20–21; Lennart Andersson, *ÖB:s klubba: Flygvapnets attackeskader under kalla kriget* (SMB, 2010), sid. 143–144, in part based on the same source.
25. War diaries Headquarters Military District South and Naval Base Karlskrona; Per Andersson, 'U 137: Verkligheten är aldrig som den ser ut att vara', *Tidskrift i Sjöväsendet* 4, 2021, pp.493–511, on p.500. Lindén, 'I sista minuten', p.90, who was in command of the coastal defences, mentions the alleged intrusion of the *SS-30* only in passing, outside his main narrative, and reasserts that the task force reached the border at 9:00 p.m. and then halted.
26. Leif Åström,'Förhindra fritagning av grundstött sovjetisk ubåt U-137!' *Ikaros: Flygvapenmusei årsbok 2010*, pp.45–60, on p.50; personal communications from Leif Åström, January-February 2016.
27. Leif Åström, "AJ 37 och AJS 37 i tjänst", Ulf Edlund and Hans Kampf (eds), *System 37 Viggen* (Stockholm: SFF, 2009), pp.85–102, on pp.94–96; additional information from Leif Åström, January-February 2016.
28. Kjell Öfverberg, "Filip Röd och U137…", Göran Jacobsson (ed.), *Fältflygare: Från dröm till verklighet* (np: Norlén & Slottner, 2009), pp.144–145, on p.145.
29. Aleksandr Rozin, *Deystviya Baltiyskogo flota po okazaniyu pomoshchi sevshey na mel' v shvedskikh vodakh PL 'S 363' (U 137) osen'yu 1981g*. (web site, http://alerozin.narod.ru/U137.htm). Rozin served in the Soviet Emergency Rescue Group (*Avariyno-Spasatel'naya Partiya*, ASP) which manned the salvage task force.
30. Hellberg and Jörle, *Ubåt 137*, pp.126–127; Ljung, *Överbefälhavare Lennart Ljungs tjänstedagböcker 1978-1983*, pp.185–186.
31. Stefenson, *Krishantering: U 137-krisen*, pp.16, 19.
32. Hellberg and Jörle, *Ubåt 137*, p.133; Besedin, *Inifrån U 137*, pp.54–55; Hultgren, 'KA 2 och händelsen med ubåt 137', p.94; war diary, BK Fo 15. That the submarine crew raised the alarm was later confirmed by then Ensign Erling Holmberg, who was there. Jörle, *U137: Vi som höll gränsen*, p.69.

Chapter 7

1. Hellberg and Jörle, *Ubåt 137*, pp.161–162.
2. Stefenson, *Krishantering: U 137-krisen*, p.28.
3. Stefenson, *Krishantering: U 137-krisen*, pp.52–53.
4. Hellberg and Jörle, *Ubåt 137*, pp.265–266; Stefenson, *Krishantering: U 137-krisen*, p.65. This conclusion is supported by Herman Fältström, 'U 137-incidenten: En fallstudie', Gunnar Artéus and Kent Zetterberg (eds), *Högsta ledningen: Förhållandet mellan regeringen och överbefälhavaren under det kalla kriget* (Stockholm: Försvarshögskolan, Försvaret och det kalla kriget (FoKK) 26, 2010), pp.113–128, on p.118.
5. Ljung, *Överbefälhavare Lennart Ljungs tjänstedagböcker 1978-1983*, p.187.
6. Stefenson, *Krishantering: U 137-krisen*, p.19. Swedish cabinet meetings are not always recorded in minutes, possibly as a means to save cabinet ministers from being held accountable for their actions. See, e.g., Michael Fredholm von Essen, 'Briefing the Swedish Policy Maker: The Analyst-Policy Maker Relationship in a Small Country', *Journal of Intelligence History* 20: 1 (2021), pp.25–44.
7. Stefenson, *Krishantering: U 137-krisen*, pp.14–16.
8. Fälldin, in Stefenson, *Krishantering: U 137-krisen*, p.15.
9. Hellberg and Jörle, *Ubåt 137*, pp.150–152.
10. Stefenson, *Krishantering: U 137-krisen*, p.7.
11. *Sydsvenska Dagbladet*, 18 November 1981; Hellberg and Jörle, *Ubåt 137*, pp.149–150.
12. Hellberg and Jörle, *Ubåt 137*, p.150.
13. Hultgren, 'Hävdande av rikets integritet', p.146.
14. Interview with Ulf Jansson, *Sydöstran*, 27 October 2001.
15. Hellberg and Jörle, *Ubåt 137*, p.149.
16. Stefenson, *Krishantering: U 137-krisen*, 23; Hellberg and Jörle, *Ubåt 137*, p.179.
17. Bjarne Darwall, *Myran: En hemlig anläggning går ur tiden* (Kallinge: Blekinge Flygflottilj, 2000), p.137; Darwall, *Luftens dirigenter*, pp.140–141.
18. Försvarsstaben, *Ubåt 137 på svenskt vatten*, p.3.
19. Interview with Björn Hamilton, *BLT*, 29 October 2001; Björn Hamilton, '1981: Ett särdeles händelserikt år på ubåten Neptun', *Årsbok för Marinmusei vänner 2010* (Karlskrona: Marinmuseum, 2010), pp.56–76, on pp.69–71.
20. Interview with Björn Hamilton, *BLT*, 29 October 2001; Hamilton, '1981', pp.72–73.
21. Kapitanets, *Na sluzhbe okeanskomu flotu*, pp.509–512; cited by Rozin, *Deystviya Baltiyskogo flota*.
22. Interview with Björn Hamilton, *BLT*, 29 October 2001; Hamilton, '1981', p.73.
23. Gennadiy Ivanovich Zakharov, 'Rutskogo v "Lefortovo" ya soprovozhdal sam', *Vlast'* 14, p.16 April 2002; cited in Rozin, *Deystviya Baltiyskogo flota*.
24. *Expressen*, 29 March 2018 (https://www.expressen.se/kvallsposten/sovjetiska-specialstyrkor-skulle-kapa-svenskt-fartyg/).
25. Christer Bjurman, 'Håll gränsen, löd statsministerns order', *Vårt försvar* 4, December 2014, pp.20–22. Published in the magazine of a Swedish patriotic society established to promote the defence of the country, this is a highly dramatic account which incorrectly dates the event to the night between 28 and 29 October and includes anachronistic elements, primarily the Prime Minister's order which only came later.
26. Two attempts: Karl Andersson, in Stefenson, *Krishantering: U 137-krisen*, p.7. One attempt: Försvarsstaben, *Ubåt 137 på svenskt vatten*, p.4.
27. Sune Thomsson's blog at the web site, www.newsmill.se, 31 October 2011. Thomsson was a retired naval officer who among other duties served as commanding officer on a minelayer.
28. *Svenska Dagbladet*, 27 October 2006.
29. Besedin, *Inifrån U 137*, p.57.
30. While the full story is given by Besedin in his memoirs, it was first published in *Izvestiya*, 10 December 1991.
31. Besedin, *Inifrån U 137*, pp.58–59.
32. Besedin, *Inifrån U 137*, pp.5, 59–60.
33. Besedin, *Inifrån U 137*, p.60.
34. *Dagens Nyheter*, 31 October 2009.
35. Kocherov and Mozgovoy, 'Dolgiye posledstviya', p.12.
36. *Svenska Dagbladet*, 27 October 2006; Anders Jörle (ed.), *U137: Vi som höll gränsen – kustartillerister berättar om sin del av insatsen och sina upplevelser de dramatiska dagarna 1981 då en kärnvapenbestyckad sovjetisk ubåt står på grund i Karlskrona skärgård* (np: Page One Publishing, 2021), p.76. We do not know how Lieutenant Colonel Elming expected the sniper to make this assessment.
37. Hellberg and Jörle, *Ubåt 137*, p.189.
38. Karl Andersson, handwritten memoir, dated 18 November 1981.
39. Grahn, *Om svensk signalspaning: Kalla kriget*, p.102.
40. *Expressen*, 13 November 1981, p.12; Darwall, *Myran*, p.136; Besedin, *Inifrån U 137*, p.76.
41. Darwall, *Luftens dirigenter*, p.141.
42. Hellberg and Jörle, *Ubåt 137*, pp.177–178.
43. Besedin, *Inifrån U 137*, p.60.

Chapter 8

1 Hellberg and Jörle, *Ubåt 137*, p.184.
2 Hellberg and Jörle, *Ubåt 137*, p.174.
3 Hellberg and Jörle, *Ubåt 137*, pp.182–183; interview with Beckman in *Expressen*, 6 November 1981.
4 Karl Andersson, handwritten memoir, dated 18 November 1981.
5 Besedin, *Inifrån U 137*, pp.61–62.
6 Hellberg and Jörle, *Ubåt 137*, p.184.

ABOUT THE AUTHOR

Professor Michael Fredholm von Essen is an historian and former military analyst who has published extensively on the history, defence strategies, security policies, intelligence services, issues related to terrorism, and energy-sector developments of Eurasia, and lectured, during conferences or as visiting professor, around the world. He has published a large number of books, including *The Goths* 1-2 (Society of Ancients, 2021-2022); *Afghanistan Beyond the Fog of War* (NIAS Press, 2018); *Transnational Organized Crime and Jihadist Terrorism: Russian-Speaking Networks in Western Europe* (Routledge, 2017); several books on Cold War intelligence, and many books for Helion & Company Publishing.